Gendered Spaces and Ruptured Identities

Representation of Women in African Literature

Gendered Spaces and Ruptured Identities

Representation of Women in African Literature

Editors

Hem Raj Bansal

Roshan Lal Sharma

AUTHORSPRESS

Worldwide Circulation through Authorspress Global Network
First Published in 2022
by
Authorspress
Q-2A Hauz Khas Enclave, New Delhi-110 016 (India)
Phone: (0) 9818049852
E-mail: authorspressgroup@gmail.com
Website: www.authorspressbooks.com

Gendered Spaces and Ruptured Identities:
Representation of Women in African Literature
ISBN 978-93-5529-094-6

Printed in India at Thomson Press (India) Limited

Preface

> The feminist novel is a form of protest literature directed to both men and women. Protesting against sexism and patriarchal power structure, it is unapologetically propagandist or strident or both. It demands that its readers, whether the male oppressors or the female oppressed, be aware of ideological issues in order that it may change their attitudes about patriarchy. For a novel to be identified as feminist, therefore, it must not just deal with women and women's issues but should also posit some aspects of a female ideology. (Ogunyemi qtd. in Arndt 44-45)

African women's profoundly genderised space stands largely invaded due to unwarranted control of their bodies, agency and lives at large. Their literary and cinematic representations too have either been commodifying them as objects of sexual gratification, or relegating them as transgressors, and submissive/ unquestioning/ silent physical entities. As a consequence of such oppressive control over their bodies, lives and destinies, African women's identities as human beings have been belittled and reduced to the extent that they have become utterly inarticulate. Emmanuel Ngara aptly observes:

> In most novels of the early period, i.e. novels written before, say, 1970, the hero is almost inevitably a male member of the African intelligentsia – Camara in *The African Child*, Waiyaki in *The River Between*, Obi in *No Longer at Ease*, Odili in *A Man of the People* and so on. In all these and other novels of the time women play a secondary role in the affairs of society and the principal female characters are portrayed as adjuncts to the main male characters. (Ngara 34)

The arrival of African women writers in the literary arena may be viewed as a major intervention into the citadel of male-centric/-dominated African literary tradition that largely served the male interests, and thereby rendered a great disservice to women. If we begin with initial but prominent female voices like that of Flora Nwapa, Buchi Emecheta, Grace Ogot and Mariama Ba, we may notice how their fictional corpus significantly contributed to African women's literature. Apart from this, the major contemporary young feminist voices like Chimamanda Ngozi Adichie also strike hard at the core of female stereotypes through their works. Female genital mutilation, barrenness, polygyny, and the bride price are a few among several other culturally sanctioned African traditions that have been questioned and critiqued by these authors.

Gendered Spaces and Ruptured Identities: Representation of Women in African Literature is about female agency, choice, activism, assertion, and identity. As a concerted effort to decode the vast fictional and poetic array of African female writers, we believe that the anthology will prove to be a pivotal contribution to the existing body of research. At a time when most of the traditions have been termed as anti-female and anti-humane, African societies still advocate them to privilege a particular sex. This, in fact, does not resonate well with true democratic spirit characterised by equality and freedom. The angst of African women novelists against patriarchal and anti-women mindset has been strongly voiced in the literary essays in the book.

Works Cited

Arndt, Susan. *African Women's Literature, Orature and Intersexuality: Igbo Oral Narratives as Nigerian Women Writers' Models and Objects of Writing Back*. Eckhard Breitinger Bayreuth University, 1998.

Ngara, Emmanuel. "The Portrayal of Women in African Literature." *Kunapipi,* vol. 11, no. 3, pp. 33-40, 1989.
<at:https://ro.uow.edu.au/kunapipi/vol11/iss3/10>

Contents

Introduction

African literature is quite diverse and brings to fore not only various cultural manifestations but also the pain, suffering and subdued voices of women. Though colonisation of the continent during the Scramble for Africa did effect it immensely in terms of racial oppression, gendered discrimination remained an unquestionable reality. While people suffered under the colonial actors and continue to overcome the psychological scars, women in particular still face bleak future in terms of domestic violence and cultural oppression. Combating racial discrimination, cultural repression, patriarchal dictates, and inhuman traditions is still a haunting reality for African women. Even the literature produced by men either portrays them as passive conduits of patriarchal victimisation or as non-active, non-performing uncreative beings that need constant guidance and care. African feminism is about agency, activism and choice:

> African feminism gets to the bottom of African gender relations and the problems of African women – illuminating their causes and consequences – and criticises them. In so doing, African feminism aims at upsetting the existing matrix of domination and overcoming it, thus transforming gender relationships and conceptions in African societies and improving the situation of African women. (Arndt 32)

African feminist literature, thus, speaks more to inherent societal gendered spaces than to colonial ones. It largely questions androcentrism which considers the male-viewpoint and opinions as touchstones for deciding women's destiny and their roles in society. Biological differences between men and women, for example, were exaggerated widely to make the latter internalise inferiority and believe themselves better suited to domestic roles than creative ones. It finds ample reflection in the literature produced by men and the myths promulgated about women.

In *Things Fall Apart* (1958), the central character Okonkwo beats his youngest wife for not offering him lunch on time. He breaks the rule of the Week of Peace when Earth Goddess Ani does not allow any violence to be perpetrated against anyone. On the second occasion, Okonkwo nearly shoots his wife Ekwefi for having broken some banana leaves from the courtyard. These two incidents are emblematic of countless such incidents where black women remain victims of their husbands' unwarranted cruelty in particular and of men in general. The legitimacy given to polygamy and the practice of bride price in African societies makes the gender violence appear quite natural against women as men can always look for other women as prospective wives.

However, *Things Fall Apart* also embodies another important aspect of women empowerment. For example Okonkwo's exile to his motherland and his maternal uncle Uchendu's address to other people is also significant in stressing the importance of the motherland. He clearly tells that Nneka implies "Mother is Supreme" and it shows the high importance given to women/mothers in Nigeria. He enlightens all that during the bitter times, it is only the motherland which accepts the victims with open arms. It signals that not everything about African societies is bad as there are some pro-women practices in place. Nevertheless, given the gravity of anti-women traditions in African societies, the good ones fade in comparison to the uglier ones. It is in this light that we need to see the issues that confront women in Africa today.

Women writers in African literature have sought to voice their concern against gender discrimination in their works. Apathy and suspicion of men of letters towards women's creative and intellectual ability is clearly voiced by Ama Ata Aidoo in her essay "To Be an African Woman Writer." She writes that while the oppression of colonisation was endemic in the lives of third world peoples "some scholars are interested only in male African writer" (514). Aidoo goes on resenting that Prof. Dieter Reimenschneider came for a lecture in Harare and he did not mention any female writer and when asked, he responded that "it was natural" (515) and she wonders how could it be natural to ignore African women writers. Publishers as well male academicians remained suspicious of women and even Gerald Moore in *Seven African Authors* (1962), again republished as *Twelve African Authors* (1980) did not include any female writer. Lloyd Brown writes: "African women writers are the voices unheard, rarely discussed and seldom accorded space in the repetitive anthologies and predictably male-oriented studies in the field" (qtd. in Aidoo 515).

Roseanne P. Bell in "The Absence of the African Women Writer" points to such discrediting of women writers even by the publication houses in Africa. She writes: "In the early sixties, out of roughly sixty-four writers published by Heinemann Educational Books in their African Writers Series, only four of those authors were women" (491). Similarly, Elechi Amadi's (1934-2016) *The Concubine* (1966) also abounds in negative references to the protagonist Ihuoma who is said to be like "a quiet dog that eats up the hens' eggs without a bark" (204).

Simone de Beauvoir's (1908-1986) key argument that the women's oppression lay in their social and cultural construction as other is true in the African context too. Each of the African woman writers wrestles with this cultural problem that manifests itself through regressive traditions. Shulamith Firestone (1945-2012) in her work *The Dialectic of Sex* (1970) predates gender oppression before race and class and sees it embodied in the natural reproductive difference between men and women. For her, it is rooted in the glorification of natural sexual division by patriarchy which then gets translated into labour division. The labour division in this case goes on in the idealisation of femininity, gender roles, marriage and motherhood. Maryse Conde writes:

> I simply believe that the personality and the inner reality of African women have been hidden under such a heap of myths, so called ethnological theories, rapid generalisations and patent untruths that it might be interesting to study what they have to say for themselves when they decide to speak... When so many women can stand up and shout slogans for emancipation or deliver political addresses for the benefit of the political parties, what prevents them from taking a pen and writing about themselves? (132-33)

Traditions, if well-received, constructive, valuable and meaningful, provide solidarity and cohesion to society. Though traditions as such are not to be scoffed at/derided, their continuing praxis should be ascertained by their usefulness to all. Using these socially validated practices as defence-shields for launching an offensive against women and inhibiting their growth is what needs to be questioned in contemporary times. Among such various undignifying societal norms, the bride-price, polygamy, child-marriage, post marriage virginity tests/rituals and female genital mutilation remain highly accountable for women's subservient position. The bride price, for example, is like a price tag which ascertains/fixes the value of a prospective bride. While it is evidently a violation of human dignity/worth, it is nearly akin to slavery where African slaves were weighed and sold like articles of consumption. Though there are many votaries of bride-price in Africa, their arguments to defend this practice seem very hollow. For example, they see it as an empowering practice to girls as compared to India where girls' parents have to give dowry to the prospective groom. However, even in the case of Africa, parents cherish their girls only as long as they bring them enough bride money. The real affection in this case remains missing. It is clearly visible in a few novels. Buchi Emecheta, for example, has written a novel titled *The Bride Price* (1976) to show the adverse effects of this custom on women. Through the elopement and eventual death of Aku-nna due to child birth complications, the novelist exposes how the fear is instilled in the minds of African women to follow such practices in letter and spirit.

Polygamy is another widely practiced tradition in Africa which has caused enormous pain to women. It gives an unquestionable right to a husband to marry another woman at will, without taking consent even from the former wife. Tom Brooks in his article "The Problem with Polygamy" writes that "defense of polygamy reduces marriage to only a sexual relationship... Women in polygamous marriages are at higher risk of low self-esteem, as well as depression, than women in non-polygamous relationships" (112). Moreover, the husbands with multiple partners often turn away from their pregnant wives, thus causing depression to women. Apart from this, the responsibility of raising children falls more on women in polygamous marriages. Literature by African women writers also voices dissent against such practices. Not only such wives but the offspring in polygamous marriages also face emotional starvation and a sense of powerlessness as the "children of polygamous families experience a higher incidence of marital conflict, family violence, and family disruptions than do children of monogamous families" (Elbedour et al. 256).

Barrenness is another stigma that women in nearly every societies face. While in countries where polygamy is not sanctioned by law, men cannot turn to other wives, in Africa, turning to other women for child fulfilment is completely accepted and highly encouraged by customs. In Flora Nwapa's *Efuru* it is clearly visible as even after delivering a baby girl, she is not deemed to be a complete woman. African societies expect women to bear more and more children, and especially the male ones. Even when after her second marriage, Efuru fails to deliver children, she is considered a man than a woman. The women in the village gossip about Efuru and her husband Gilbert, "We are not going to eat happy marriage. Marriage must be fruitful" (139). Moreover, another woman Omirima's blaming of Efuru shows how she herself has internalised the patriarchal notions of polygamous marriages, "Why does she not allow her husband to marry another wife when she is barren... But can't the husband do anything about it? He is to blame for letting a woman rule him" (175). Finally even Efuru is made to accept that it is a bad woman who wants her husband only for herself and does not let him marry another girl. She, therefore, goes looking for a girl for her husband when her hopes to conceive shatter.

Apart from this, numerous regressive gendered societal customs arrest women's growth, individuality and freedom. "Custom insists upon the dissolution of a family when a father dies, because a family is simply not a family without the male in it" (Bazin 9). It shows how important a male is considered in the African societies for controlling a family. Unfortunately, the surviving wife is inherited by the husband's brother, whether she is willing to do so or not. Such traditions further forbid menstruating girls not to visit the stream and other places in the house as it would pollute everything and would bring bad luck to the inmates.

The oldest way to exert control over women is through violence. Afraid of being hit and silenced by force, many women choose to remain the silent victims of physical assault. Carol Anne Douglas in her article "Gender Violence in Africa: African Women's Response" writes: "Many countries in East and Southern Africa have high rates of wife beating. Some societies have the idea that women are foolish and childlike, and need to be beaten to be corrected" (9). Many women feel "that men have the right to discipline their wives by beating. The women who are beaten often feel that it is their fault. Even many matrilineal and matrilocal societies accept men beating their wives as correction" (Douglas 9). Rape is another way to exercise violence on women as Douglas says, "Under traditional law in much of southern Africa, a rapist is required to pay bride wealth and to marry the victim; the same is true in Eritrea. No one considers this a further injury" (9).

It is this male-centred literature and cultural practices which have largely kept women at bay from expressing their concerns. Role of women writers in Africa is really significant to speak against the so called endeared traditions which have been detrimental to women's mental and physical health and well-being. While polygamy has kept them subservient thinking the husband to be their lord, self-incurred inferiority has also been one of the reasons for such a degraded social state. Many women act against women, become the enemies of co-wives, and perpetuate gender discrimination through such internalisation of patriarchal dictates. Ossai, for example in *Efuru* does not go against her husband even after he deserts her. Nnu Ego in *The Joys of Motherhood* also comes up with the same realisation after suffering badly at the hands of her sons: "We women subscribe to that law more than anyone. Until we change all this, it is still a man's world, which women will always help to build" (187). The law being referred to is that of women blindly following patriarchal cultural dictates of keeping their destiny tied to that of their children and husbands.

African women writers have appeared on the literary scene to set this gender imbalance right. Flora Nwapa (1931-1993), Bessie Head (1937-1986), Ama Ata Aidoo (b. 1942), Buchi Emecheta ((1944-2017), Nadine Gordimer (1923-2014), Chimamanda Ngozi Adichie (b. 1977) are a few powerful writers whose works permeate with lived experiences and hence, offer powerful critiques of gender oppression. Flora Nwapa is a Nigerian novelist who has been instrumental in exposing gender bias in Africa. While *Efuru* (1966) attacks polygamy, the bride price, and female genital mutilation, *One is Enough* (1981) is about the protagonist Amaka choosing a life of happiness over a life of desertion and dejection. After being consistently subjected to oppression by her in-laws and husband over her barrenness, she decides to leave him. Having later a relation with another man, she declines his marriage offer, "I don't want to be a wife … A mistress, yes, but not a wife … As a wife, I am never free" (132). The novel is, thus, an attack on the institution of marriage and a celebration of independent life. *Edu* (1970), *Never Again* (1975), and the posthumously published *The Lake Goddess* (1995) are other significant fictional works of the writer.

Buchi Emecheta is another female writer from Nigeria whose fictional and non-fictional works do not only question regressive customs but also create a distinct identity of women. Writing stories based on her life for *The Statesman*, the same were woven later in the novel *In the Ditch* (1972). *The Second Class Citizen*, *The Bride Price* (1976),

The Slave Girl (1977), *The Joys of Motherhood* (1979), *Destination Biafra* (1982), and *Double Yoke* (1982) are other key fictional works of Emecheta which deal with women's varied concerns like bride price as a new form of slavery, mothers ending up being alone and joyless even after delivering many children, gender and race oppression, treatment as second class citizens in England and as wives at home, and finally the emergence of new women characters. Simone Gikandi calls Buchi Emecheta as one of "Africa's rebellious women writers" (240) for her strong feminist stance in her works, challenging the male-hegemonic discourse.

South African-born and Botswana settled writer Bessie Head weaves her bitter memories during the Apartheid legislation in her novels, especially *Maru* (1971). By casting a Masarwa woman called Margaret as the protagonist of the novel, Bessie Head critiques race and gender prejudices. Moreover, by making an African chief Maru marry Margaret, she questions the social inequalities as getting social approval from the village fold remains a distant dream for them. Head's novels *Maru, When Rain Clouds Gather* (1968) and *A Question of Power* (1973) are set in *Serowe,* the largest village of Botswana where she settled permanently after suffering mixed race-prejudices in South Africa throughout her childhood and post-marriage phase. *A Question of Power* dwells on what drives women mad. Largely autobiographical, the novel discusses the protagonist Elizabeth's school experiences; and the teacher's insensitive revelation about her mother's identity, "Your mother was insane. If you are not careful, you'll get insane just like your mother" (16) shatters her to the core. It is such incidents in the novel and the real life of Head which drive her insane amidst such alienating environment. *The Collector of Treasures and Other Botswana Village Tales* is a short-story collection by Head which was published in 1977.

Ghanian author Ama Ata Aidoo is another major force to reckon with in African literature. *Our Sister Killjoy: or Reflections from a Black-eyed Squint* (1977) is her most acclaimed novel. *Changes: a Love Story* (1991) is another significant work that traces the issues of polygamous marriages. Apart from this, she also wrote a play, poetry and two major short-story collections titled *No Sweetness Here: A Collection of Short Stories* (1970) and *The Girl Who Can and Other Stories* (1997). Various facets of her writing have been beautifully described by Natalia Saldarriaga in the following words:

> Aidoo's writing reflects various central aspects of Africa's social and economic history – the heritage of slavery, the consequences of oppressive political regimes, as well as brutal gender and racial conflicts. Above all, Aidoo's work is representative of her own life and her struggle to find her identity as a free, independent woman within Africa's rather patriarchal society. (Saldarriaga n.pag.)

Chimamanda Ngozi Adichie is another powerful voice in African literature in the present who does not only attack the adverse effects of colonialism on Africa in general and Nigeria in particular but also lashes hard on stereotypes against women in her culture. "We Should All Be Feminists" is her long essay that lambasts against gender discrimination in Africa. Accepting tip only from the males, forbidding women entering hotels alone, barring them from becoming class monitors even after scoring the best grades, going out with boys as a mark of sexual promiscuity or depravity are a few such stereotypes against women which are attacked by the novelist in this work. *Purple Hibiscus* (2003), *Half of a Yellow Sun* (2006), *Americanah* (2013) dwell on colonial Christian religion as a disruptive force, race and racism as a never ending reality, a pride in national identity in the light of Biafran identity, and female subjugation as the oldest forms of injustice to silence women. She does not consider marriage to be an achievement for women but education as can be seen in her work *Dear Ijeawele, or A Feminist Manifesto in Fifteen Suggestions* (2017). Her recently published short story "Zikora" (2020) is again a strong statement on women's commodification as sexual objects. Zikora, the protagonist, recalls her mother and cousin's painful married life in Nigeria and how now she herself gives birth to a baby when deserted by her lover. This literary piece lays bare "many injustices women – especially black women – still face, often at the hands of a black patriarchy" (Law n.pag.).

These women writers and many others have contributed immensely to African literature through multiple literary representations. The issues of colonialism, neo-colonialism, race, culture, and identity find ample representation in relation to gender. These literary endeavours unearth varied socio-cultural layers of oppression of women and thus attempt to stitch together the identities which have been ruptured due to the said subjugation.

II

This anthology brings forth fifteen research articles on various African writers examining diverse issues that African women grapple with in their society. Neha Arora in her paper "Erasure and Re-writing: Reading Female Identity in Adichie's *Purple Hibiscus*" critiques neo-colonialism and simultaneously questions oppressive African traditions. Through the central characters of Ifeoma, Adichie shows the importance of education to women for their empowerment. Bipasha Som Gune in "Re-Imagining the Masculine: A Reading of Bessie Head's 'The Collector of Treasures'" traces the feminist theories of Luce Irigaray, and the power discourse of Foucault to show how patriarchal constructs normalise power relations. She critiques the patriarchal utilitarian philosophy where women are traded/exchanged as commodities by men.

The institutionalisation of religion and the forced conversion of people into accepting one or another religion and its detrimental effect on women is the thrust in Shweta Tiwari's article "Religion and Gender Dynamics: A Study of Chimamanda Ngozi Adichie's *Purple Hibiscus*." Contrasting African unwritten religion with the Western religions, she analyses how Christianity dealt a blow to traditional African spirituality. The religious conflict is presented through the characters of Papa Nnukwu, Eugene and Ifeoma and how Ifeoma's university job empowers her through liberating ideas. Shikha Thakur in her analysis of Chimamanda Ngozi Adichie's short story "A Private Experience" brings out the intense moments of religious turmoil of a Christian Igbo and Muslim Hausa woman. She shows how while protecting themselves from ethnic riots outside, these women connect on the basis of race, region and gender. The author describes how the situational identity lends fluidity to otherwise fixed/singular identities of these two women as sister and mother.

Deepshikha Sharma in her paper "'The Look' in El-Sadaawi's *Woman at Point Zero*" draws a bleak picture of Islamic patriarchy through the central character Firdaus who is battered by her sixty-year-old husband, and all other men who come in her life, finding outlet in her murder of a pimp who tries to pin her down. Firdaus does not only expose her father who would ill-treat her mother but also the corrupt Imam and her husband who make her reach a state of near neurosis. As an interesting read on gaze in relation to women, the paper draws on and simultaneously contests Sartre's existentialism. Evil and ugly elements of Igbo culture are interrogated by Vinod K. Chopra in his article "Igbo Culture as a Tool of Women's Repression and Mortification: A Critical Study of Buchi Emecheta's *The Bride Price*." Widows forced to wear only "old smoked rags", widows being inherited by husband's brother, forced marriage of sisters to pay for the education of brothers with the bride price so earned, and the eventual fear spread through the death of Aku-nna for eloping without paying the bride money are a few regressive traditions among others which are exposed by the author. Roshan Lal Sharma and Prakash Kumar Meher have analysed Beryl Subia Awuor's debut poetry collection, *Black Moon* from the viewpoint of issues concerning female identity, its denial and politics involved therein.

Pallavi Mishra studies the African female poets in her article "The Reconstruction of Myth, Memory, History and the Element of Resistant Aesthetics in the Postcolonial Women Poets of Africa," to discuss their rich legacy and contribution to African literature. She shows how memory serves as a strong tool in reclaiming the lost culture and interrogating the past abuse. History, as retained in the memories of the people, is infused with symbolic power as they become the symbolic projections of hope, values, fears and aspirations of people. Subhash Verma's analysis of *David's Story* reveals the plight of Black South African women during (post)Apartheid era and explores the theme of oppression in all its ramifications. As a blend of history and fiction, the novel delineates the world of liberation movements, a world filled with betrayal and danger, and also highlights the fact that stereotypical representations of women lead to violence on their bodies and any attempt at an accurate representation, paradoxically, will lead to violence as well, especially to violence through language. The novel illustrates how impossible it is to represent trauma and violence through language and thus confirms the post-structuralist realisation that language always fails.

Archana Thakur and Hem Raj Bansal in their paper "Reading Buchi Emecheta: Invalidating the Myth of 'Complete Woman' in *The Joys of Motherhood*" look at the idealised/glorified patriarchal institution of motherhood in a critical way. Despite bringing up her children with too much affection, Nnu-Ego's desertion by her children and death exposes that a woman still remains incomplete and vulnerable even after becoming a mother. "Representation of Women Suffering under Regressive Traditions in African Literature: A Reading of Buchi Emecheta's *The Bride Price*" is another article by Priti Paul Verma and Roshan Sharma that exposes the ugly face of African traditions. It is an incisive critique of African society whose age old traditions are not in sync with the modern democratic societies and cause immense agony to women. Kanupriya and Sheelpa Sweety also analyse Buchi Emecheta's novel *The Bride Price* to contest how some orthodox inhuman customs in Nigerian society prevent women from exercising choice and enjoying autonomy in their article "Autonomy and Agency of Women in Buchi Emecheta's *The Bride Price*." Khem Raj Sharma in his paper titled "Violent Times, Vexed Lives: Surfacing of the Innate African 'Female' in Jennifer Nansubuga Makumbi's *The First Woman*" dwells on the attainment of the noble 'female' self by relying on Elaine Showalter's proposition concerning it. It examines Kirabo's dismissal of the 'mwenkanonkano', a la, Feminism in the narrative. Further, it sees how the protagonist's quest for finding her biological mother and understanding the myths of motherhood makes her identify that she is not 'squeezed inside.'

Varnika and Hem Raj Bansal in "Education as Empowerment: Exposing the Real Infertility in Lola Shoneyin's *The Secret Lives of Baba Segi's Wives*" expose how three wives hide their husband's impotency in order to save their marriage and have children with sexual relation with other men. However, the fourth university educated wife shatters this whole edifice of lies and exposes her husband's infertility by subjecting him to medical examination. Prajya Mishra and Roshan Sharma in their article "Ruptures, Wounds and Convalescence: Analysing Complex Contours of Slavery in Yaa Gyasi's *Homegoing*" interrogate slavery as a disruptive force. As a powerful tale of Mamme and her two daughters Effia Otcher and Esi Asare, the novel delves deeper into the effects of slavery on these three women who remain dispersed in different places and undergo a life of drudgery.

Works Cited

Achebe, Chinua. *Things Fall Apart.* Penguin UK, 2001.

Aidoo, Ama Ata. "To Be an African Woman Writer." *African Literature: An Anthology of Criticism and Theory*, edited by Tejumola Olaniyan, and Ato Quayson, Blackwell Publishing, 2007, pp. 513-520.

Arndt, Susan. "Perspectives on African Feminism: Defining and Classifying African-Feminist Literatures." *Agenda: Empowering Women for Gender Equity*, no. 44, 2002, pp. 31-44.

Bazin, Nancy Topping. "Feminism in the Literature of African Women." *The Black Scholar*, vol. 20, no. 3-4, 1989, pp. 8-17, *JSTOR*.

Beauvoir, Simone de. *The Second Sex*, edited and translated by H. M. Parshley, Jonathan Cape, 1953.

Bell, Roseann P. "The Absence of the African Woman Writer." *CLA Journal,* vol. 21, no. 4, pp. 491-498. *JSTOR*,

https://www.jstor.org/stable/44329402?seq=1#metadata_info_tab_contents

Brooks, Thom. "The Problem with Polygamy." *Philosophical Topics*, vol. 37, no. 2, 2009, pp.109-122.

Conde, Maryse. "Three Female Writers in Modern Africa: Flora Nwapa, Ama Ata Aidoo and Grace Ogot." *Presence Africane*, no. 82, 1972, pp. 132-43. *JSTOR.*

Douglas, Carol Anne. "Gender Violence in Africa: African Women's Response." *Off-Our Backs*, vol. 30, no. 9, 2000, pp.9 &19. *JSTOR.*

Elbedour, Salman. "Effect of Polygamous Marital Structure on Behavioral, Emotional, and Academic Adjustment in Children: A Comprehensive Review of the Literature." *Clinical Child and Family Psychology Review,* 2002, pp. 255-71.

Elechi, Amadi. *The Concubine.* Heinemann International Literature & Textbooks, 1966.

Emecheta, Buchi. *The Bride Price.* George Braziller, 1976.

---. *The Joys of Motherhood.* Heinemann, 1979.

Flora, Nwapa. *Efuru.* Heinemann, 1966.

Gikandi, Simon, ed. *Encyclopaedia of African Literature.* Routledge, 2003.

Head, Bessie. *A Question of Power.* Davis Poynter Ltd.,1974.

Kolawole, Mary E. Modupe. "Women's Oral Genre." *African Literature: An Anthology of Criticism and Theory*, edited by Tejumola Olaniyan and Ato Quayson, Blackwell, 2007, pp. 92-97.

Lauretta, Ngcobo. "African Motherhood – Myth and Reality." *African Literature: An Anthology of Criticism and Theory*, edited by Tejumola Olaniyan and Ato Quayson, Blackwell, 2007. pp. 533-541.

Law, Katie. "'Zikora: A Short Story' by Chimamanda Ngozi Adichie Review: A Taut Tale of Sexism and Single motherhood." *Evening Standard.* 30 Oct. 2020, Accessed on 22 June 2021.

Saldarriaga, Natalia. "Ama Ata Aidoo." *WOWOIRE,* 30 April 2011. Accessed on 28 Sept. 2021.

CHAPTER 1

Erasure and Re-writing: Reading Female Identity in Adichie's *Purple Hibiscus*

Neha Arora

Socio-Cultural Setup of Nigeria: Political Background

The military rule in Nigeria has greatly impacted the economy of the nation and has also "fractured (the nation) along religious and cultural lines" (Obeke and Chukwuka 98). Almost 30 years of military regime has paralysed the development, and has scarred the nation with violence, riots, coups, call for democracy etc. It has created an environment where "opposition and diverse opinions are muzzled, favouritism replaces meritocracy, and the public good is subordinated to the selfish interests of the ruling military junta" (102). Even after the nation gained independence in 1960, the word 'democracy' rings aloud in the political (as also in literary) culture of Nigeria.

Native Culture vs Colonial Baggage

Post-independence, we witness a shift in the Nigerian culture – from the traditional African to the Western culture. The new elite class, armed with the weapons of colonial culture, began the movement to subjugate the native masses, to prove its allegiance to the European masters. The indigenous practices – social, cultural, political – suffered much with the imposition of cultural imperialism and widened the cultural gap between the generations. The Western ideology became the normative way of life for the new generation of Nigerians.

The Politics of Gender

Amid the frequent ethno-political conflicts and the simultaneous struggle with the colonial forces, certain other significant concerns go unnoticed. This paper engages with the lens of African Feminism to bring forth the patriarchal set-up of Nigerian society. The argument is based on the reading of African Feminist literature in general, and on examining the corpus of Adichie in particular. The primary text taken is her debut novel *Purple Hibiscus* that blends the political and the woman issue perfectly well. To emphatically highlight Adichie's concern for her women, a brief trajectory is drawn, of gender politics in Africa, and also of the rise of new band of women writers who have emerged as the champions of female cause.

Rule of Patriarchy

The Nigerian society practices traditions that favour their males. For instance, preference for a boy-child, rearing him to be the representative of family/community, granting men the license for spouse-beating, and polygamy etc. are certain rituals to permit the subjugation of women. On the other hand, woman has to be the epitome of values, a dutiful daughter and a loyal wife and an affectionate mother who would be responsible for instilling cultural values in her children; marriage is an indispensable part of a woman's life as only the husband can accord respect/dignity/acceptability to her, and therefore, there is no place for a divorcee (woman) in the Nigerian society. And unfortunately if the husband dies, his widow is put through other ordeals, such as the traditional mourning ritual and even dispossessing the bereaved family of inheritance. Interestingly, besides all these qualities for being the 'good woman', the society also expects women to bear many children to her husband, else the man is permitted to take another woman to carry on his clan.

"But You Are a Woman. You Do not Count."

The words by Papa Nnukwu to his daughter, Ifeoma in *Purple Hibiscus* clearly bring home the message of the exclusion of women in the African world. Adichie and other women writers grieve upon the colonial practice of 'othering' reflected in the patriarchal set up of the native culture. It is a system that approves of controlling and subjugating women as the accepted norm. Only a man (read, 'husband') could provide anchorage and dignity to a woman, that 'a husband crowns a woman's life' are the indoctrination a woman is subjected to since her birth, hence marriage is suggested as the obligatory act for women. African Womanism questions such cultural practices that make women just a plaything for men, to adorn his home. Also, it endeavours to create a positive agitation in their minds to transform their beings.

The Practice of Phallagocentrism

The proposed study aims at taking the attention towards the body of African literature, which was predominantly phallocentric. The writers (male) were so preoccupied with the political issues that they failed to give due space to women characters; the issues of women got overshadowed by the socio-political concerns. The exclusion of women concerns and also of women writers presented an incomplete picture of African literature. Also, the native culture could not be condoned for acting accomplice in creating and propagating the patriarchal structure of the society. Udumukwu writes:

> The latter part of the twentieth century witnessed the growth of an enormous volume of literature written by women and for women. This literature has underscored the view that the images of women usually found in literature have been created by men without any true reference to the peculiarity of women's experiences. In African literature, for instance, men have mostly written of women in their own context as sexual objects, as mothers of children as daughters and as mistresses and goddesses. These female stereotypes turn out to conform with the traditional patriarchal view of the woman as inferior to man. (5)

In the present paper we shall discuss certain practices of the Igbo culture that make women subservient to men. Such rituals are scathingly criticised by the women writers who have developed their own definition of 'Feminism' and are using the tool of their Womanism to create strong women characters.

African Womanism – A New Dawn

> African feminism... recognises a common struggle with African men for the removal of the yokes of foreign domination and European/American exploitation. It is not antagonistic to African men but challenges them to be aware of certain salient aspects of women's subjugation which differ from the generalised oppression of all African peoples... [It] recognises that certain inequities and limitations existed/exist in traditional societies and that colonialism reinforced them and introduced others... It acknowledges its affinities with international feminism, but delineates a specific African feminism with certain specific needs and goals arising out of the concrete realities of women's lives in African societies... [It] examines African societies for institutions which are of value to women

> and rejects those which work to their detriment and does not simply import Western women's agendas. Thus, it respects African woman's status as mother but questions obligatory motherhood and the traditional favoring of sons... It respects African woman's self-reliance and the penchant to cooperative work and social organisation... [It] understands the interconnectedness of race, class, and sex oppression. (Davies 8-10)

The distinct Womanism of Africa has overhauled the literary landscape of the continent. Earlier the writers were primarily engaged with the pre-colonial and colonial past of the land; their chief agenda was to invoke the readers to retaliate against the European powers and to re-instate the indigenous culture. However, the skyline of earlier African literature missed out on the women cause and now with African Womanism, the firmament of Africa can be seen proudly shining brightly with women writers as stars. While the crusade against colonisation continues in their works too, they are also writing powerfully on women-centric issues. Ogunyemi defines the holistic nature of Womanism as

> ... black centered, it is accommodationist. It believes in the freedom and independence of women like feminism; unlike radical feminism, it wants meaningful union between black women and black men and black children and will see to it that men begin to change from their sexiest stand. (65)

Rational, not Radical Writers

> Many of the writers have confessed that they are motivated to write by the impulse to change the status quo, interrogate patriarchy, imperialism and Western Feminism. This is closely related to the desire to liberate African women, change their consciousness and create a positive self-perception to enhance progress. (Kolawole 153)

Talking about the band of new writers (women), I would draw on the concept of Nego-Feminism (no-ego feminism) given by Obioma Nnaemeka to elucidate the nature of African Feminism. It is more mature and in sync with the demands/nature of the native culture, believing more in the co-existence, participation and negotiation of both the sexes. The writers do not resort to acidulour vocabulary against men. At the same time, we should in no way ignore Africa's status of being a Third World. The politics of appropriation in the postcolonial protest does not give space to its women to speak differently from their male counterparts. Also, the 'otherness' practiced by cultural imperialism and Western feminism as well, excludes the issues of Third World women completely, (something brought forth by theorists like Spivak and Chandra Talpade Mohanty) thus emanating the necessity of having a distinct 'feminism' of the Third World, to answer back to the Eurocentric feminism. As in India, we have a separate Dalit Feminism, likewise, in Africa, the female critics/writers are challenging the patriarchal institutions and are promoting individuality over stereotyped image. To cite Filomina Chioma Steady, a distinct African Feminism is needed as for African women, gender oppression is always, "fused with liberation from other forms of oppression, namely slavery, colonialism, neo-colonialism, racism, poverty, illiteracy and disease" (34). So to say that Feminism is 'unAfrican' would be a fallacy, in fact the African women have moulded the concept to suit their cultural environment. Whether it be Acholonu's 'Motherism' or Molara Ogundipe-Leslie's STIWANISM (Social Transformation Including Women in Africa), it is very much clear that the African women writers are not just ripping Nigerian patriarchy apart, but are critiquing Western feminism as well. The rationality that they display in their approach of keeping their 'Africanism' intact is commendable, to use Kolawale's words, "any African woman who has the consciousness to situate the struggle within African cultural realities by working for a total and robust self-retrieval of the African Woman is an African Womanist" (34).

A Counter to Sexual/Textual Politics

> Women writers write about women because when we wake up in the morning and look in the mirror we see women. (Aidoo 163)

The traditional African society practices 'systematic subjugation of women' and the hegemony of the male permeates into literature too. It is worth noticing that the entire corpus of African literature is predominantly male-centric, so much so that the women are conditioned into accepting the male point of view on life and they hardly ever questioned this set up. The contemporary women writings interrogate the power structure of the highly patriarchal society by which the males earn the licence to marginalise women. They question the patriarchal practice of colonial discourse of 'othering.' Doing away with the erstwhile objectification of women of androtexts, the women writers are adamant to reverse the equation (in fact, to dismantle the vertical hierarchy between the two sexes).

The 'Happy Feminist' Adichie: The Voice of African Women

> When people ask me rather bluntly every now and then whether I am a feminist, I not only answer yes, but I go on to insist that every woman and every man should be a feminist – especially if they believe that Africans should take charge of African land, African wealth, African lives and the burden of African development. It is not possible to advocate independence for the African continent without also believing that African women must have the best that the environment can offer. For some of us, this is the crucial element in our feminism. (Aidoo qtd. in Nnaemeka 47)

This is how Ama Ata Aidoo summarises her idea of African feminism, while delivering her Keynote Address, "The African Woman Today." And Adichie imbibes this very idea of Africa's true liberation and develops her idea of 'Happy Feminist.'

Born on 15 September 1977, Chimamanda Ngozi Adichie is one of the prominent female writers of Nigeria. In her writings she paints a realistic picture of contemporary Nigeria, struggling with neo-colonialism, civil war, corruption etc, besides raising the issues of Nigerians in diaspora, at the same time, she is very honest about portraying the condition of women in her society. No doubt, all her works have the structural framework of the political atmosphere of Nigeria, yet her discussions do not escape the gender issues.

Her oeuvre comprises of novels like *Purple Hibiscus* (2003), *Half of a Yellow Sun* (2006), *Americanah* (2013) and also a collection of short stories, *The Thing around Your Neck* (2009). Among the many awards that she has won, some are: the Orange Broadband Prize for fiction for her second novel *Half of a Yellow Sun* (2006), the 2005 Commonwealth Writers Prize for *Purple Hibiscus*, the winner of 2008 MacArthur Foundation Fellowship.

Critiquing Neo-colonialism and Patriarchy

As said earlier, the emergence of the neo-elites is read as a blow to indigenous habits. In the blind race of imitating the West, the country is trapped in another phase of colonialism. In *Purple Hibiscus*, Papa is so critical of his native traditions that he disowns his own father unless the latter converts into Christianity; he even imposes his fanatic ideology on his wife and children. Not just this, he abstains from using Igbo language with his people or follow the local customs. Father Benedict is the White missionary who had come with the 'white man's burden' of civilising the savage. He uses his 'religion' to expand the imperialist intentions.

As a contemporary writer, it is impossible for Adichie to completely do away with the socio-political atmosphere of her country, but the dexterity she exhibits in blending the two issues is laudable. She exposes and critiques the misdoings of neo-colonialism, at the same time, she is equally unhesitant to question her native culture too that practices and promotes such biased customs. In her entire oeuvre, she tries to interrogate the social structure of Nigeria that leads to the subjugation of women. In her seminal work, "We Should All Be Feminists", she says:

> These Nigerians have been raised to think of women as inherently guilty. And they have been raised to expect so little of men that the idea of men as savage beings with no self-control is somehow acceptable. (13)

Questioning the Oppressive Structures

Recalling her own experiences, Adichie produces ample evidences of the oppressive patriarchy stifling women. Whether it being the class monitor or an employee, the society very casually 'assumes' man to be in the charge, because, to quote her, "The sad truth of the matter is that when it comes to appearance, we start off with men as the standard, as the norm" (14). Her "We Should All Be Feminists" is replete with a very unabashed portrayal of the pro-male Nigerian society. She is pained to tell the world that her society does not permit a woman to enjoy the pettiest thing, like the pleasure of going to a hotel alone (as it labels her a sex worker); a woman does not deserve respect if she is in a senior designation in job; a girl is trained right from the beginning to please men. Adichie strongly recommends a mental overhaul of her people to see the two sexes as complementary.

Celebrating African Women

African women writers are feminist, but their works are more inclusive in nature. Their women are not confined to the household chores, rather, are equal participants at the national and social front. Adichie empowers her women to combat oppression of all kinds. She is not a radical feminist, i.e., she is not anti-male; for her man and woman are complementary entities for a just society. She celebrates African women, the 'real' African women, thus deconstructing the prevalent 'Mother Africa trope' of the African androtext. Her women come out of the Madonna/Whore binary practiced in society and imposed through literature.

No Misandry/ Re-defining Feminism

Adichie fashions a new definition of 'feminism', bringing it out from the narrow and negative notions of 'unhappy woman who cannot find a husband' or the one who hates men or the one who does not wear make-up or who does not have a sense of humour and is always angry. ("We Should All Be Feminists"). She agrees with bell hooks that "we are socialised from birth to accept sexist thought and action" (viii) and seeing the stratified society we all are living in, she cannot but create a new self for women, rational women, who, instead of living on the extremes (of either being submissive or dominant), opt to co-work with men for a better future. Her call is for an inclusive society.

Chiselling New Woman

Adichie is the ardent believer of assertive and bold women, for this, she emphatically advocates 'Education for Women.' Her women draw strength from education, long denied to them by patriarchy. She sees education as a liberating tool to empower women, intellectually as well as financially. After her husband's demise, Aunt Ifeoma (in *Purple Hibiscus*) could take the charge of her children, and even her father, due to her professional background. She neither does re-marry nor does she go back to her brother Eugene/father or to her in-laws. On the contrary, she herself champions the cause of women education and is disheartened to see how patriarchy is institutionalising marriage as a necessity for girls. Quite a number of her female students drop their studies and opt for settling down with a man as marriage promises security. In marriage, she says, "the husbands own them and their degrees" (*Purple Hibiscus* 36). In fact, many a times we see her counselling Beatrice (Mama) to walk out of the abusive marriage and the illusionary life. This 'ownership' of woman in marriage is strongly denounced by Adichie. As a mother, Ifeoma dons the role perfectly well in carving out independent and liberated children; as an academician she is vocal against the wrongs happening in the university and in the country; as a dutiful daughter, she takes charge of her father till his last breath; and as a life-giver, she gives new hope to Beatrice and her children. She is Adichie's defiant voice, or as Moyana describes her, "Women who refuse to be compartmentalised into the chiseled up roles" (30). In Ifeoma, Adichie chisels a new woman who would be her representative for the entire women community.

Purple Hibiscus

Published in October 2003, *Purple Hibiscus* won the Huston/Wright Legacy Award in 2004 and was short-listed for the Orange Broadband Prize for Fiction. It was also awarded the Commonwealth Prize for the Best First Fiction Book 2005. 'Intolerance' is one word that describes the entire novel, and we see it working at various levels – political, social, religious and family/domestic. The setting is Adichie's hometown, Enugu, and she authentically replicates its socio-political-cultural environment. Adichie has an art of running the political and the personal threads together to weave the fabric of Nigeria; in *Purple Hibiscus* the unrest of the country does get foregrounded (in Papa's controversial newspaper, *The Standard*, in the cold blooded murder of Ade Coker, in the students riots and continuous strikes of Nsukka University etc), but the issue of domestic violence too emerges significant. In Kehinde's words,

> Adichie makes a call for an all-inclusive public sphere in Nigeria society. The novel is a political satire that makes a call for change in a nation that is stunted due to failed promise of the public sphere... Eugene is intolerable and disallows his family members from the public sphere of his household. (43)

The novel provides valuable insights to understand how patriarchy operates at the family level, and how it has been made 'acceptable' by the native cultural practices. Adichie approaches the women question using Home as a symbol. Her protagonist, Kambili is a thirteen-year-old girl of a rich father (Eugene), whose philanthropic and generous acts have even been rewarded by the *Amnesty World* but whose brute patriarchal dominating self is unknown to the world. Kambili narrates the existence of herself, her mother Beatrice (Mama) and her brother Jaja enveloped in the loud silences created by Papa. This silence develops a crack by the children's visit to their Aunt and finally the crack opens wide in the death of Papa. In the conclusion of the novel, Adichie highlights the psychological denouement of the three, celebrating the birth of a new freedom.

Home: A Microcosm of Nation

By intertwining the political and the personal, Adichie complicates the narrative in the novel. The home emerges as a microcosm of the nation where the members are grappling for freedom. When the entire country was struggling with the military brutalities and oppression of the masses, Eugene (Papa) comes out as the dictator, stifling the voices of the family. The impending fear of being targeted and victimised that had become the norm of the land could well be felt within the four walls of the house. Moreover, the acquiescence of the victims makes it easier for the oppressive forces to operate. Mama (Beatrice) silently endures the harassment, Kambili and Jaja forget the language of words, Eugene, the autocrat deprives his family of any decision-making power. The everlasting silence or the measured talks, the regimented life (for example, the schedule made for the children by Papa) indicate the prison-like existence. Interestingly, the occupying and division of the space is also very neatly done as per the patriarchal norms – domestic space for Mama and the public domain for Papa. But looking deep inside, it would be clear that even domestic world is not exclusive to them as Papa intervenes, dictates and controls it completely. Papa's inhuman behaviour developes bitterness in Beatrice, resistance in Jaja and isolative inclinations in Kambili. Like the dictating political system, the family structure too believes in gagging the weak, and any kind of dissent is punished severely by Papa. The claustrophobic environment of the nation gets resonated in their home where the suppressed masses lack the nerve to resist the unchallenged centrality of the powerful.

The juxtaposition of Enugu and Nsukka is purposeful. Adichie makes the readers re-think the definition of home, beyond the physical structure of concrete walls. The warmth of relations in Nskukka is in sharp contrast to the pervading coldness of Enugu, where despite all luxuries, the humane element is missing. The wild garden of Aunt Ifeoma with assorted flowers, 'roses and hibiscuses and lilies and ixora and croton grew side by side like a handpainted wreath' (53-54) exudes more happiness than the shiny marble of Papa's world. While 'Home' is equivalent to confinement, Nsukka offers them freedom. Their home, with "yard enough to hold a hundred of people...The compound walls, topped by coiled electric wires, were so high" (8) to curtail any kind of connection with the outside world.

Violence: A Tool of Corrective Measure

Violence does not always come in the form of physical torture in the novel, in fact, mental persecution is often used by Papa to supplement the agony of Mama, Jaja and Kambili; he adopts all methods to 'correct' his family. Eugene, the 'unchristian Christian' is guilty of not only accruing violence on his immediate family, but is also culpable of murdering his unborn children (violating Beatrice in her pregnancies and causing miscarriages). Kambili recalls one of the miscarriages, neatly 'executed' by Papa. Incapable of walking upto Father Benedict's house, the pregnant Mama tries to excuse herself, unknowing the severe repercussions she would have to face later in the day. "Let me stay in the car and wait, *biko*," Mama said, "I feel vomit in my throat." Papa turned to stare at her... "Are you sure you want to stay in the car?" Papa asked. Mama was looking down... "I asked if you were sure you want to stay in the car." Mama Looked up. "I'll come with you. It's really not that bad" (17-18). Hardly did she know that once home, the 'swift, heavy thuds' on their hand-carved bedroom door and the blood trails on the floor would mark the end of their unborn child.

Another such brutality we read towards the end of the novel when the pathetic Beatrice comes to Ifeoma's home, losing yet another child.

> Mama was climbing out of a yellow unsteady-looking taxi. What was she doing here? What had happened? Why was she wearing her rubber slippers all the way from Enugu? She walked slowly, holding on to her wrapper that seemed so loose it would slip off her waist any minute. Her blouse did not look ironed. Mama sat carefully at the edge of a cane chair. Her eyes were glazed over as she looked around.
>
> "You know that small table where we keep the family Bible, *nne*? Your father broke it on my belly."
>
> She cried for a long time. She cried until my hand, clasped in hers, felt stiff. She cried until Aunty Ifeoma finished cooking the rotting meat in a spicy stew. She cried until she fell asleep, her head against the seat of the chair. (111-112)

In fact, all through the novel, she appears either limping or scarred, black and blue swollen eyes, bleeding etc. The terror of angering Eugene and also the fear of society if she is abandoned by her husband overpowers her rationality to think for herself and for the children. The effect of mental/physical sadism affects them psychologically. Instead of speaking properly, with confidence,

Kambili is left with stutters, muttering, mumbling, frozen words etc. The fear is omnipresent, as she recalls, "Fear. I was familiar with fear, yet each time I felt it, it was never the same as the other times, as though it came in different flavours and colors" (91). Interestingly the word 'fear' itself occurs in almost fifteen pages of the novel, besides the implied and subtle existence and its companion 'silence' recurs on almost twent-two pages.

Kambili and Jaja too are not forgiven for any slightest deviation from the set rules. They are beaten badly by belt when she dares to eat corn flakes before the Mass to avoid her period cramps. Again, upon their return from Nsukka, when Papa discovers their grandfather painting with them, he just could not control his wrath:

> He started to kick me. The metal buckles on his slippers stung like bites from giant mosquitoes. He talked nonstop, out of control, in a mix of Igbo and English, like soft meat and thorny bones... The kicking increased in tempo... I curled around myself tighter, around the pieces of the painting... The stinging was raw now, even more like bites, because the metal landed in open skin on my side, my back, my legs. Kicking. Kicking. Kicking. Perhaps it was a belt now because the metal buckle seemed too heavy. Because I could hear a swoosh in the air... More stings. More slaps. (96)

When he was merely ten, Jaja suffered one of the most inhuman punishments by his father. His little finger was chopped off by the brute father only because "he had missed two questions on his catechism test and was not named the best in his First Holy Communion"' (68). Kambili vividly recalls how the maniac Papa "took him upstairs and locked the door. Jaja, in tears, came out supporting his left hand with his right, and Papa drove him to St. Agnes hospital" (68). Papa would devise newer methods to penalise them. On their visit to Nsukka, they stay in the same house with their 'pagan' grandfather as the latter was not keeping well and Aunt Ifeoma brought him to take care of him. For this, 'unintentional sin', both the brother and sister are made to stand in the bath tub, with hot water scalding their feet. In the perfect world of Papa, there is no place for deviation. The daily schedule that he pins at the study desk of Jaja and Kambili registers another example of the psychological trauma. He does not forgive Kambili for having secured second position in her class and tortures her mentally.

Violence becomes an accepted norm in the house, so much so that none of the three ever question or blame Eugene. Silence and violence are the two extremes on which their world rests. There is no place for NO in this set up. Eugene's authoritative behaviour controlls and monitors their lives; when and what to study, when to pray, whom to meet, what to say, etc, all is regimented. They are not allowed to stay back with class mates after the school hours, and are barred from meeting their grandfather beyond the allotted time, in brief, all and every kind of socialisation is prohibited. This violence, though not visible overtly, does much damage to their psyche and stunts their growth– the rationality.

The novel identifies religion and domestic violence as the two structures devised (and appropriated) by patriarchy to oppress women. The instances such as Beatrice sharing her fears with Ifeoma about losing Eugene if she does not bear more children; the reference to preferring the male child in taking the family name further; polygamy; the definition of a happy married life; the significance of marriage in the lives of women, etc. corroborate the biased society to marginalise women. And all such practices get the sanction of religion – native or colonial. The novel is replete with examples of Eugene's religious fundamentalism with which he controls his family. To Hewett, his personality is that of "a strict catholic who lives within the Manichean dictates of unforgiving faith." Among many of his fanatic fits, the one that hammers the final nail in the coffin is throwing of the missal to hit Jaja when the latter adamantly refuses to join the family for the Mass. The manner, the purpose and the intensity with which it is hurled, Ogaga Okunyade compares it to a missile, that loses its sanctity by the very use it is put to.

Silence: A Metaphor for Incapacitation

> There is a sharp contrast between the real woman in postcolonial Africa. Far from being the source of comfort and rest (the sweet mother as she is perceived in popular imagination), the "good" woman in sub-Saharan Africa happens to be the one who suffers the effects of oppression, and neglect; and who must maintain a silence and passivity in order to remain good. Silence and passivity are two principal features of the good woman. In the media presentation of images from troubled regions of Africa, for instance, it is this "good" woman who bears the wicked children of war and disaster. Apart from being passive and silent in the face of radical change, she is also the embodiment of culture and tradition. The important issue, however, is that her passivity and docility have turned out to be potent fodder for her objectification by patriarchy. In other words, she is good because she naturally fits into the mould shaped for her by patriarchy (Udumukwu 3).

Beatrice stands for the ideal woman in Nigerian culture, who would fake contentment but would not dare to walk out of marriage. She endures all kind of ill treatment – from physical bashing to the emotional trauma of a series of miscarriages (because of being thrashed by Papa) yet her world revolvs around him. Her limp, swollen eyes, scars, bleeding, tears are in sharp contrast to the towering image of Papa. She is circumscribed by society and cannot think of her existence beyond her husband:

> Where would I go if I leave Eugene's house?... Do you know how many mothers pushed their daughters at him? Do you know how many asked him to impregnate them, even, and not to bother paying a bride price? (112)

Her silence does not only affect her, in fact, it becomes dangerous for the children too. She always acts as a mute spectator whenever Eugene bullies Jaja and Kambili; her allegiance to them is communicated only by her tears and in nursing the wounds. Despite everything, Mama stoically bears everything in her marriage lest her husband should take in another woman.

Silencing is another means to traumatise and *de-identitise* anyone. It is done in such an organised and systematic manner that after a time it becomes so powerful for one to hear silence speaking. D'Almeida writes, "Silence represents the historical muting of women under the formidable institution known as patriarchy, that form of social organisation in which males assume power and create for females an inferior status" (199). Uwakwe too has similar opinion: "Silence comprises all imposed restrictions on women's social being, thinking and expressions that are religiously or culturally sanctioned. As a patriarchal weapon of control, it is used by the dominant male structure on the subordinate or muted female structure" (n.pag.). And this silence percolates down to the children as well. It affects their psychology and personality to the extent of being labelled 'abnormal', 'backyard snob' etc.

Adichie reads Beatrice's repeated pregnancies as hope building in the family, to break through all the fetters, and conceive a new world, a better world, but every miscarriage (as a result of Papa's bullying her) thwarts their desire and brings back the perpetual and cyclical despair.

Nsukka: A Place for Deliverance

> I watched every movement she made; I could not tear my ears away. It was the fearlessness about her, about the way she gestured as she spoke, the way she smiled to show that wide gap. (37)

....

> That night, I dreamed that I was laughing, but it did not sound like my laughter, although I was not sure what my laughter sounded like. It was cackling and throaty and enthusiastic, like Aunty Ifeoma's. (42)

The 'fearlessness' in the world of 'fear', the sound of 'laughter' amidst silence – this is the consequence of Kambili's first interaction with their Aunt Ifeoma. And this brief meeting signals the metamorphosis that was to come in/through Nsukka. The children who were 'conditioned' to feel happy, now realise the existence of their repressed desires. Also, it is the beginning of replacing their ideal – Papa, who could never do any wrong, by Ifeoma, the fiery, outspoken one.

I argue that by presenting Nsukka as a contrasting image of home (Enugu), Adichie triggers the still waters in the mind of the children. The very first visit to Nsukka (and subsequent other trips) opens a new and democratic world to them. They learn to behave as human beings, in contrast to the robotic life they had been conditioned to by their father. Nsukka actually becomes as a place of deliverance for them that values the diverse opinions and gives space/acceptability to diversity – be it flowers or furniture or crockery or viewpoints – the 'mismatching' is the beauty of Ifeoma's home. The laughter and talks give a blow to the looming unending silence Jaja and Kambili were accustomed to. Their Aunt's home provides a vent to the subdued feelings – even Mama (Beatrice) is 'permitted' to cry herself out fully. Whereas the affluence of Papa's world subsumes their identity, stifles their voice, the poverty of Aunt Ifeoma's home gives them wings of rationality and freedom to soar high. Not just the contrast in the spatial terms, the two 'homes' bring forth contrasting characters too. The submissive, meek Beatrice is juxtaposed to the assertive, outspoken, independent Aunt Ifeoma; the stutter of Kambili stands in opposition to her cousin Amaka's uncontrolled questions; Jaja's reticence and Obiora's fiery thoughts are also dissimilar; and moving beyond family, we get to see the two different approaches to religion: Father Benedict and Father Amadi; while the former represents a fearful picture of the ever-monitoring and interfering religion, Amadi introduces the benevolent and all-accommodating version of God, of which Kambili and Jaja were completely oblivious. Each individual at Nsukka contributes in his/her capacity in the psychological evolution of Mama, Jaja and

Kambili. It is Nsukka that teaches them the existence and worth of diversity – colours, words and laughter.

In material context, they bring from Nsukka, an incomplete painting of their grandfather and a few twigs of purple hibiscus, but in truth, they come back armed with the knowledge of the language of defiance to invert the autonomy of Papa and thus to create a counter narrative.

Journey: A Motif for Resistance

> Sometimes life begins when marriage ends. (36)

The three, Mama, Jaja and Kambili herself, do not know how to respond to Papa's extremities, the journey to Nsukka helps them to confront reality. They learn the language of words, the significance of voice, the melody of laughter, the necessity of aspirations, the meaning of life. The motif of journey is exploited by Adichie to comment on the metamorphosis in the three, the unlearning of the old style of life and to tutor them into the alternate way of living. The caterpillar has to come out of its case to let the butterfly take birth. The physical journey of the three enables them to embark on a psychological expedition to find answers to their shackled existence.

Saying 'enough' to the brutalities of Eugene, Beatrice thinks the unthinkable – she plans and executes his murder by poisoning his tea. Although Jaja takes the blame on himself to prevent his mother going to prison, this extreme step of her speaks for itself how prolonged and agonising her married life had been. Not only this, a marvellous change is observed in her – the way she carries out herself and the house after Eugene's death and Jaja's imprisonment – she dares to deviate from the traditional rituals of mourning practices of *umunna* and seems quite confident. Okuyade writes, "She steps out of her enervating state, fractures the patriarchal social structure and demystifies the idealised traditional images of the African woman" (255).

Jaja, though in prison, takes a sigh of relief in not becoming like his father. In the beginning of the novel also, we see him much considerate, when he says that he will 'protect' his unborn sibling. The feeling of shielding gives away much about the harm done by Papa. Kambili, who has learnt to laugh and speak, in the company of Father Amadi and her aunt's family, takes over the role of financial supporter of the house and even could now plan for their future. A new approach to religion is introduced to them – far removed from the fundamentalism of Papa to a more accommodating Lord. Cynthia R. Wallace sees Ifeoma and Amadi as "surrogate parents" for the children as they both help them heal and evolve (474). The journey from Enugu to Nsukka becomes a journey from ignorance to knowledge. Ironically, the new place provides them with the comfort of 'knowing' themselves.

Things Fall Apart

> "Being defiant can be a good thing sometimes," Aunty Ifeoma said. "Defiance is like marijuana – it is not a bad thing when it is used right" (67).

Things fall apart only to create something new. The long denied and the much needed outlet was provided by the journey/s to Nsukka; it allows the three to discover the real self that had been eclipsed by the intimidating image of Papa. Jaja's refusal to join the family for communion is the first mark of resistance, followed by many. In fact, the timing of the narrative (on and around Palm Sunday) cannot be overlooked. In the Bible, Palm Sunday holds significance as it symbolises the victory of loyalty over betrayal, of good over evil. It marks the beginning of the Holy Week with which the period of Lent comes to an end. The entry of Jesus into Jerusalem before his arrest on Holy Thursday and crucifixion on Good Friday can be read in parallel to the family member's retaliation (i.e. indicating a closure to the mourning period and 'resurrection' of a rightful existence). Jaja's 'NO' registers the beginning of protest to encourage Kambili and Mama also to come out of the cocoon of fear and silence. The future which is withheld from them in the 'life of Papa's schedule' was waiting for them with open arms; though still they use fewer words and the silence is very much a part of their lives, this silence is sans fear. It is the dissolution of the dark clouds with the shower of optimism.

> The new rains will come down soon. (136)

Conclusion

The Visionary Adichie

> Gender matters everywhere in the world. And I would like today to ask that we should begin to dream about and plan for a different world. A fairer world. A world of happier men and happier women who are truer to themselves. And this is how to start: we must raise our daughters

> differently. We must also raise our sons differently. ("We All Should Be Feminists 10-11)

Adichie's writings are with a mission. To read her works merely as feminist or political documents would be a reductionist approach. In her works, she keeps the indigenous African culture alive too. She holds high respect for her heritage and through her books, she lets the world and the future African generation know of its richness. However, the visionary in her is critical of the practices that oppress women: women circumcision, polygamy, abandoning the widow, looking down upon a single woman, castigating a divorcee, preferring the male child, respecting women who could produce many children, etc. She calls for reform; for restructuring the mindset of the society. 'Democracy', both at the national as well as at the domestic front, is the concern that runs in her writings. Her feminist stand is never divorced of her political commitments. Aunt Ifeoma's garden, with multicoloured and unorganised flowers symbolises polyphony at every level; eschewing some and letting the one dominate would take away the beauty of the garden. Adichie creates real women in her works; her women are not anti-male, nor do they spew venom against the other sex. They aspire for a just society, a society that believes in integrating the women too into its fold. She voices for getting rid of the customs through which suppression of women is propagated. Her women are educated, intellectual, liberated, rational, not tied with the patriarchal fetters. *Purple Hibiscus* projects her idea of erasing the old silenced woman and re-writing/re-creating a liberated new woman. Adichie also presents 'new man' in the form of Jaja, who defies the patriarchal notion of controlling women. Unlike his father, he is compassionate and understanding, to his mother, to his sister, to his grandfather, to his aunt's family and even to his unborn sibling. Instead of radical feminism, Adichie advocates a democratic set up. Through the characters of Jaja and Father Amadi, Adichie conveys her message straight that the men in her society are waking up to their responsibilities to rectify the wrongs being done to the women, also through her female characters she urges the women not to surrender to the meaningless customs and start striking back. Self-esteem and self-assertion are the rule of the day.

Works Cited

Adichie, Chimamanda Ngozi. *Purple Hibiscus.* Fourth Estate, 2009.

---. "We Should All Be Feminists." Fourth Estate, 2014.

Aidoo, Ama Ata. "Literature, Feminism and the African Woman Today." *Reconstructing Womanhood, Reconstructing Feminism*, edited by Delia Jarrett-Macauley, Routledge, 1996, pp. 156-74.

Barr, Okeke, and Ugwu Chukwuka. "Nigerian Polical Culture: The Saga of Militarism." https://www.longdom.org/open-access/nigerian-political-culture-the-saga-of-militarism-2315-7844-1-124.pdf. Accessed 21 April 2020.

Davies, Carole B and Adams Greeves A, editors. *Ngambika: Studies of Women in African Literature*. Africa World Press, 1986.

D'Almeida, I. *Francophone African Women: Destroying the Emptiness of Silence*. University Press of Florida, 1994.

Heather, Hewett. "Finding Her Voice." *The Women's Review of Books*. Old City Publishing, 2004, pp. 10-11.

hooks, bell. *Feminism is for Everybody: Passionate Politics*. Pluto Press, 2000.

Kehinde, Ayo. "Rulers Against Writers, Writers Against Rulers." *African Development*, vol. 35, no 1-2, 2010, pp. 27-53. *AJOL*.

https://www.ajol.info/index.php/ad/issue/view/8477. Accessed 30 April 2020.

Kolawole, Mary. *Womanism and African Consciousness*. African World Press, 1997.

Moyana, Rosemary. "Men and Women: Gender Issues in Dangarembga's *Nervous Conditions* & *She No Longer Weeps*." *African Literature Today*. James Currey Ltd., 1996, pp. 25-34.

http://ir.uz.ac.zw/bitstream/handle/10646/536/moyana-gender-issues.pdf?sequence=1&isAllowed=y

Nnaemeka, Obioma, editor. *Sisterhood, Feminisms, and Power: From Africa to the Diaspora*. Africa World Press, 1998.

Ogunyemi, C. O. "Women and Nigeria Literature." *Perspectives on Nigerian Literature,* edited by Y. Ogunbiy. Guardian Books, 1998, pp. 60-67.

Okuyade, Ogaga. "Changing Borders and Creating Voices: Silence as Character in Chimamanda Adichie's *Purple Hibiscus*." *The Journal of Pan African Studies*, vol. 2, no. 9, 2009, pp. 245-259.

Steady, F. C., editor. *The Black Woman Cross-Culturally*. Schenkman Publishing Company, 1981.

Udumukwu, O. *Signature of Women*. Onii Publishing House, 2007.

Uwakwe, A. P. "Debunking Patriarchy: The Liberation Quality of Voicing in Tisitsi Dangarembga's *Nervous Conditions*." *Research in African Literature*. vol. 26, no. 1, 1995, pp. 75-84.

Wallace, Cynthia R. "Chimamanda Ngozi Adichie's *Purple Hibiscus* and the Paradoxes of Postcolonial Redemption." *Christianity & Literature*, vol. 61, no. 3, June 2012, pp. 465-483, doi:10.1177/014833311206100311.

CHAPTER 2

Re-Imagining the Masculine: A Reading of Bessie Head's *The Collector of Treasures*

Bipasha Som Gune

African women's writing, like female writings in the rest of the world, concerns itself with the history of women in a given cultural and political context and their experiences through centuries. Women's writing provides a much needed 'Other' side of the grand narrative of the canonical 'mainstream' literature that often silences the mini-narratives on its margins. Bessie Head's *The Collector of Treasures* is a landmark text in the field of African female writing. In African writing in general, where female voices are still not heard much, where even stalwart postcolonial writers are allegedly not much concerned about feminist issues of the society and nation, the mere act of writing from a female vantage point is revolutionary enough. Bessie Head has done that. Fiercely feminist as her works are, there is another reason for which her works are often quoted, especially with respect to the title short story "The Collector of Treasures." It can be said that this story is a remarkable feat in itself. Most of the short stories included in *The Collector of Treasures* deal with the theme of double marginalisation of women as victims of both gender oppression as well as colonisation. They focus on the condition of women mainly in and around the village of Botswana. Her short narratives give voice to so many unheard and often strategically silenced accounts of suffering and victimhood. She focuses on the complexity of human relationships as well as social injustices. Her stories are remarkable for their candid accounts of women's socio political as well as colonial experiences.

The history of feminism is inexorably connected with the history of discourse. Feminist theories are generally concerned with power relations in a given social structure and the way women as individuals and as members of groups negotiate with that relation. Feminists have tried to modify Foucault's work on discourse. They have made some of the political potential of his work more overt. The fact that Foucault's discourse theory is concerned with theorising power makes it useful to feminist theorists because feminists too are concerned with power relations from a gendered perspective. Recent feminism has moved away from the concept of simple female passivity or victimhood in the hands of patriarchal oppressive mechanisms and has started focusing more on the complexity of power relations that keep those mechanisms running. The study of such multi-layered power relations also includes race, class and other such variables. The concept of confessional discourse is an interesting case in point. Michel Foucault (1926-1984) in his *Discipline and Punish* (1975) explains the development of a disciplinary society. He argues that such a society gradually evolves where the tendency to use punishment as a way to warn people of social deviance gradually gives way to the system of using reformation as a means to make people internalise disciplinary regime. Confessional practice, he says in *The History of Sexuality*, had a "central role in the order of civil and religious powers" (Foucault 56). While this is true that confessional discourses are potentially oppressive forms of discussion, feminist scholars point out that there is a possibility that they can serve as sites of resistance as well. Many times the so called personal failures and difficulties of anyone in general and of women in particular, can be seen as structural or institutional in nature. Hence, within a given context, asserting those difficulties during such discourses may be empowering instead.

The very structurality of the frame of femininity as well as of heterosexuality is another important aspect of feminist and discourse theory that is relevant in this discussion. The main difference between seeing femininity as an imposed ideology and seeing it as a discourse is that in the first case femininity is considered homogenous. But the practices that oppress women are not uniform, nor are the reaction of women to that. Their reactions range from compliance to negotiations or even amassing of power from a seemingly powerless situation. Here discourse theory becomes useful. Women take part in the discourses of femininity that are mutli-layered and mutli-dimensional and in order to address the issues of oppression and agency in a more complete way, it is important that we consider them within the framework of discourse theory.

As Luce Irigaray in her work "When the Goods Get Together" comments on the commodification of women in an economy dominated by men, she comes up with an interesting analogy. The utilitarian philosophy of patriarchy regarding women is defined as a trade that considers women as goods. Women are commodities handled and exchanged by men and among men. The essence of kinship among them is achieved through exchange of women among them. As the capitalist set up is controlled and driven by men, trade of products, services and even women takes place. Or in other words, in such an exchange based social organisation, men are socially linked through mutual swapping of women as goods. Irigaray problematises this relationship among men and brings in subtle yet powerful dimensions of homosocial and homosexual relationships. Homosociality and homosexuality, as they refer to relations among people of same sex without and with sexual interest respectively, are important concepts in this context. Irigaray talks about the overlapping as well as mutual exclusiveness of both. There is a continuum between them and they both are present in society. On the one hand, homosexuality among men is considered a taboo; on the other hand, the masculine relationship among men is sometimes overlooked and sometimes even encouraged depending on the situation. In fact, she points out that homosociality among men is promoted. Homosexuality is not. But it may often be underlying the apparent homosocial relationships among them. She asks the question "Why is masculine homosexuality considered exceptional then, when in fact the economy as a whole is based upon it? Why are homosexuals ostracised, when society postulates homosexuality?" (Irigaray 192). Homosocial cultural order is at the heart of men's system of trade and economy. On the other side of the picture, women are generally not allowed any space for any such homosocial engagement. Traditional male-homosocial economy depends upon an exchange/use continuum. So naturally it has a fear around the notion of female unity. Homosexual engagements among women or what she calls a 'female libidinal economy' is an absolute taboo and not allowed at all, or allowed only to the extent it satisfies male fantasy, in pornography for example. In fact, it feels threatened by the possibility of females trying to 'get together', because the use and traffic of women is the very foundation of masculine homosociality. And female homosexual or even homosocial relations will be like the goods refusing to go to the market-place for exchange. Hence, that is forbidden. Women in this system, have only 'exchange value.' They are limited to the territory of heterosexuality wherein they are assigned not productive roles like men, but only reproductive roles instead. Women cannot bring change to this male homosocial network no matter how much they add their voice to it. Women need to establish their own homosocial and homogenous relationship among themselves so that the 'phallus' loses power. Relation between male homosocial and female homosocial structure is an important link in the understanding of complex power dynamics in a gendered context.

We are living in a time and a world where on the one hand, the increasing awareness of the politics of power has made women more resistant to it, and on the other, patriarchal frameworks have become stronger with more vindictiveness and urgency in the face of the increased resistance. When we look around we often see a clash of ideologies between radical feminist ideas and radical patriarchal philosophies where the latter, sometimes express itself by denying its own existence. So in such a situation it is really important that there are texts that can point society's power dynamics out to the readers rather than simply casting women as passive victims of oppression. Bessie Head's *The Collector of Treasures* does that wonderfully. That is undoubtedly one of the reasons to celebrate the text.

Another thing that draws our attention to this text is something that brings both discourse theory and the theory of Irigaray into play. This is related to identity politics, especially in the context of discourses in conflictual relations. The politics that is used to create an identity is a complex one. When we see that the different markers of identity formation are carved out by a society about a part of society, we know it is carved out by people from their position of hegemony. One of the millions of examples can be the way female body is described in poems or movies or advertisements or magazines and the way these descriptions aim to construct an ideal or even an exoticized female body. And these are used to control and finally define women. This is how the hegemonic centre defines a section of society and this is how the said section identifies itself as well. The fact that different parts of the entire structure work hand in hand in collaboration with constructing the identity of women from the vantage point of male agency, ensures that whatever happens, happens through the male gaze.

Now, most of the successful feminist writings try and resist this kind of image formation. We often talk about different tools of identity formation and see that different writers resist image formation of different marginalised sections in different ways. Ama Ata Aidoo's "The Girl Who Can" is an exercise in resistance that provides voice to the African women struggling and trying to find their rightful place in society. The child protagonist in that story finally succeeds in breaking out of the body obsession of her society that considers women merely as baby-producing machines. In case of Bessie Head, we see that in a story of apparent and total victimhood where the protagonist has been a sufferer throughout and ends up in prison with new types of confinement and oppression, the author manages to put up a rather interesting kind of resistance to the unjust demands of society on women in multifarious ways. One of the ways is that of the confessional discourse. Going back to the confessional discourse theory one can point out the inherent sense of resistance and agency that undermines the process of the formation of an apparently compliant subject through a confession. One example would be Dikeledi 'çonfessing' her crime to her friend in prison ""'Do you feel any sorrow about the crime?' 'Not really,' the other woman replied. 'How did you kill him?' 'I cut off all his special parts with a knife,' Dikeledi said" (Head 154).

While this is a classic example of 'confessions' incorporating more resistance than compliance, we can say that Head in her story goes beyond mere resistance. She goes on to mimic the construction process of the patriarchal hegemonic structure and creates an almost identical but reverse counterpoint to it. She attempts a construction of masculinity, a unique discourse for male identity formation which is equally structural in nature. While descriptions of and opinions about men are common in the texts of female authors, an executed ideological structure functioning with the aim of re-constructing masculinity through a female gaze is what makes Head's work stand apart. This story of an oppressed African woman creating and propagating narratives of a new construction of the African male from the vantage point of female agency makes a unique and interesting construction in itself. As we know, this kind of identity formation can take multiple paths and ways. There can be direct attempt at inscribing masculinity through overt mechanism or there can be other more covert ways of the production of masculinity. The author here takes both the overt and the covert ways and even more. On the one hand, she gives direct description of how men are, especially in Africa. She describes two types of men. A careful study brings to notice the fact that the difference between these two types is made mainly on the basis of two concepts: the psychoanalytic and feminist idea of phallocentrism and the main pillar of Head's feminist vision of a liberated family man. On the basis of these, there are two types of men, the phallocratic misogynist and its other, the liberated ideal man. She says "here are really two kinds of men in society" (162). The first kind is characterised as the type that creates misery and chaos and can be broadly damned as evil. He lives near the animal level and behaves just the same. He accepts no responsibility for the young, he procreates like animals. He is in the majority in society. He is responsible for the complete breakdown of family life. He dominates the government and political life. "He regards sex as a means of exerting power over his wife and is not faithful. He has sex with his women like dogs, out of pure carnal lust" (162).

On the other hand, the liberated ideal man is described as: "…another kind of man in the society with the power to create himself anew. He turned all his resources, both emotional and material, towards his family life and he went on and on with his own quiet rhythm, like a river. He was a poem of tenderness" (163). Head also adds that these second types of men have tender feelings and they make sexual life enjoyable for their wives.

Though this rather blunt comparison and description is quite simplistic in appearance, the fact that Head assumes the agency to define masculinity and form a vision of an idealised new African male is what makes it exceptional. As a post-colonial writer, gender issues are never divorced from political ones for her. As 'personal is political' for her, she has surveyed the impact of generations of colonial rule on African men as well. She says that history can explain the origin and characteristics of this type of man who can be analysed across three time frames. "In the old days, before the colonial invasion of Africa, he was a man who lived by the traditions and taboos outlined for all the people by the forefathers of the tribe. He had little individual freedom to assess whether these traditions were compassionate or not" (162).

She further adds: "The colonial era and the period of migratory mining labour to South Africa... broke the hold of the ancestors. It broke the old, traditional form of family life and for long periods a man was separated from his wife and children while he worked for a pittance... to pay his British Colonial poll-tax" (162). Accordingly, the African male moved from a status of primacy in the tribe to a status of inferiority. He then became merely 'the boy' of the white man.

Independence, she says, provided the first occasion for family life of a new order. But men of this kind started a new process of wild destruction and dissipation. The new jobs and the higher salaries brought corruption and moral decay. Decades of deracination frequently left the postcolonial man "a broken wreck with no inner resources at all" (162).

Such discussions and opinions about the evolution of African male in the text make a sensitive reader conclude that Garesego is a postcolonial aberration, not the traditional ideal for African manhood. However, the fact remains that even in pre-colonial Africa things were not very good for women either. As Head points out that in the pre-colonial Africa their "ancestors made the big mistake of relegating a superior position to the men in the tribe and women were regarded as an inferior form of human life. This made the women very unhappy" (162). So, though colonialism is not the only or even the primary reason for the lopsided power relations in African society, it surely has a role to play in it.

There is another and subtler way of identity formation. Romantic stories and songs or movies have given us examples in plenty of this kind. The narrative of female beauty, being a part of the powerful discourse to construct the female subject, more often than not, exoticizes or even fetishizes the female. Starting from the sublime romantic poems where the beloved is like a 'red red rose' to the modern movies where our algebraized mind often fails to notice the absurdity of shiffon saree clad heroines dancing on a snow-covered mountain, the narratives created by patriarchal institutions are replete with objectified or even fetishized female body. Even in famous superhero films like *The Avengers* (2012), woman's body or even soul are constantly show-cased under the male gaze which is mesmerised by the 'beauty' of those women. In *The Avengers,* for example, the camera focus lingers on the character of Black Widow in an objectifying manner almost every time she appears on screen. As a 2015 film review article by Elyce Helford on an online platform suggests, Black Widow is fetishized through emphasis on specific body parts. Unlike the unrevealing costumes of the male superheroes, with the exception of Hulk of course, the superhero bodysuit of Black Widow is left zipped down to expose cleavage, with a clear purpose of sexualising her image; even though it betrays the sheer impracticality of leaving a vital area of her body unprotected. As we know, such objectification bordering on fetishisation has always been a thinly veiled way of constructing female subject. In the short story "The Collector of Treasures", we see an uncannily similar thing about male identity formation, especially in the construction and presentation of the character of Paul Thebolo. Dikeledi's exotic description of Paul and his eyes mirrors a classic structure-plan for the construction of a subject from the vantage point of an authoritarian gaze.

> The man impressed her immediately when she went around….He was tall, large boned, slow moving. He was so peaceful as a person, she says, that the sunlight and shadow played all kinds of tricks with his eyes making it difficult to determine their exact color. When he looked still and looked reflectively the sunlight liked to creep into his eyes and nestle there; so sometimes his eyes were the color of shade, and sometimes light brown. (163)

After the initial introduction Paul also talks to her 'çharmingly.' He is 'the beautiful one' and he is an 'oasis of goodness.' Exoticisation of his eyes continues further and takes up an almost poetic expression when she says: "Two soft pools of cool liquid light were in his eyes and something infinitely sweet passed between them; it was too beautiful to be love" (167).

Such idealisation of male subject is possible when female to female relation is strong enough to create the agency and the vantage point needed to do that. Understandably, female friendship is given a lot of importance in the story. Be it Dikeledi and Kenalepe relation or Dikeledi and Kebonye relation in prison, examples of deep female comradeship can be seen. "It was not long before the two women had going one of those deep, affectionate, sharing-everything kind of friendships that only women know how to have" (164).

Perhaps this is what Luce Irigary implies when she says that women establishing their own homosocial and homogenous relationship among themselves can make the 'phallus' lose its power. It is indeed this relationship that makes the physical act of losing the phallus, namely castration of the phallocratic male, possible.

Dikeledi's relationship with Kenalepe and Paul undoubtedly emboldens her to take the drastic step. And this female friendship is not like the kitty party friendship. In their friendship, there is a queer mixture of femaleness and gender neutral comradeship. In a world where public opinion about woman to woman relationship largely oscillates between 'women are their own enemies' and 'kitty party friends', the statement 'women make good friends' or 'kind of friendships that only women know how to have' is a strong enough act of resistance in itself. Here the women exhibit bonding not only as women but as humans. Just like the way men do. Dikeledi and Kenalepe as well as Kebonye are friends not merely because they are all women but mainly because they love and care for each other and their ideologies match. They are not a homogenous group huddled together. In fact, such de-individualisation and huddling happens for men in this story at times where they are reduced to a homogenous horde stripped off their individual identity. "But the story took such a dramatic turn that it made all the men shudder with horror. It was some weeks before they could find the courage to go to bed with women, they preferred to do something else" (169). This is a rare space where femininity of the protagonist and her comrades is asserted, in fact their femininity is the glue that holds them and the plot of the story together but at the same time the characters rise above that womanhood and establish themselves as humans. This is possible when the centre of the structure of a discourse is too obvious to need any separate mention. When the centre is so strong it is only obvious that the margin will be discoursed from the vantage point of the centre. And this absolute power of the central hegemonic force goes, just as it does in a real life patriarchal set up, to the extent of objectification of the margin, mainly of sexual type.

In a characteristic case of turning of the table, we see fetishisation and sexual objectification of men in this story. That is already evident in Dikeledi's act of castration and thereby feminisation of her husband Garesego. As a distinctive case of, to use Luce Irigaray's terms, the 'exchange' of men as 'goods' among women where this exchange becomes the basis of their relationships, we see that Kenalepe offers to 'loan' Paul as a lover to Dikeledi, so that she can experience the sexual pleasure that her husband denies her. Though at a first glance it may seem that by this turn the story is shifting back to a world of African polygyny, closer attention to the detail of the story makes it clear that here these two women are negotiators rather than objects of exchange as Dikeledi says to Kenalepe, "I cannot accept such a gift from you" 163). It is this agency to choose to offer and to accept or not accept the 'gift' from each other that forms the basis of friendship between these two women, and not a common grief, as is often shown in many texts. As it is evident that they do not have any common grief to bond over, it can be certainly concluded that this is not a bond of victimhood. Head's idyllic feminist vision is based on a few major components, and romantic love bound by monogamous relation is one of them. So in such case it is unlikely that Head would like to shift back to an idealised polygynous set up. On the contrary she would love to turn the table and hold a mirror to it and show how it looks from the other side. In the process she presents a radical women-oriented transformation of society. In this society women are bound by a bond of agency and centrality, compared to which men appear in the periphery with their stature diminished to a great extent. The 'exchange value' of Paul becomes even more significant in this case as the author has already told us that good neighbours always "help each other at all times and mutually loan each-other's goods" (163). Interestingly, the 'ideal' man exhibits all qualities of a marginalised subject, including that of a fragile 'honour'. When Garesego goes on a character assassination spree against Paul, the latter feels quite vulnerable and almost needs protection. In this new idealised African community which Head tries to establish in her writings, the man becomes a sexual object shared by women for sexual pleasure. And it is he who loses his 'honour' for that. When Garesego publicly questions Paul's honour for what he is allegedly indulging in, the people around "half liked the smear on Paul Thebolo: he was too good to be true" (169). Idealisation and objectification goes so smoothly hand in hand that the reader almost accepts the 'exchange value' of the ideal man in the process. Kenalepe's description of her intimate life with Paul with the information that Paul is also sexually liberated and innovative, makes his sexual objectification complete. Not only does he hold the opinion that sexual intercourse is for the gratification of both men and women and therefore tries to gratify his wife in the act which makes him ideal as a man, but also the description of his sexual skill and his ability to surprise his wife every night makes him even more 'expensive.' He is pitted against Garesego. Women for Garesego are merely objects of his own pleasure. However, such objectification and sexualisation of men is quite paradoxical in general because it is men who, within a patriarchal framework of system, turn women into sex objects. In the case of this short story we see these assumptions being transferred onto the male body, be it in the exotic description of Paul or in the physical description of Garesego lying naked on his bed. Dikeledi, armed with a 'substitute phallus', i.e., a kitchen knife, not only emasculates him but also literally gazs upon the unguarded and defenceless body of Garesego as he lays on his back and even draws pleasure from it as Garesego bleeds to death. Kenalepe too gains phallic power because she too is in possession of a substitute phallus, the glorified body of her husband which she can exchange with other women of her choice.

As the definition of feminism is often mistakenly interpreted as hatred towards men, so is such a story sometimes mis-interpreted as misandric in nature. But the fact is it merely attacks the inherent misogyny in the society and what can be a better way to do that than simply turn the table and show how it looks from the other side? Bessie Head holds a mirror up to the society and we shudder to see the graphic nature of the evil prevalent in there. In such a world love is the only unguent for the anguished souls. Dikeledi Mokopi, whose very name means tears, goes through her tearful journey of life but is still open to love. This is not the patronising love of any privileged prince charming who searches for his fortunate beloved with her glass shoes in his hands. It is the universal sense of human love and respect that one human feels for another when they touch each other's heart. Gender plays hardly any role in it. Dikeledi sees that love in the eyes of Paul as well as of Kenalepe. Such a love is the real treasure of life. That is why Dikeledi looks at the plump and always cynical-looking Kebonye in the prison and smiles tenderly at her, "because she knew already that she had found another such love. She was the collector of such treasures" (156).

Works Cited

Aidoo, Ama Ata. *The Girl Who Can and Other Stories.* Heinemann, 2002.

Beard, Linda Susan. "Bessie Head in Gaborone, Botswana: An Interview," *Sage* vol. 3, no. 2, 1986.

. "Bessie Head's Syncretic Fictions: The Reconceptualisation of Power and the Recovery of the Ordinary," *Modem Fiction Studies,* no. 37, 1991.

Bruner, Charlotte H. "Bessie Head: Restless in a Distant Land," *When the Drumbeat Changes*, edited by A. Parker, Three Continents Press, 1981, p. 271.

Crous, Marius "Díkeledí's Revenge: A reading of Bessie Head's "The collector of Treasures" *Literator,* vol. 17, no. 1, April, 1996, pp.133-142.

Daymond, M.J., editor. "Inventing Gendered Traditions: The Short Stories of Bessie Head and Miriam Tlali," *South African Feminisms: Writing, Theory and Criticism*, Garland Publishing, 1996, pp. 223-239.

Foucault, Michel. *The History of Sexuality: An Introduction.* Pantheon Books, 1978.

---. *Discipline and Punish: The Birth of the Prison.* Penguine, 2019.

Fernandez, Juan Miguel. "From Periphery to Centre? *The Collector of Treasures* by Bessie Head (1977): The Translation and (Mis) reconstruction of an African Woman's Identity in Spanish, Italian and French." *Universidad de Valladolid ES, 28*, 2007-8, pp. 241-263.

Head, Bessie. *The Collector of Treasures and Other Botswana Village Tales.* Heinemann Educational Books, 1977.

Helford, Elyce Rae. "What is the difference between the male gaze and female objectification".http://screenprism.com/insights/article/what-is-the-difference-between-the-male-gaze-and-female-objectification. Accessed July 30, 2018.

Ibrahim, Huma. *Bessie Head: Subversive Identities in Exile.* University Press of Virginia, 1996.

Ingersol, Earl G. "Reconstructing Masculinity in the Postcolonial World of Bessie Head." *ARIEL: A Review of International English Literature*, vol. 29, no. 3, July 1998, pp. 95-116.

Irigaray, Luce. "Women on the Market". *This Sex Which is Not One.* Cornell University Press, 1985.

Jersen, Gillian Stead Ei., editor. *Tales of Tenderness and Power*, Donker, 1989.

Mills, Sara. *Discourse.* Routledge, 2007.

Ramraj, Victor j., editor. *Concert of Voices: An Anthology of World Writing in English.* Broadview Press, 2009.

CHAPTER 3

Religion-Gender Interface: A Study of Chimamanda Ngozi Adichie's *Purple Hibiscus*

Shweta Tiwari

Religion in Africa

Often regarded as an intangible link between human beings and God, religion is one of the most complex terms in lexicons across the globe. It can be elucidated as a socio-cultural phenomenon that comprises an array of moral, ethical and behavioral mandates. Religion surely embodies our collective consciousness but its utilitarian dimension of promoting social cohesion and cultural conformity cannot be disregarded. An individual can belong to a particular religion either by natural inheritance from ancestors or selecting it on the basis of his ideological inclination.

Though religious affiliations are governed by personal beliefs and value system, they are less spiritual and more social in nature. A celebrated religious theorist, William Robertson Smith studied religion of the Semites and observed that despite being elementary, the rites performed by the followers fostered community living. He asserts:

> We have seen that ancient faiths must be looked on as matter of institution rather than of dogma or formulated belief, and that the system of an antique religion was the part of a social order under which its adherents lived, so that the word "system" must here be taken in a practical sense, as when we speak of a political system, and not in the sense of an organised body of ideas or theological opinions. (29)

Likewise, Emile Durkheim noted that enlightenment enabled people to understand about totemism and superstitions being ordained by human beings and not supernatural forces. Ritualistic practices were used as potential medium to communicate thoughts and opinions at gatherings in order to reiterate belongingness. The collective rigor of myths and customs fused the society into a composite whole, the premise on which the concept of religion rests. Differences began to make inroads only after institutionalisation of religion and the subsequent coercion to conform or convert.

Africa, the second largest and the second most-populated continent in the world hosts a wide range of geographical and linguistic diversity. Traditional African religion was a byproduct of age-old community beliefs, cultural norms and collaborative ethics. It primarily aimed at preserving fundamental human values like respect, kindness, acceptance and empathy. Kinship was pivotal to the indigenous African cosmology and the ancestors were revered for their sagacity. In order to ensure that ancestral contribution was remembered, people used to build shrines in the name of their forefathers. This was later incorporated in the African religion. People came to believe that the deceased predecessors continue to exercise a sway in the lives of their descendants. Hence, it can be said that African religion was more spiritual and ritualistic than institutional in nature. Jacob Olupona illuminates the reason behind spiritual inclination of Africans thus:

> One of the basic reasons is that indigenous African spiritual beliefs are not bound by a written text, like Judaism, Christianity, and Islam. Indigenous African religion is primarily an oral tradition and has never been fully codified; thus, it allows itself to more easily be amended and influenced by other religious ideas, religious wisdom, and by modern development. Holding or maintaining to a uniform doctrine is not the essence of indigenous. (16)

The Africans followed their religious credos for ages but multiple imperialist intrusions jeopardised their rich legacy. It would be inaccurate to assert that Christianity was introduced in Africa only in the nineteenth century. Various written records talk about the presence of apostles in Africa much before the continent was colonialised. For example, Baur records, "The Christian Church blossomed in North Africa for six centuries before the arrival of Islam in this region. In those early centuries C.E., Athanasius, Clement of Alexandria, Anthony, Pachomius from North Africa, Origen, Tertullian, and Augustine were the pillars on which the universal Church were standing" (17). Just when people began to familiarise themselves with Christianity, the Arabs invaded Africa in the seventh century. The subtle propagation of Christian Commandments was replaced by Islamic doctrines. Islam was disseminated widely by merchants and scholars through peaceful methods. However, as the Arabs gained a strong foothold along the Swahili coast, their modus-operandi became violent. As per the *Ancient History Encyclopedia*, "Military campaigns did occur from the 14th century CE against the Christian kingdoms of Nubia... There were also sometimes violent resistance by supporters of traditional African beliefs such as animism and fetish, spirit and ancestor worship" (n.pag.).

A prolonged tussle between Christianity and Islam effected (if not remodeled) the traditional African religion. However, the indigenous culture suffered a sweeping onslaught only with the advent of European colonisers in the nineteenth century. The invaders did not inspire conversion through harmonious means but by devaluing their practices. Life led by the local population was incomprehensible to the European colonisers; hence, they branded them as savage and uncultured. They believed it was the ethical duty of the colonisers to civilise the colonised who according to them were followers of heathenry. It brings to mind the poem, "The White Man's Burden" by Rudyard Kipling in which he hinted at the moral obligation of the Whites to civilise the Oriental population:

> TAKE up the White Man's burden –
> Send forth the best ye breed –
> Go bind your sons to exile
> To serve your captives' need;
> To wait in heavy harness
> On fluttered folk and wild –
> Your new caught sullen peoples,
> Half devil and half child. (web.)

The mental configuration of the colonised population as deficient and benighted was not limited only to the colonial administrators and authors but evangelists also. Daniel Kumler Flickinger in his missionary memoir mentions, "The only reason why our theological views are not as foolish and corrupting as theirs (Ethiopians), and that we are not believers in witchcraft, devil-worship, and a thousand other foolish things, is simply because the light of Heaven shines upon us" (84). The chronicle speaks volumes about the deeply entrenched patronising attitude of the colonisers. The spread of Christianity during this time can also be attributed to the establishment of church buildings that largely facilitated Evangelisation.

The colonisers began to expand their authority by exploiting the vulnerability of the colonised population. One of the most exploitative systems was the introduction of cash crops in an agriculture-centric continent. Men lost their land to colonial masters for a paltry sum of money and were forced to work as wage laborers in tea and cotton plantations. As more than half of the male population was unable to sustain their family they had to migrate to alien lands in search of new opportunities. Christianity thus mutated from a way of living to a framework that governed the relationship between individual and society. The indigenous population found itself located at the cusp of tradition and modernity. While some Africans rejected the imposed religious identity, the others uncritically imitated it. However, it should be noted that like all other male-dominated institutions, colonisation too affected men and women differently.

Religion and Gender

It has been amply emphasised that 'sex' refers to the biological difference between men and women while gender is a socially-constructed category. Studying gender is important not only because it is pivotal to our existence but also on account of its being a major determinant of cultural, social and moral structuring. Almost every religion across the globe is androcentric, therefore, the reason behind re-reading, re-interpreting and re-writing the religious texts by postmodern women authors is not far to seek. There were no pronounced gender differences in the African societies before the advent of the colonisers. This can be attested on the basis of women's participation in several outdoor and revenue generation activities. Women used to help men in tilling, sowing, harvesting and animal husbandry apart from looking after the household. The adverse impact of Christianity on the lives of African women can be gauged by the privileges they lost in the name of religion.

Marriage in African society was not just a transaction but an institution that bestowed social stability upon women. They exercised absolute authority in the household as matrons and played a significant part in economic endeavors too. Women also had the liberty to divorce their husband in case of negligence or violence and remarry. A few scholars refute the centrality of the feminine principle in the pre-colonial African society as bride-price and polygamy were among the then prevalent norms. However, Sylvia Leith-Ross, an oft-quoted anthropologist who worked closely on the Nigerian population observes, "Nigerian women, because of their economic importance as mothers, farm cultivators and traders have been more powerful than is generally thought" (21). Hence, according to her polygamy was a means of increasing helping hands in farming and also combating infant mortality rate. Even if both the perspectives are given equal credence, it cannot be denied that the cultural codes that guided African society were different from the Western society. Therefore, to bluntly regard these practices as subjugation of women would be to misread the complexity of the African culture.

The colonialists introduced not only Christianity in the traditional African society but masculine-feminine divide also. Marriage in Christianity is upheld as a complimentary relationship in which the husband is the head of the family and wife is the supporter. The institution of marriage is even likened with the bond between human beings and God. Hence, divorce or separation from the husband began to be looked down upon. The women were asked to upkeep the marriage even if they were in an unhappy alliance. The colonisers made African women to believe that they were ancillary to men and must preoccupy themselves with the domestic chores only. The missionaries endorsed feminine qualities like modesty, coyness and restraint for women. Resultantly, the public appearance of women in congregation and community gatherings began to shrink. Young girls who attended the missionary schools were trained to be ideal Christian wives and mothers whereas boys were given practice on mining, transport jobs etc. Uchem writes, "It was the Christian missionary through control of education system transmitted perhaps, female inferiority and served discrimination in Nigerian economic and political affairs as part of Western civilisation which lowered the social status of women at that time" (47).

It can be said that African women became victims of the same systematic subordination as their white counterparts. The absence of women from fields and market led to an imbalance in the local economy also. Women were no longer autonomous entities and had to depend on men for survival. The colonial government also covertly debarred women from the administrative sphere. Important matters concerning the land were discussed with the male members of the community and one of them was appointed as the 'warrant chief' (a native agent of the colonial masters).

Purple Hibiscus: Introduction

Chimamanda Ngozi Adichie is one of the most acerbic voices in contemporary African literature. She has written three novels namely *Purple Hibiscus* (2003), *Half of the Yellow Sun* (2006) *Americanah* (2013). She also has to her credit a book length essay titled "We Should All be Feminists" (2014) and a manifesto, "Dear Ijeawele, or A Feminist Manifesto in Fifteen Suggestions" (2017). Recipient of MacArthur Foundation Fellowship, Adichie's keen understanding of her cultural heritage and political climate of the country propels her to craft a corpus that addresses barbaric tortures hurled at the Black masses from not an impassioned but a critical point. One of the most distinct traits of her novels is that the characters confront the gloomiest moments of pain and rejection with hope or solutions (whichever works in the situation). The paper intends to explore the relationship between religion and gender in *Purple Hibiscus.* It aims to analyse the impact exerted by religion in shaping, nourishing and perpetuating gendered identity. The paper will deliberately refrain from using any theoretical lens like postcolonialism or postmodernism so as to avoid an agenda-driven reading of the novel.

Set against the backdrop of a military coup, the novel is narrated by a fifteen-year old Nigerian girl, Kambili Achike who is both a participant and a critical observer in the plot. She lives with her father, Eugene (Papa), mother, Beatrice (Mama) and elder brother, Chukwuku (Jaja). Her father is an affluent factory owner and a philanthropist. He also publishes a newspaper, the only one that dares to castigate the Head of State. The social persona of Eugene is in stark contrast to his family image. He is a violent man who breaks things and beats his family members. On Christmas, the family goes to Abba to meet Eugene's father, Papa Nnukwu. Euguene does not share a cordial relationship with Papa Nnukwu for the old man refuses to convert into a Christian. At the same time his daughter, Aunty Ifeoma also pays him a visit along with her children Amaka, Obiora and Chima. She is a university lecturer who vehemently opposes the colonial regime and Eugene's use of his social reputation to coerce her into remarrying. As the military coup engenders public strikes and violence, Eugene sends Kambili and Jaja to his sister's house. The mediocrity of Ifeoma's household dejects both Kambili and Jaja but they are taken aback by the liberal ideas of their aunt and their familial bliss despite the financial constraints. In the meanwhile, Papa Nnukwu's health begins to deteriorate and Ifeoma brings him to her home. Eugene is infuriated to know about the presence of his father in his sister's house along with his children and he brings them back to Enugu. He inflicts corporeal punishment on Kambili and Jaja for looking at the painting of their grandfather. Ifeoma criticizes a government-appointed administrator and as a consequence her apartment is plundered and she loses her job. She later relocates to America along with her children. Eugune continues to subject his wife and children to domestic abuse. Jaja is disquieted at the increasing brutality of his father and retaliates on Palm Sunday. Eugene dies under mysterious circumstances. An autopsy report confirms the presence of poison in his body. Beatrice tells her children that she had been gradually poisoning their father as she was desperate to get rid of the abusive relationship. Jaja takes the responsibility of the murder and safeguards his mother. He is released later as the pro-democracy groups blame the former regime for Eugene's assassination. The whole episode leads to Bethanie's psychological breakdown but exercises an enabling effect on Kambili. She visits Nsukka only to breathe the freedom that the place embodies even though her aunt no longer lives there.

Religion and Its Shades

The importance of religion in the novel is unmistakable as it is divided into three timeframes namely "Palm Sunday", "Before Palm Sunday" and "After Palm Sunday." Palm Sunday is a Christian fest that falls on the Sunday before Easter. It marks the entry of Jesus Christ into Jerusalem.

The novel foregrounds contrasting religious worldview through the characters of Papa Nnukwu, Eugene and Ifeoma. Papa Nnukwu is a traditionalist and embodies the indigenous Nigerian value system. Eugene represents the transition from religious ignorance to supposed civilisation. Ifeoma and Father Amadi epitomize a balanced amalgamation of both the philosophies. Papa Nnukwu lives in Abba and adheres to customary practices by keeping a little shrine there. Much to Eugene's dismay, he refuses to convert into a Christian despite multiple persuasions by him. To retaliate, Eugene calls Papa Nnukwu a "heathen" and also restricts his interaction with his family members to just fifteen minutes at a time. They are also forbidden from eating and drinking in his house so that they do not imbibe any anti-Christian ideals. Papa Nnukwu is disempowered by Eugene much like the colonisers marginalised the natives. However, it is interesting to note that the ineptness of the colonised subject to grasp or appreciate the religion of the colonisers challenges their absolute authority to some extent. Papa Nnukwu is not a follower of Christianity, hence, for him the crucifixion of Christ does not signify redemption but violence. He believes that the colonisers are vicious and brutal because their religion preaches so. He questions "who is the person that was killed, the person that hangs on the wood outside the mission? They said that he was son, but that the son and the father are equals. It was then that he knew that the white man was mad" (*PH* 84). Kambili and Jaja have a close encounter with Papa Nnukwu when he falls ill and Ifeoma brings him to Nsukka. Kambili had noticed that her father's prayer to God predominantly revolved around either instilling sense in Papa Nnukwu or sparing everyone from the tortures of hell. She is exposed to an alternate way of praying by her grandfather and aunt. The joy and hope in Papa Nnukwu's prayer leaves her surprised.

Eugene, on the other hand, is a victim of the "cultural bomb." According to Ngugi wa Thiongo, "The effect of cultural bomb is to annihilate a people's belief in their names, in their languages, in their environments, in their heritage of struggle, in their unity, in their capacities and ultimately in themselves" (3). He is a devout Catholic who blindly follows all the religious practices of the colonisers and coerces his family into doing so. The most predominant spectacle of the Achike household is violence. The colonisers made use of violence in order to suppress the autochthonous population and Eugene unconsciously applies the same tactic to ensure the submission of his family. The novel opens with his questioning Jaja about not going to the altar on a particular Palm Sunday. The reason cited by Jaja is "The wafer gives me bad breath... And the priest keeps touching my mouth and nauseates me" (6). His transgression petrifies Kambili:

> Had something come loose in his head? Papa insisted we call it host because "host" came close to capturing the essence, the sacredness of Christ's body. "Wafer" was too secular, wafer was what one of Papa's factories made – chocolate wafer, banana wafer, what people bought their children to give them a treat better than biscuits. (7)

The response of Jaja and Kambili is the outcome of their gendered conditioning. One of the widely held stereotypes about women is that they are more emotional than men. Though psychological analyses over several decades have failed to reach a consensus but it cannot be denied that an individual's response to negative stimuli or arousing stressors is largely shaped by his/her immediate environment. The patriarchal nature of Eugene has a direct bearing on the emotions and expressivity of his children. Kambili says, My shocked eyes begged him to seal his mouth, but he did not look at me" as opposed to Jaja who defiantly remarks, "Then I will die" (8). Kambili cannot dare to defy the religious terms dictated by her father but Jaja criticizes Christian practices that are upheld as sacrosanct. His refusal to accept his father's religion does not only jeopardize Eugene's autocracy but also brings to the mind Papa Nnukwu. The subsequent reaction of Eugene is described thus, "He picked up the missal and flung it across the room, towards Jaja. It missed Jaja completely, but it hit the glass étagère, which Mama polished often" (7). It is ironic that Eugene throws the missal (a book comprising prayers and sermons that are read in Catholic Mass throughout the year) at Jaja to penalise him for not attending the Mass. On another occasion when Beatrice does not meet Father Benedict citing nausea, Eugene beats her into miscarriage. The overpowering presence of Eugene in Kambili's life does not let her realise the full potential of her being. The internalisation of fear of her father is best rendered by the lines, "I had never considered the possibility that Papa would die, that Papa could die... He had seemed immortal" (199). Upon returning from Nsukka, Kambili carries a painting of Papa Nnukwu as a token of her stay with him. Eugene misreads such a harmless act as disobedience and beats Kambili so violently that she has to be hospitalised. The merciless treatment meted out to Kambili by Eugene is explained graphically as, "The stinging was raw now, even more like bites, because metal landed on open skin on my side, my legs. Kicking. Kicking. Kicking" (211). Thus, it can be said that Eugene's parochial understanding of Catholicism cloaks his vision and he (in)advertently follows patriarchal violence to guarantee the allegiance of his family members. In this regard, Oshindoro notes, "Papa's conception of religion is such that confession of sin and supplication alone do not suffice to receive forgiveness. Beyond penance, there must be restitution; he makes his household pay for their transgressions" (211).

Gender discrimination can also be witnessed in how threatened Eugene feels by Papa Nnukwu and Ifeoma. He is not rattled by Ifeoma as she is a woman. He wants her to convert to Christianity for her own good. In the past, he agrees to help Ifeoma only if she joined the missionary, stopped wearing make-up and sent Amaka to a convent school. He also forces her to remarry as a single woman with children is supposedly a misfit in the normative Christian order. However, Papa Nnukwu who is the male head of the family offers a stiff resistance to Eugene's religious beliefs and undisputed power. The latter is aware that Papa Nnukwu can instill a liking for Igbo culture in his children and hence, he keeps them away from him.

The women characters in the novel are situated at different social-economic intersections in postcolonial Nigeria. Aunt Ifeoma is Eugene's widowed sister. She is a strong-willed woman who works at the University of Nigeria in Nsukka and raises her children on her own. Ifeoma exhibits a consummate balance between her cultural roots and Christianity. Igbo words and songs are a part of her daily routine. She attends masquerade festivals and visits Papa Nnukwu despite her brother's caution against it. She is aware that Eugene is impervious to alterations yet she criticizes his use of material influence to inspire conversion among people. Hence, she can be regarded as the antithesis of Eugene. She is bold and assertive and explicitly points out to Betraice, "Eugene has to stop doing God's job. God is big enough to do his own job. If God will judge our father for choosing to follow the way our ancestors, then let God do the judging, not Eugene" (68). The courage and resolve displayed by Ifeoma speaks volume about her character which is opposite to what is expected from women in a male-centric society. Another salient feature that sets her apart from Eugene is the efficient management of her household. Eugene claims to be the in-charge of his house but he miserably fails to make it a home. On the contrary, Ifeoma's household bustles with energy and commotion which implies that along with being thinking individual she is also a doting mother who provides space for her children to err and grow. In the end of the novel, she transplants herself in the United States along with her children but Kambili continues to visit Nsukka even after that as the place provides a sense of relief and liberation to her.

It is safe to conclude that religion and gender are inextricably linked and so is the power-nexus that follows thereafter. Adichie identifies the complexities encountered by her people especially when they are faced with choices. The characters in the novel side with the option which resonates with their personal thoughts. However, a deeper probing of the plot with respect to gender also reveals that the characters possess subtle nuances that cannot be classified under fixed gendered identities and roles. Eugene wreaks havoc in the house yet he feels apologetic about it even though occasionally. Similarly, aunt Ifeoma embraces her cultural identity but only along with Western education which unconsciously implies that an exposure to the outer world is necessary to be able to appreciate the inner world. The novel ends on an optimistic note that the population that was once colonised can transcend gender-race-class barriers if it is firmly determined.

Works Cited

Adichie, Chimamanda Ngozi. *Purple Hibiscus.* Algonquin Books, 2003.

Baur, J. 2000 *Years of Christianity in Africa.* Pauline Publications, 1994.

Carson, Dana. *The Five Watersheds of History and Theology : A Fresh Look at 21st Century Christianity in Light of Cultural Distortions and the Kingdom of God.* Kingdom Publishing, 2019.

Chiorazzi, Anthony. "The Spirituality of Africa." *The Havard Gazette*, 6 Oct. 2015. Web. 15 June 2020.

Denkyi-Manieson, G. Agyeiwaa. "*Purple Hibiscus*, *Half of a Yellow Sun* and *The Thing Around Your Neck* by Chimamanda Ngozi Adichie: A Thematic Study." *Africology: The Journal of Pan African Studies*, vol. 11, no. 1, 2017, pp. 52-65. Web. 17 June 2020.

Durkheim, Emile. *The Elementary Forms of the Religious Life.* Dover Publications, 2008.

Kipling, Rudyard. "The White Man's Burden." *Kipling Society*, http://www.kiplingsociety.co.uk/poems_burden.htm. Accessed 28 Sept. 2021.

McIntosh, Marjorie Keniston. *Yoruba Women, Work, and Social Change.* Indiana UP, 2009.

Smith, William Robertson. *Religion of Semites.* Transaction Publishers, 1907.

Thiongo, Ngugi Wa. *Decolonising the Mind: The Politics of Language in African Literature.* James Curry Limited, 1986.

Oshindoro, Michael Eniola. "Solidarity between Women in Chimamanda Adichie's *Purple Hibiscus.*" *Africana Studies Student Research Conference*, 2019, pp. 1-20.

Ross, Sylvia Leith. *African Women: A Study of the Ibo of Nigeria.* Routledge & Kegan Paul, 1965.

Uchem, Rose N. *Overcoming Women's Subordination in the Igbo African Culture and in the Catholic Church: Envisioning an Inclusive Theology with Reference to Women.* 2001. Dissertation.com, 2001.

CHAPTER 4

Interrogating Colonial Politics: An Analysis of Chimamanda Ngozi Adichie's "A Private Experience"

Shikha Thakur

> Being born white in South Africa or anywhere in the empire and Commonwealth automatically conferred this special status. You had no problem finding a place to live, a job, trade union membership, access to social services. Being white, speaking English, you were accepted as English, entitled to all the rights of citizenship.
>
> Peter Abrahams (n. pag.)

The chapter seeks to explore Chimamanda Ngozi Adichie's short story "A Private Experience" to explore ways in which African voice contests colonial voice. Amidst this contestation, strategic tool such as 'quid pro quo' has been employed to expose the colonial cultural politics. The story is set against the backdrop of a violent riot between the two ethnic groups, the Igbo and the Hausa in Nigeria. Two women, Chika – a Christian Igbo and mid-aged-woman – a Muslim Hausa, seek refuge in a deserted store. The time span of three-hours, sharing mixed experience of similarity on race, region, gender while still infused with dense religious bigotry, lays the foundation of the chapter. The staggering contrast between the interior-store blurring religious boundaries and the exterior-streets broadening religious violence is deeply analysed to question the fixedness of ethnic and religious identity of a person. Derivatively, this fixity of identity is used as a cudgel by the colonial literature to perpetuate its supremacy, and concomitantly, depreciate the peripheral voices. Apparently, the study endeavours to examine the arbitrariness of identity which has otherwise been created by the ascendancy of colonial voice. And while projecting the negation of the commonwealth literatures by the colonial powers – prompting laceration of colonised countries at the hands of Britain; this chapter intends to bring to surface the socio-political situation of Nigeria (yet another British colony). Thus, while building on the elementary stance of commonwealth literatures, the chapter gradually moves from examining colonial discourse in terms of colonial policy of 'divide and rule' to contest as well as question the colonial supremacy.

Introduction

Commonwealth literatures refer to literatures written in the former colonies of Britain. The online dictionary, *Vocabulary.com*, while elaborating on the origin of commonwealth literatures states that it is "comprised of the roots *common*, meaning 'belonging to all,' and *wealth*, meaning 'happiness or riches,' the word *commonwealth* [thus] originally referred to the government of England from 1649 to 1660" (n.pag.). Clearly, since then the literature coming from Britain was initially termed as the British Commonwealth literature, though the term commonwealth was first used by Oliver Cromwell in 1649. Drawing the historical timeline based on a 'USAD Literature Resource Guide', it states:

> The Commonwealth of Nations is a body comprised of fifty-three member states that were previously territories of the British Empire. It was formally constituted by the London Declaration in 1949 and has England's Queen Elizabeth II as its head. The Commonwealth was, primarily, a way to define the relationship of England with its colonies that had gained their independence from the British Empire in the twentieth century. It survives largely as a vestige of colonialism. According to political writer James Astill, as quoted in the BBC article 'What Is the Relevance of the Commonwealth Today,' the Commonwealth today is 'a large and somewhat anomalous club, which devotes most of its energies to maintaining its strange existence. (48)

However, later in the 1900s when erstwhile British colonies – Australia, Africa, Asia, Caribbean, realised the need to design the curricula in English, they started to write their literature in the Standard English language. Such that the new emerging literatures then shaped-reshaped the cannon, writing about the super colonial power-Britain and its colonial policy of divide and rule. Building on Himadri Lahiri's lecture on "Salman Rushdie's *Imaginary Homelands*," he discusses how gradually the emerging peripheral voices began to go against the norms set by Britain, apparently, transforming British

Commonwealth literatures to commonwealth literatures. The 1980s was marked as the revolutionary time in the history of commonwealth literatures, which collapsed the nucleus – British literature by threatening its supremacy, cogently surfacing the new literatures (Lahri 00:01:15-00:2:15). S. Mohan Raj in "Commonwealth Literatures – An Outline," explains the shared socio-cultural setting of the commonwealth literatures also called the new literatures, plausibly interrogating the cultural politics of the nomenclature of 'commonwealth literatures' (Raj, slide 2-10). Comprehensively, the study advances understanding the commonwealth literatures, not only as a 'Third World Literature' but also as a 'Post-colonial Literatures in English', attempting to establish the link between Empire and the standard English-language literature, by using the same standard English language to incisively unearth the rancorous cultural politics of colonial literature. Following is an attempt made to discuss one such British colony, Africa, and its literature (commonwealth literature) fervently offering a curative-means to contest the multiple jeopardy of women in Nigeria specifically.

African continent, colonised on the basis of race, by the major super-powers ranging from France, Portugal, Dutch etc., however, remained an important colony of Britain for the longest period of time in history. The British, while on a privileged perch, claimed to have refined artillery and an advanced technology, thus justifying its right to colonise Africa and exploit its resources. *Encyclopedea.com* in an article titled, "Africa: British Colonies," cogently explains:

> Colonialism by its very nature has racist connotations. British colonialism in particular was structured as a dictatorship, using violence to pacify the colonial subjects and to maintain order. There was no input from the colonised in the way that they were governed: The British Colonial Office in London made all the decisions concerning the colonies. The British also tended to choose a preferred ethnic group over all the others in the countries that they colonised. These preferred groups, usually a conservative minority within the country, were supported to the extent that they worked against the interests of their fellow Africans. For example, the British chose the Arab minority to lord it over the majority Africans in the Sudan and favored the Fulani in Nigeria. (n.pag.)

Conflict being a focal point of concern in colonial rule, has zealously widened the interaction between Christianity and African traditional religion. Consequently, as per the British colonial policy 'to divide and to rule,' the British in Nigeria practiced its vicious cycle by broadening the religious gulf between Northern Nigeria centralising

– Hausa Muslims and Southern Nigeria centralising-Igbo Christians. Derivatively, Muslims looking up to *Sharia* Law under the tutelage of colonial force led to wanton massive obliteration. Moses Onchonu in an article titled, "The Roots of Nigeria's Religious and Ethnic Group," states:

> Modern Nigeria emerged through the merging of two British colonial territories in 1914. The amalgamation was an act of colonial convenience. It occurred mainly because British colonisers desired a contiguous colonial territory stretching from the Arid Sahel to the Atlantic Coast, and because Northern Nigeria, one of the merging units, was not paying its way while Southern Nigeria, the other British colony, generated revenue in excess of its administrative expenses. It made practical administrative sense to have one coherent British colony rather than two. It also made sense to merge a revenue-challenged colonial territory with a prosperous colonial neighbour, so the latter can subsidize the former. (n.pag.)

Subsequently, Northern Nigeria being the centre of pre-colonial Islamic empire named, the Sokoto Caliphate, held the Middle East governance practising *Shariat* in high regard. Evidently, the differences became the means of antagonism since colonial times, well reflected by Moses Onchonu in his article, "Northern Nigerian Muslim Nationalist Leader Declared Nigeria 'the Mistake of 1914' while a Prominent Southern Nigerian Christian Nationalist Figure Called Nigeria 'A Mere Geographic Expression' " (n.pag.).

The broadened ethnic diversity imposing a singular forced identity has generatively fomented violence and terror. Men in southern and Northern Nigeria were multiply jeopardised on the basis of race, region, religion, while adding to the cauldron women were additionally jeopardised on the basis of gender too. Clearly, the following thematic analysis discusses Chimamanda Ngozi Adichie's attempt to examine the distorted identities of two Nigerian women – each belonging to a rival ethnicity, for the surgical implantation of singular identity in each.

Thematic Analysis

Chimamanda Ngozi Adichie (b. 1977) is a contemporary budding writer in the domain of gender space, with acute penchant towards women in Africa. She, along with Sylvia Tamale (b. 1963), Buchi Emecheta (1944-2017), Grace Ogot (1930-2015) etc., has been in the list of industrious scholars on account of her immense contribution in the discipline of emancipating African women. Adichie, grown as the fifth of six children in an Igbo family, has globally gained distinction for her massive contribution to African literature. Besides, voicing her revolutionary ideas in various writings – fiction, short story and non-fiction, she has majorly spoken on issues related to African women's quandary. Chimamanda Ngozi Adichie's eponymous official site lucidly states, "Her 2009 TED Talk, *The Danger of A Single Story*, is now one of the most-viewed TED Talks of all time. Her 2012 talk *We Should All Be Feminists* has started a worldwide conversation about feminism, and was published as a book in 2014" (n.pag.). From amongst the platter of her enormous works, the study builds on her less-known short story, "A Private Experience," comprised in her classic collection titled *The Thing Around Your Neck* (2009). The story, based on Adichie's personal growth as an Igbo in Hausa majority Nigeria, portrays the turbulent ethnic relations incisively sabotaging the identity of two women – Chika, an Igbo Christian and mid-aged woman (referred to as woman in the story), a Hausa Muslim.

An American scholar, Larry Diamond (b. 1951) limpidly explains in his scholarly work, *Class, Ethnicity, and Democracy in Nigeria* (1988): "When Southern Nigerians migrated to the North, whether they were Yoruba, Igbo, or an ethnic minority, Northern Muslims were forbidden on religious and administrative grounds to [not to] associate with Southerners, whom they [Northern Nigerians] were taught to regard as pagans and infidels" (26). Perspicuously, Adichie sets the story in the ancient city of Kano blazing riot between Southern Igbo and Northern Hausa. Setting the grounds for a spiteful riot, "when a man drove over a copy of the Holy Koran that had been dropped on the roadside, a man who happened to be Igbo and Christian" (5), the chapter intends to analyse the colonial policy. Chika, who is studying medicine in America and has lately come to visit her aunt in Nigeria (Chika's birthplace) with her sister Nnedi, suddenly loses the track as religious riots break in the market. Unable to come to terms with the abrupt conundrum, "Riot! Trouble is coming, oh! They have killed a man!" (4), she drops oranges and handbag to climb the store window to seek refuge. Ignorant of the reason for the hasty outburst outside, Chika accidently bumps into another mid-aged woman clambering in the same store after her. Comparing the inner space – the store marked with the two women at a "silent stand-still" and the outer space – the market, marked with the chaotic "shouting, running, overturning... pushing" (4), this chapter prompts to contest the fixed identity roles naturalised by the colonial power to legalise its illegal lacerating policy. Donileen Loseke (1954) in *The Study of Identity as Cultural, Institutional, Organisational, and Personal Narratives* (2007) explains four levels of identity:

> Cultural identities, located at the macrolevel, are the imagined characteristics of disembodied types of people that construct symbolic boundaries around types of social actors. Similarly, at the meso-level, a large-scale political process creates institutional identities, which also reflect imagined characteristics of certain people;in this case, the people are often the intended targets of policies. The chosen characteristics serve to justify policy decisions and legitimise institutional arrangements. (661-662)

Situating on the above societal conditioning, the fixed religious identity describing a Muslim northerner from "narrowness of her face, the unfamiliar rise of her cheekbones;... the scarf", while a Christian southerner from "her light complexion and the silver finger rosary... and her accent (2), surfaces the contested colonial discourse. The colonial discourse that imposes singular religious identity results in an uncontrolled violence. "Hausa Muslims hacking down Igbo Christians with machetes, clubbing them with stones" (44), considerably illumines Amartya Sen's (b. 1933) observation in *Identity and Violence* (2006), "Violence is fomented by the imposition of singular and belligerent identities on gullible people, championed by proficient artisans of terror" (2).

The escalated ethnic-religious animosity – underpinning the colonial discourse to sustain British hierarchy – has been the legalised norm in Nigeria. Opeyemi Adedoyin Çancı, in an article titled, "Ethnic and Religious Crisis in Nigeria" meticulously delineates:

> Historically, identities have played a significant role in the Nigerian political process during the colonial period and in the post-colonial era. During the colonial period, the administrators allowed the emergence and aggravation of an 'us' versus 'them' syndrome, where Muslims were pitted against Christians, Northerners against the Southerners, Hausa-Fulani, Yoruba and Igbo against each other, and so on. (n. pag.)

However, this chapter judiciously examines 'quid pro quo'; help for help, as a tactical technique to combat colonial strategy of 'to divide and to rule. Chika and woman's three-hour peaceful conversation in the dilapidated store, while the world outside was tearing apart, enlightens their assisting suggestions to collectively fight the havoc. The inner space exchanging dialogues from: woman assuaging Chika, "This place safe," (1), to woman "untying her green wrapper and spreading it on the dusty floor...

(offering Chika to) Come and sit" (6), to finally woman curing Chika's bleeding leg by "tying the wet headscarf around it, knotting it at the calf" (17), blurs religious boundaries. Furthermore, Chika's cordial efforts to solve woman's perplexed query on feeling dryness and painful sensation on nipples, "After you feed the baby, you have to use some lotion. And while you are feeding, you have to make sure the nipple and also this other part, the areola, fit inside the baby's mouth" (11), projects Chika and woman's proclivity towards 'quid pro quo'; help for a help. Evidently, irrespective of the established signifiers-northerner Hausa-Muslim and southerner Igbo-Christian; inner space defies the signified-religious-ethnic hatred as they cooperatively connect with each other. Based on Chika's knowledge of medicine, she offers curative measures to woman who is illiterate and poor, "having five children" (11) and is suffering from much-ignored painful nipples. Chika, on immediately connecting woman's misery with her (Chika) own mother who also suffered the same pain, satisfactorily suggests woman to apply, "Cocoa butter. The cracks heal fast" (12). Besides, their mutual discontentment on outside brutality and barbarity, clearly collapsing the ethnic cleavage, the woman says "Every time when they are rioting, they break market" (10). The repetitive usage of the pronoun, 'they', refers to her aversion to riots no matter who organises it – the Igbo Christians or Hausa Muslims. Later Chika's wild search for Nnedi in the bloody streets of Kano further corroborates the central idea, rupturing the ethnic-religious dichotomy. Adichie writes:

> She will look at only one of the corpses, naked, stiff, facedown, and it will strike her that she cannot tell if the partially burned man is Igbo or Hausa, Christian or Muslim, from looking at that charred flesh. She will listen to BBC radio and hear the accounts of the deaths and the riots – "religious with undertones of ethnic tension" the voice will say. And she will fling the radio to the wall and a fierce red rage will run through her at how it has all been packaged and sanitised and made to fit into so few words, all those bodies. (16)

Subsequently, the demonstrative pronouns: 'that charred flesh', 'it' and 'those bodies' create a topoi abounding in Chika's consciousness to argue the arbitrariness of singular ethnic identity. The arbitrariness between the signifier – headscarf, holy rosary; and the signified – northern Muslim Hausa and southern Christian Igbo respectively, defies the fundamental nuance of conditioned religious ethnic identity. Drawing minimal attention to the established hierarchy, rather emerging as each other's saviours in the times of crisis, interestingly lays the foundation of the chapter: contest 'to divide and to rule' by 'quid pro quo.' Derivatively, the women supposedly nemesis, despite cognizant of the diametrical religious and ethnic differences, congenially share a space illumining an elemental humanistic tendency which outdoes the religious bigotry asserted by colonial regime. Furthermore, woman while in the store looking up to an optimistic energy to rescue her, opens her headscarf, sits on her knees, "facing Mecca... " (14), "praying with her head to the dust floor" (52), brings "tears, a private experience, and she (woman) wishes that she could leave the store" (14). Here the headscarf plays an important role in defining religious identity – wearing a headscarf outside is a singular Islamic identity, while offering the headscarf as tourniquet to help the injured and using the same scarf to offer namaz seeking positive energy inside, is a chosen multiple identity depending upon a situation. Carly Campbell in the thesis titled, "There is no Other: Situational Identity in Adichie's 'A Private Experience'," vividly observes how in the story the ethnic and religious identity of Chika and woman are situational, while their only fixed chosen role remains that of a sister and a mother respectively. Hence, as Chika and woman's three-hour short encounter comes to an end as the outside space becomes silent marked with bloody carnage, the chapter studies the antipodal inner space reflecting agency to display multiple identities over the outer imposed singular identity.

The analysis further shifts to accessing the role of Standard English language as yet another colonial tool to continue dense colonial chauvinism. The British literature authorised Standard English language as the only means of expression, such that any other language was looked down upon. Apparently, the colonised countries wrote their literature attempting to match up to the parameters set by the British literature. However, despite various attempts to emulate the British literature, the commonwealth literature was never accorded due reverence and authorisation. Thus, the commonwealth literature eulogised its native English language to contest the Standard English language. Chimamanda Adichie projects woman and Chika as vertical parallel representing native English language – a metaphor of illiteracy and barbarism, and Standard English Language – a metaphor of literacy and civilisation, respectively. Woman poor and illiterate, not able to even differentiate between a university and a school, asks Chika "Where you go school?" (7), while Chika studying in the States "wonders if the woman even knows what going to university means, and responds, we are at the University of Lagos. I am reading medicine. Nnedi is in political science" (7). Plausibly, colonial discourse in an attempt to promote its language credits the sense of acceptance only to the countries that centralise colonial language, thus naming – Standard English language. Derivatively, the idea of literacy – usage of Standard English language is associated with a developed country like America (though another former colony of Britain), such that Africa (Nigeria) is projected to be a gorge of barbarity. Salman Rushdie (b. 1947) while taking the subject position of a peripheral voice, endeavours to glorify the cultural heritage of the colonised while ardently challenges the superiority of white people's language. Salman Rushdie in his landmark essay, "Commonwealth Literature Does not Exist," (1983) prudently states:

> But its (commonwealth literature) present-day pre-eminence is not solely – perhaps not even primarily – the result of the British legacy. It is also the effect of the primacy of the United States of America in the affairs of the world. This second impetus towards English could be termed a kind of linguistic neo-colonialism, or just plain pragmatism on the part of many of the world's governments and educationists, according to your point of view. What seems to me to be happening is that those peoples who were once colonised by the language are now rapidly remaking it, domesticating it, becoming more and more relaxed about the way they use it-assisted by the English language's enormous flexibility and size, they are carving out large territories for themselves within its frontiers. (64)

Conclusively, Rushdie prompted commonwealth literatures to transgress literary ghettos – the standards of English language set by British empire; and emerge with the English language of their own (just like Indian English language – a means to combat colonial policy: through language and subject). Therefore, the use of Black-folk-English language in African literature, "I (woman) am looking for my daughter. We go market together this morning. She is selling groundnut near bus stop, because there are many customers. Then riot begin and I am looking up and down market for her" (12) refers to Adichie's concern to attain linguistic self-assertiveness and bitterly condemn language imperialism.

Conclusion

There have been various researches conducted on Adichie foregrounding different perspectives in African literature. The major chunk of research has investigated the devastating role of women in Africa, however, her rarely discussed short story "A Private Experience" has not been studied that diversely. Clearly, this chapter has intended to examine 'a private experience' between two women laying ground for generosity, kindness and helpfulness resultantly disintegrating their social singular identity. This chapter, hence, carves a niche by contesting 'to divide and to rule' by 'quid pro quo'; analysing African women's issue in the light of commonwealth literature. The concomitant tendency to battle the legalised odds of the colonial discourse, the chapter provides fresh insights to combat pandemonium – colonial strategy and colonial language.

Works Cited

Abrahams, Peter. "Commonwealth Quotes." *Brainy Quotes.* brainyquote.com/quotes/peter_abrahams_718879?src=tcommonwealth. Accessed 29 May 2020.

Adichie, Chimamanda Ngozi. "A Private Experience." *Chimamanda Ngozi Adichie.* 2008. Accessed 2 May 2020.

"Africa: British Colonies." *Encyclopedea.com.* 1 May 2020. encyclopedia.com/sosciences/encyclopedias-almanacs-transcripts-and-maps/africa-british-colonies. Accessed 8 May 2020.

Campbell, Carly. "There is no Other: Situational Identity in Adichie's "A Private Experience." April 2013. Accessed 29 May 2020.

Çancı, Opeyemi Adedoyin. "Ethnic and Religious Crisis in Nigeria." *Accord.* accord.org.za/ajcr-issues/ethnic-religious-crises-nigeria/. Accessed 28 May 2020.

"Chimamanda Ngozi Adichie." *©2020 Chimamanda Ngozi Adichie.* chimamanda.com /about-chimamanda/. Accessed 20 May 2020

"Commonwealth." *Vocabulary.com.* vocabulary.com/dictionary/commonwealth. Accessed 24 May 2020.

Diamond, Larry J. *Class, Ethnicity, and Democracy in Nigeria: The Failure of the First Republic.* Syracuse University Press, 1988.

Lahiri, Himadri. "Salman Rushdie's *Imaginary Homelands.*" *Youtube.* 10 May 2020 Youtube.com. Accessed 15 May 2020.

Loseke, Donileen R. *The Study of Identity as Cultural, Institutional, Organisational, and Personal Narratives: Theoretical and Empirical Integrations.* London, 2007.

Ochonu, Moses. "The Roots of Nigeria's Religious and Ethnic Conflict." *TheWorld.* 10 March 2014. pri.org/stories/2014-03-10/roots-nigerias-religious-and-ethnic-conflict. Accessed 25 May 2020.

Raj, S. Mohan. "Commonwealth Literatures: An Outline." *Slideshare.* slideshare.net /MohanRaj632/commonwealth-literature-an-outline. Accessed 10 May 2020.

Sen, Amartya. *Identity and Violence.* Penguin Books, 2006.

Tunca, Daria. "The Chimamanda Ngozi Adichie Website." *Universite de Liege.*28 December 2019. cerep.ulg.ac.be/adichie/index.html. Accessed 10 May 2020.

"USAD Literature Resource Guide." 2015, Literature-Resource-Guide%20(1).pdf. Accessed 10 May 2020.

CHAPTER 5

'The Look' in El-Sadaawi's "Woman at Point Zero"

Deepshikha Sharma

Introduction

A woman's body is pivotal to her identity. A political battlefield, it is often conquered, violated, and medicalised beyond its entitled "domestic" niche. Loud expressions of this uterine identity are prominent in art created by women. They whisper their confessions, narrate their experiences, and scream about their suffering and trauma. Feminist literature has been an age-old medium to promote empathy towards the entire womankind, despite being situated on different intersections of the society. While Celie in Walker's *The Colour Purple* ponders over her sexuality as a woman of colour in a heteronormative society, Atwood's *The Handmaid's Tale* paints a bleak picture of a dystopian reality where women are sexual slaves. Despite being under various kinds of subjective jeopardy, these characters illumine a fragment of the different phenomenological realities experienced by womankind.

The Egyptian writer Nawal El-Sadaawi's *Woman at Point Zero* successfully captures painful bodily experiences of the protagonist within a brief canvas of 114 pages. Firdaus, the pro-tagonist, takes the narrator through her life on the eve of her hanging, when she finally thinks she is "free." Imprisoned for such bold words, El-Sadaawi exposes the hegemonic patriarchal quicksand that suffocates women since birth. This text depicts traumatic events like genital mutilation, child marriage, domestic violence, sexual assaults that drive the protagonist to become a prostitute and finally, a murderess. One of the most prominent symbols in this book, in relation to the body, is that of the eyes. Other scholars have fleetingly mentioned it in terms of "the gaze" (Saiti 158) and the theme of "surveillance"

(Balaa 242), but never in detail. My intention in this paper is to deeply examine this aspect of the novel, as I will relate it to existentialist philosophy. I shall mostly be drawing from Jean Paul Sartre's *Being and Nothingness* but shall also resort to other theories of the gaze when required.

A psychiatrist by profession, Nawal El-Saadawi when conducting research on "women suffering from neurosis" (ix) met Firdaus at the Qanatir Prison who inspired her to jot down this work of "creative non-fiction" (Cooke vii). The story starts off with the narrator feeling disheartened by the refusal of Firdaus to *see* her, as she questions her self-worth equating it to the rejection by a lover. On the eve of her hanging, she summons the narrator to recount her life with urgency, as she pronounces, "… Do not interrupt me. I have no time to listen to you" (9). Firdaus takes the narrator and reader on the journey of her life – from a young girl to a murderess, her accounts reflect the oppressive matrix she sifted through, battered yet stronger after every experience.

Patriarchal Expositions in the Plot

While recalling her childhood memories, she closely associates her father with the other men who praised the Imam for his Friday sermon, invoking Allah's name, despite being hypocrites who sinned. A wife-beater, her father punished her mother when a male child died but not when a female one perished. While the rest of the household slept empty-stomach, her father chewed on every morsel of food while her mother washed his legs. Firdaus spent her days burdened with chores like filling earthen jars with water, sweeping sheds and making dung cakes, and kneading the dough. Her uncle would creep up his hand to her thighs to a spot where she once experienced pleasure when playing "bride and bridegroom" with her friend Mohhamadain, but could no more due to the genital mutilation ordered by her mother.

Soon after the death of her parents, her uncle takes her to Cairo with him till he enrols her into a boarding school for girls due to his wife's persistence. There she fancies a teacher named Iqbal, but denies it due to the heteronormative ideals of the Egyptian society. Despite excelling in school, Firdaus is married off to a sixty-year-old man at the tender age of eighteen by her uncle to pay off his debts. He takes her back to her husband's place when she returns to him after a beating, reassuring her that "All husbands beat their wife" (46).

After being abused multiple times, she runs away from home to be held captive by a man named Bayoumi who she meets in a restaurant. Bayoumi allows his friends to sexually abuse her till she escapes with the help of a neighbour who calls a carpenter to break open the door.

When seated on the banks of the river Nile, she comes across Sharifa Salah el Dine who takes her home to clean and feed her, and employs her as a prostitute. Fawzy, the pimp reveals that Sharifa is merely using her to make money, as he engages in a fight with Sharifa, giving Fir-daus the chance to escape. Realising the power of economic independence, she decides to start serving clients under her own management. Despite her booming success, after an insult from a journalist, calling her profession "not respectable", she gives up prostitution to go look for a new job with her secondary certificate. Initially content with her new job, she soon realises that, "As a prostitute, I had been looked upon with more respect, and been valued more highly than all the female employees. My body was never hemmed in by other bodies in the bus, nor was it a prey to male organs pressing up against it from in front and behind. Its price was not cheap" (81).

Further, she falls in love with a revolutionary called Ibrahim in the company fighting for workers' rights as she joins his campaign. She willingly gives her heart and body to this man, to eventually discover his engagement with the company's owner. This disillusionment leads her to the epiphany: "A successful prostitute was better than a misled saint. All women are victims of deception. Men impose deception on women and punish them for being deceived, force them down to the lowest level and punish them for falling so low, bind them in marriage and then chastise them with menial services for life, or insults, or blows" (82).

As a high level prostitute, Firdaus lives life on her terms – refusing even those who threaten to imprison her. She soon comes across Marzouk, the pimp who confiscates a large amount of her earnings. He conspires with the police and the jury to subvert women whose bodies are his "capital" (101). When he prevents her from leaving, the two wrestle with Firdaus killing the pimp as she "struck the knife into almost every part of his body" (104). After getting picked up by an Arab prince, she tears all the money that he pays her in a way to reject all the men she has come across. She soon confesses she has killed a man as the prince orders for her arrest, and when they arrive she declares: "You are criminals, all of you: the fathers, the uncles, the husbands, the pimps, the lawyers, the doctors, the journalists, and all men of all profession" (110).

Even when the prison doctor asks her to beg for pardon she refuses, feeling exalted and triumphant. When the narrator drives away, she is left with the feeling of Firdaus being better than all men and women out there.

Many Arab critics accuse El-Sadaawi of using Orientalist stereotypes in her work to appear as a champion of women's rights in the West, Luma Balaa disagrees. She argues that El-Sadaawi "occupies a space in-between in which she at times employs stereotypes but at other times challenges them" (Balaa 237), using intersectionality to show the multiple layers of oppression Afro-Arabian women go through, entailing issues of class and the female sexuality.

While a number of arguments can be raised as to whether Firdaus liberates herself from the system while exposing its latent corruptness (Gohar 182) or whether the story clarifies the incomplete definition of feminism as the right to choose, as the lack of options drive her to such limits (Salami 2015), one cannot deny the persistent pervasion of the male gaze present throughout the story.

Theories of Gaze

An umbrella term, the gaze and the theoretical discourse surrounding it cannot be traced back to a movement; rather it has been scattered as concepts in philosophy, psychoanalysis, discourse studies, and film studies. (Geetha & Sarulatha 2). John Berger's (1926-2017) influential book *Ways of Seeing* (1972) served as a stage for the development of this idea. His notorious claim that "men act, women appear" (47) implicates a model of heterosexuality in which men look and women are looked at. Laura Mulvey picked up this association of vision with the masculine and popularised the term "male gaze" in her article "Visual Pleasure and Narrative Cinema" (1975). With ideas borrowed from psychoanalysis, she extends the theory to gender politics. She argues that the gaze enables the construction of a male subject and a female object further leading to the "active/passive heterosexual division of labour" (20). This division leads masculinity to be associated with activity and femininity with passivity, informing the subject-object dichotomy, making man with locus of subject hood and woman the lacuna for him to carry out his activity. To quote Simone de Beauvoir (1908-1986): "He is the Subject, he is the Absolute. She is the Other" (26).

Following this, the visual metaphor has enjoyed the privilege of being the ideal mode of thought following the "male logic" (Keller & Grontowski qtd. in Storr 62). Another film theorist Jane Gaines argues, "Some groups have historically had the licence to 'look' openly while other groups have 'looked' illicitly", labelling the "right to look" (39) as a privilege. If this is so, "the prevalence of vision and the gaze in philosophical works may well play an important role in philosophy's privileging of the masculine" (Storr, 12). This can especially be seen in Jean Paul Sartre's existentialism

The Sartrean Gaze

The Nobel laureate introduces *Being and Nothingness* (1965) as his single greatest articulation of his existentialist philosophy, as "an essay in phenomenological ontology" (xxxv). At the centre of this ontological treatise, in a section called "Le regard" or "The Look," Sartre (1905-1980) creates a small narrative moment of dubious virtue from which he is able to resolve one of the truly vexing problems of phenomenology up to that time, i.e., the problem of the Other. For Sartre, the Other-as-subject is not a subject known through oneself but is solidified by an oscillation of intersubjectivity. With "the look" of the Other rendering one to be exposed as an object, the latter's vulnerability generates fear, pride, and especially shame, eventually causing the Other's perspective to intertwine with one's own sense of self. Sartre proposes that this results in the establishment of a relation that confirms the existence of the other along with granting one reflective self-consciousness.

Prior to the interpretative task at hand, it is necessary for the complete understanding of the article, to familiarise oneself with Sartre's ontological structure. Distinguishing between two principle characters of being, Sartre attributes in-itself (*en-soi*) as self-identical, independent, un-created, passive, and unchanging, and hence uses it to characterise the existence of worldly ob-jects, while he believes for-itself (*pour-soi*) active, dynamic, transcendent, and the surpassing of the in-itself on which it is dependent, hence equating this character as consciousness.

Positing it to be the ground for intersubjectivity, Sartre comes to speak of the body in two ontological modalities. Firstly, the body as being-for-itself is the mode through which the body is transparently lived-through, a means through which the world appears. In the state of being-for – itself, one is the body and cannot regard it as an object, resulting in its invisibility when engaged intentionally with the environment. Secondly, the body for others is the mode through which one's body "is utilised and known by the other", as the Others' perspective leads one to realise its objectual nature situated in the world, amongst many other bodies. Noteworthily, Sartre distinguishes between the first two ontological dimensions of the body as he asserts that they are incommunicable and cannot coexist.

Despite the use of his gender-neutral (pro) nouns, Sartre equates subjecthood, consciousness, and activity with looking, resulting in the implicit equation of looking with masculinity. For him, as stated above, to be a subject is to be 'being-for-itself' rather than 'being-in-itself.' With existentialism embedded in phenomenology, consciousness, and hence subjecthood is the start-ing point of a Being's enquiry. As mentioned above the subject extrapolates its consciousness by generating shame or fear, leading to the othering of this 'being-in-itself', making it an object.

However, if this other looks back, one may become an object for this other. Hence, leading to abattle of the looks for the protection of their subjecthood from annihilation or nothingness by the Other's look. This conflictual nature of the look, where one contends to be the subject, and not the object, leads to the establishment of a binary of the looker-looked at, active-passive, and mind-body. Drawing from Foucault's (1926-1984) *Discipline and Punish: The Birth of Prison* (1975), the gaze becomes an instrument of power based upon the social dynamics of power relations, and social dynamics of disciplinary mechanisms, such as surveillance and personal self-regulation. And this power struggle manifests in *Woman at Point Zero.*

The Gaze in *Woman at Point Zero*

Saiti in his article "Paradise, Heaven, and Other Oppressive Spaces: A Critical Examination of the Life and Works of Nawal El-Saadawi" comments on how the gaze constantly haunts Firdaus throughout the novel. He classifies the gaze into two kinds: first being kind and maternal and the second being "dangerous and threatening to [Firdaus's] survival" (Saiti 258). When sharing looks with Miss Iqbal or Ibrahim, Firdaus gets what Saiti claims a kind of "illusionary happiness" that eludes her time and again. Balaa points out that the author uses "the eye motif to symbolise the theme of surveillance" (Balaa 242). However I'd like to make an ambitious attempt to analyse all the instances of the gaze through a Sartrean lens.

Firdaus when talking about the men resembling her father says, "they watched what went on around them with wary, doubting, stealthy eyes, eyes ready to pounce, full of an aggressiveness that seemed strangely servile" (11-12), and a repetition of these words when strolling the streets of Cairo (42) show, in a Sartrean mode of thought, a being which is ready for combat for claiming its subject-hood by annihilating the Other through "the look."

When recalling her mother's "two rings of intense white around two circles of intense black" (16), she remembers them following her wherever she went despite the "contradictory forces" (16) that kept pulling her in different directions. "Two eyes that alone seemed to hold me up" (15) seems to show a positive dependence of the being-in-itself on the being-for-itself, as she acknowledges her mother in return. Celine Sciamma's recent movie, *Portrait of a Lady on Fire* tries to depict the oscillating intersubjectivity yet shared equality in terms of subject-hood integral to the exchange of a female gaze. However, in terms of the intertwining of the one's sense of self with the Other's perception, led her mother to internalise the patriarchal norms leading to the clitoridectomy of her own daughter.

After watching a kissing scene in the cinema with her uncle, Firdaus could "no longer look into his eyes" (21), perhaps intuitively picking up on her status of a "body for others", after witnessing what had happened on the screen. He sexually exploits her till he marries someone with eyes which "were large, and black with an extinguished vitality that left nothing but pools of dark, sleepy indifference" (22).

When sharing a moment with Miss Iqbal, Firdaus remarks, "I could see her eyes looking at me, observing me, despite the darkness. Every time I turned my head, they were after me, holding on to me, refusing to let me go. Even when I covered my face with both hands, they seemed to see through them into my eyes" (28). A repetition of this experience is seen later when Firdaus is a working woman, and shares a moment with Ibrahim, and El-Sadaawi uses the identical words with changed gender pronouns to depict the similarity of her vulnerable experience. In the Sartrean paradigm, Firdaus becomes alienated from her sense of self, as she is caught crying in the playground/office. She ceases to be the act, as "my consciousness sticks to my acts, it is my acts... My attitude... has no 'outside" (Sartre 259), but becomes a seen object, losing her subjecthood.

However, Sartre's assertion of "apprehension of a look turned toward me appears on the ground of the destruction of the eyes which 'look at me.' If I apprehend the look, I cease to perceive the eyes" (Sartre 258) seems to fail in this case as Firdaus describes in detail the eyes of both Iqbal and Ibrahim. Following Saiti's prompt, perhaps this idea of shared subjecthood con-stitutes her "illusory happiness", to be disillusioned later by the power-play inherent (as per Sartre) in visual relations. She does indeed feel the internalised homophobic shame for fancying Iqbal when she claims "How could I be in love with a woman?" (32), or the disappointment she feels when she realises Iqbal looked at her "always in the same way as she looked at any other of her pupils" (30). After Ibrahim's betrayal, the deceit pushes her to return to prostitution. In Sartre's words, "Shame reveals to me that I am this being, not in the mode of 'was' or of 'having-to-be' but in-itself" (Sartre 262).

Firdaus runs away to the streets of Cairo on knowing through eavesdropping about her arranged marriage to a man forty years her senior. She does not seem to realise the matrix of domination she's placed in, as she's taken herself to be a "being-in-itself", an object, a (ironically) no*body* as she states "No one noticed me as I stood there alone. And because they did not notice me I was able to observe them" (42). She acknowledges the subjecthood of the Other, just like Sartre does in the park where he recognises "a spatiality which is not my spatiality, for instead of a grouping toward me of the objects, there is now an orientation which flees from me" (Sartre 254). Just as Firdaus starts thinking "I had become one of them" (43), she comes across two eyes or rather feels them moving towards "me very slowly, closer and closer. They dropped their gaze with slow intent down to my shoes, rested there for a moment, then gradually started to climb up my legs, to my thighs, my belly, my breasts, my neck and finally came to stop, fastening themselves steadily in my eyes, with the same cold intent" (43-44).

She feels, in the words of Sartre "disintegration of the universe (Sartre 256) where her subjecthood in relation to the world is annihilated. The shudder which she calls, "fear of death, or like death itself" (44) is "the triumph of the point of view of the Other over the point of view which I am toward myself" (Sartre 540). El-Sadaawi relatably writes, "For after all I was not confronted with a hand holding a knife or a razor, but only with two eyes, nothing but eyes" (44). The eyes which carry the look seem to compromise Firdaus' entire being. She remains scared of the look springing up from anywhere to threaten her again.

When married, her husband fixates his look on her the entire time. Firdaus recalls, "He kept looking at my plate while I ate" (45) or "All day long he remained by my side in the house, or in the kitchen watching me as I cooked or washed" (46). He keeps asserting his unwavering subjecthood as a form of domination over Firdaus. When jumping on her and demanding, "Why do you turn your face away from mine?... Why do you keep at a distance whenever I come near you?" (47), he is demanding the acknowledgment of his subjecthood, his dominion over the object that he thinks she is. A thinking like this leads to domestic violence between the two, till she runs away.

While there are many instances in the novella, where the eye-look split, as mentioned above, of Sartre does not apply, it is perfectly applicable to the case of Bayoumi. While she initially thinks his eyes are "resigned and calm. They did not seem to me like the eyes of someone who could kill" (49), the gaze he gives her later which "travelled with an infinitely slow movement over my face, and my neck, and then dropped downwards gradually over my breast, to settle somewhere just below it, between my thighs" (52), makes her apprehend the look over the eyes, the "subject" over the object. "I kept my eyes closed and abandoned my body" (53), shows what Sartre calls the "alienation" felt.

Although I shall be grossly over-simplifying the complexities of Lacanian psychoanalysis, I'd like to refer to his "Mirror Stage" to better explain the gaze and the concept of a subject in *Woman at Point Zero.* In what he calls the "Mirror Stage", a toddler who sees his image in the mirror, it mistakes this unified whole for a superior self. "The infant internalises this image as an ideal ego and this process forms the basis for all other identifications, which are imaginary in principle" (Flitterman-Lewis qtd. in Morin 324). Hence, this exteriority of the mirror image is internalised by the subject (Morin 324). The child while recognising the "Ideal-I", is like recognising oneself as the other. The gaze in this context, hence, is an almost self-alienating awareness of being looked at.

The first time Firdaus looks at herself in a mirror is when she is a school girl in Cairo. This rhetoric correlates with the formation of Lacan's Ideal-I, as she "had the feeling of looking out (of her eyes) for the first time... was being born a second time" when looking at the mirror. She re-calls staring at her face and her heart sinking – "I neither liked the look of my nose, nor the shape of my mouth. I thought my father had died, yet here he was alive in the big, ugly, rounded nose" (19). She internalises the exteriority of the genes of the patriarch. The feeling of this self-alienation fills her with a "deep hatred for the mirror" (20). She stays subservient, despite having a rebellious streak, due to the idea of being compiled of her mother and father. However, the character development results her to confront the mirror at Sharifa's place where she claims, "I realised that now I was being born again with a new body, smooth and tender as a rose petal" (57). This change in the frame of her mind makes her value herself, as she internalises her objectual reality to constitute her subjecthood.

Her awakening is heightened when she is paid for her services after running away from Sharifa's. Financial independence, which society made her feel was the forbidden fruit, makes her feel like a being-in-itself. She claims:

> From that day onwards I ceased to bend my head or to look away. Walked through the streets with my head held high, and my eyes looking straight ahead. I looked people in the yes, and if I saw someone count his money, I fixed it with an unwinking gaze. (73)

She gallantly states:

> How many were the years if my life that went by before my body, and myself became really mine, to do with them as I wished? How many were the years of my life that were lost before I tore my body and myself away from the people who help me in their grasp since the very first day? (74)

She maintains her subjecthood firmly, as she does the task "without looking at him, without even trying to glimpse something of his features" (75) without even granting the customer an object-hood, and completely refusing to partake in the battle of the looks.

When finally having faced the journalist who declares "You are not respectable", she feels herself return "to a moment of time which now belonged to the past" (77), as she again feels objectified. Lacan's comment about how "*Le regard* or the look can include non-visual phenomena like the rustling of the leaves," (Morin 324) fits here, as her subjecthood slips by the aural phenomenon unlike the usual visual one. Deeming the "veil to have lifted from her eyes", Firdaus conforms to the subject's opinion, wanting to take agency to become a "respectable" being-for-itself. When working for the company she could "read every day in the eyes of the higher level executives when they looked at the lesser female officials" (82) that "all of us were prostitutes who sold themselves at varying prices"

(82). Heartbroken, she finds her eureka moment, claiming herself to be a "free woman" who has "cut all relations with the world around her" (95). However, this turns out to be a short-lived freedom as the pimp keeps her as a sex slave. Wanting to be a master and not a slave (which can be related with Hegel's dialectic, but in a separate paper), she tries to leave. And hence the battle of the looks commences:

> I continued to look straight at him without blinking. I knew I hated him as only a woman can hate a man, as only a slave can hate his master. I saw from the expression in his eyes that he feared me only [as] a master can fear his slave, as only a man can fear a woman. But it lasted for only a second. Then the arrogant expression of the master, the aggressive look of the male who fears nothing, returned. (104)

Ending the war of the looks by stabbing him, she is triumphant, for in the words of Sartre, "To die is to lose all possibility of revealing oneself as subject to an Other" (Sartre 297). However, after claiming her status as subject and freeing herself of this totalitarian regime of the look (Morris, 104), she herself is sentenced to die as they are "afraid" (110) of her. Freeing herself, living her truth, she realises that "My life means their death", as she could finally disentangle herself from the oppressive male gaze. When she takes the action, she becomes the "being-for-itself", realising sometimes counter-violence is the action that's required. And this "truth is like the death in that it kills" (112).

Conclusion

Choosing Sartre whose existentialism "offers a space for expressing a terror on the part of men in relation to women's bodies which provides the basis of an ontologicocarnal hierarchy between masculine and feminine" (Le Doeuff qtd. in Storr, 62) might seem paradoxical for the analysis of a feminist text. I could have relied on Mulvey, or Irigay, or Atwood, or De Beauvoir. However, this attempt of mine may be summarised by the idiom – killing two birds with one stone. This would be an attempt to highlight the sexist undertones in Sartre's existentialism that privileges the visual logic erecting the dichotomy of "looking-looked at, active-passive, subject-object, mind-body, masculine-feminine" (Storr 101) while asserting the validity of the patriarchal apparatus of the gaze that haunts our daily lives and feminist literature. The use of this ideology emphasises the plight of the protagonist, almost serving as a confession of the tactics of terror. Foucault rightly said that "The gaze that sees is the gaze that dominates" (39), as throughout the novel oppressive factors "patriarchy, capitalism, domestic violence, hypocritical religion, classism, sexual slavery, heterosexism, surveillance and others" (Balaa 249) are all mediated by the gaze – whether Sartre's visual one, or Lacan's non-visual phenomenon.

The problem of this Sartrean gaze which snowballs into serious issues is present throughout the world, varying as per one's spatio-temporal paradigm. Rather than the triumph of one of these ontological modalities, we need to disable such constructions of thought which generate binaries. At the time when El-Sadaawi wrote this novel, even a dark light of acknowledgment and tolerance was rising in many places, though Egypt was suffering from this old malady. This daring work of art by El-Sadaawi caused severe antagonism without any sympathy in her homeland but praises and admiration for her gallantry throughout the world. In this way she certainly deserves to be the object of admiration and the subject of the mantle of change, regarding the condition of her fellow-women.

Works Cited

Balaa, Luma. "El Saadawi Does Not Orientalise the Other in *Woman at Point Zero*" *Journal of International Women's Studies*, vol. 19, no. 6, 2018, pp. 236-253, 2018.

Beauvoir, Simone De. *The Second Sex*. Vintage Classics, 2010.

Berger, John. *Ways of Seeing: Based on the BBC Television Series with John Berger*. British Broadcasting Corp., 45-49, 2012.

Deschanel, Broey. *What the Portrait of a Lady on Fire Tells Us about "the Gaze." YouTube* https://www.youtube.com/watch?v=DMUC584ppNQ&t=573s

Dolezal, Luna. "Reconsidering the Look in Sartres: Being and Nothingness." *Sartre Studies International*, vol. 18, no. 1, 2012, doi:10.3167/ssi. 2012.180102.

Foucault, Michel. *The Birth of the Clinic*. Routledge, 2003.

Gaines, Jane. "White Privilege and Looking Relations: Race and Gender in Feminist Film Theory." in *Screen*, vol 29, no 4, 1988, pp. 12-26.

"Gaze." *Wikipedia*, Wikimedia Foundation, 6 Apr. 2020, en.wikipedia.org/wiki/Gaze.

Geetha, N, and D Sarulatha. "Theories of The 'Gaze.'" *International Journal of Creative Research Thoughts (IJCRT)*, vol. 5, no. 4, 2017.

Gohar, Saddik. "Empowering the Subaltern in *Woman at Point Zero*." *Journal of International Women's Studies*, vol.17, no. 4, 2016, 174-189.

Housham, Jane. "*Woman at Point Zero* by Nawal El Saadawi Review – Classic Feminist Novel". *The Guardian*, Guardian News and Media, 6 Nov. 2015, https://www.theguardian.com/books/2015/nov/06/woman-at-point-zero-by-nawal-el-saadawi-review

Mulvey Laura, 'Visual pleasure and narrative cinema', in Bill Nichols (ed.), *Movies and Methods*, vol 2, University of California Press, 1985, pp. 303-15

Morin, Pauline. "Foucault and Lacan: The Gaze and Its Operation within Historiography." *89th ACSA Annual Meeting*, 323-327, 2001.

Salami, Minna. "An Egyptian Classic of Feminist Fiction." *The Guardian*, Guardian News and Media, 7 Oct. 2015, www.theguardian.com/books/booksblog/2015/oct/07/an-egyptian-classic-of-feminist-fiction.

Sadaawi, Nawal El. *Woman at Point Zero*. Zed Press, 2007.

Saiti, Ramzi. "Paradise, Heaven, and Other Oppressive Spaces: a Critical Examination of the Life and Works of Nawal El-Saadawi." *Journal of Arabic Literature*, vol. 25, no. 2, 1994, pp.152-174., doi: 10.1163/157006494x00059.

Sartre, Jean-Paul. *Being and Nothingness: an Essay in Phenomenological Ontology*. Citadel Press, 1964, pp. 221-339.

Sciamma, Celine, Director. *Portrait of a Lady on Fire*. 2019.

Storr, Melinda Jill. "The Gaze in Theory: the Cases of Lacan and Sartre." *Thesis (PhD)*, 1994, pp. 10-74.

CHAPTER 6

Igbo Culture as a Tool of Women's Repression and Mortification: A Critical Study of Buchi Emecheta's *The Bride Price*

Vinod K. Chopra

So much is written in the form of novels, drama, poems, essays and short stories about societal problems and aesthetic dimensions of life. It is society that influences the writers to write something. Significance of cultural context cannot be disregarded while interpreting a work of literature. Buchi Emecheta's most acclaimed novel, *The Bride Price* reflects the particular concerns of that place and time when the novel was written. It shows how society leaves a lasting imprint and influences the writers and their work. Hence, it is important to consider a work's cultural context. Authors do have in their mind the beliefs, customs, values and activities of different groups in society that stimulate their creativity. The values and mores – good or bad – find mention in writings overtly or covertly. As good indexes of values, works of literature mirror the culture of a particular region in-depth. In a way consciously or unconsciously whatever is bad is attacked and good is held in high esteem.

Tylor defines culture as "that complex whole which includes, knowledge, belief, art morals, law, custom and any other capabilities acquired by man as a member of society" (Bhushan and Sachdeva 769). Culture denotes acquired behaviours, which are shared by and transmitted among the members of society. The purpose of this paper is to analyse *The Bride Price* keeping in mind the cultural context of Igbo people. Igbo culture is considered rich culture by the people of south eastern Nigeria. The age old practices are still prevalent in that part of Nigeria, though new concepts are added to the Igbo culture owing to the external influences. While reading Buchi Emecheta's *The Bride Price,* one easily concludes that Igbo culture is used in that patriarchal society to subjugate and torture women. There is no denying the fact that Igbo culture inflicts violence of various kind, – physical and psychological on women. And this interest in perpetuating violent cultural practices against women has been one of the significant features of present day traditional setting in South-East Nigeria. Though the Igbos are, no doubt, culturally gifted and they espouse their unique way of life with pride, one has to admit the fact that some of the cultural practices Igbos follow honestly have been very outdated, dangerous, and destructive to the psyche of women (Chukwu et al. 49).

Like many other patriarchal societies across the world, the Igbo cultural customs and values are meant to use, control, subdue and repress. Ritzer has rightly pointed out that women's oppression was basically cultivated through patriarchy just for the purpose of commandeering women to achieve the intents of the so-called power structure (Chukwu et al 50). Buchi Emecheta is one of the famous Nigerian-born African women novelists who highlights female subordination and subjugation in her novels. Besides, she also contemplates female subservience and conflicting cultural values in modern Africa. In *The Bride Price*, Emecheta reveals how culture is used as an instrument to humiliate and repress women in patriarchal society, thus exposing the gender politics in patriarchy.

Custom demands in Igbo culture that a woman must produce more and more sons. Girls are not valued much. If a woman fails to do so, she has to undergo hardships and humiliation. Ma Blackie, the mother of the protagonist, Aku-nna, is such a victim of crude custom that demands more children, especially sons, from a woman. Though Ma Blackie has two children, she is humiliated as childless. This so-called childlessness is often a cause of tension between Ma Blackie and her husband, Ezekiel Odia.

> Aku-nna had heard over and over again Ma Blackie and her Nna quarrelling over this great issue of childlessness. Nna would go on and on, talking in that small, sad voice of his, telling Ma, reminding her, that he had had to pay double the normal bride price before he was able to take Ma as his wife….He would remind Ma Blackie that having paid this heavy bride price he had had the marriage sanctified by Anglicanism. And what had he to show for it all – an only son. (9)

It is all due to the custom that Aku-nna is considered too insignificant to be regarded as a blessing to the unfortunate marriage of her parents. The demand of custom is so pressing that she decides to go home to their town Ibuza to placate their river goddess Oboshi into "giving her some babies" (8). Here custom ruins the life of Ma Blackie as she has to leave behind her two children who are not mature enough to look after themselves. On the other hand, the children, too, become victims of custom that demands more children from their mother who is forced to please the gods in her native place. In the absence of her mother it is fourteen-year-old Aku who has to cook for her father and brother. There is also a reference to Okolie who deserts his wife only because she failed to bear a male child. He relates the story of his life:

> My first wife ran away because I beat her up. My second wife died when she was having a child. My third one had to go, because I fed her for seven entire years and she bore me no child.... I also want a child. A male child as fat as a plump yam to inherit all my properties. (111-12)

Everyone knows that the old man, Okolie has nothing but his grass-covered mud hut, his loin cloth and a pipe organ. Marriage is considered as a devout institution that allows men and women to have a blessed family life. It is a stable relationship in which a man and a woman are socially permitted to have children (Bhushan and Sachdeva 331). But here it seems that marriage is solemnised so that the male members of society may satisfy their ego by beating their wives and to beget more and more children brushing aside callously what the wives want. Wife beating is not peculiar to any society but is common to patriarchy all over. A husband – the protector and lover of his wife often beats her. It really becomes a horrendous experience for a woman when she is ill-treated, assaulted and humiliated by none other than a man whom she trusts the most (Chopra 117).

Pre-colonial Nigerian culture had been famous for her tradition and African cultural values that were imparted to the inhabitants and coming generations. These values included practical life skills, such as farming, fishing and trading. Besides, community beliefs and philosophy were inculcated through instruction by parents, blood relatives, surrogate parents and extended family relations. Nigerian culture was celebrated for industry, independence, honesty, co-operation and responsibility. One of these tenets included the position of women as subordinate to that of men and tradition

(Umeh 1). Numerous other inhibiting manifestations of traditional culture determined and enforced by men find mention in *The Bride Price* (Frank 483). Widowhood and polygamy have been used as instruments to impose subordination on women. Emecheta explains, through her novels, the darker side of African culture that inflicts psychological and physical pressures upon the weaker sex through contentious customs like polygamy and widowhood. Even today these customs are used as institutionalised forms of male oppression.

The life of a widow – *isi mkpe* – according to Igbo culture is full of trauma, humiliation and ostracism. *Nwanyi isi mkpe* is the term used for a widow that means a woman without the head, the deceased husband being the head (Chukwu et.al 50). Wailing and mourning under a customary formula is tiresome for a widow. For days together she has to wail and this kind of bitter wailing is expected to go until the deceased is buried. Women suffer owing to the mourning and burial rituals when a man dies. The days following the death of husbands present a traumatic, painful and regrettable experience all over the world but in countries like Nigeria the situation is worse due to the obnoxious practices and rituals (qtd. In Inekwuaba and Anthonia 49). In *The Bride Price* Emecheta tells us how Ma Blackie leaves Laos for her native place, Ibuza, where

> Young men got together and in less than two hours erected the hut in which Ma Blackie was to stay and mourn for her dead husband for nine full moons. The length of mourning was longer than the usual seven moons because Ezekiel Odia, to ensure that his wife would always be his, had taken the precaution of cutting a lock of hair from Ma Blackie's head and keeping it as evidence. Once a man had taken this step, his wife could never leave him, for to do so would be to commit an abomination....So testing was this period for a widow that, before it was over, she might herself die and this would be treated as a clear indication that she had been responsible for her husband's death. (71)

In this way a widow is not only subject to ill-treatment and loneliness but a stigma is also attached to her life in the form of responsibility of her husband's death. The psychological violence that she undergoes is enough to shatter her whole self and makes her lose her pride and glory that she enjoyed earlier. Ma Blackie's pitiful state as a widow is degraded by some cultural beliefs, norms and dispossessions. The physical and psychological violence inflicted on widows leaves them most of time traumatised and battered. Similar is the agonised self of Ma Blackie who "was to remain alone in this special hut; not until the months of mourning were over could she visit people in their homes. She must wear continually the same old smoked rags" (71). Obviously Ma Blackie, like innumerable widows, is reduced to the status of cattle that can be driven anywhere as male member of society wish them to drive.

In all the patriarchal societies like Nigeria women are viewed just as appendages to their husbands. They are devoid of the right to own property and are subject to inhuman treatment and practices resulting from harmful customs. The day her husband dies, the widow loses her identity, free will and independence. Besides, as far as children of widows are concerned, the death of the father means death of parents as mother, as per the custom, does not exist anymore. Emecheta herself explains in *The Bride Price*:

> It is so even today in Nigeria: when you have lost your father, you have lost your parents. Your mother is only a woman, and women are supposed to be boneless. A fatherless family is a family without a head, a family without shelter, a family without parents, in fact, a non-existing family. Such traditions do not change very much. (28)

The Bride Price delineates how Ma Blackie suffers after the death of her husband. She cannot take any independent decision about her children and her own life. She does not allow her daughter to choose a husband of her choice as neither the custom will grant permission to do so neither will Ma Blackie's new husband ever agree to it. She is bound to obey the orders of Okonkwo, her new husband. Likewise, polygamy is an equally hateful tradition that guarantees male authority and anarchism. In *The Bride Price* as soon as Aku-nna reaches her native village, Ibuza, her cousin, Ogugua, gives her a rather appalling information, "You are almost fourteen years old now and you still don't know the customs of our Ibuza people? Your mother is inherited by my father, you see, just as he will inherit everything your father worked for" (64). Not only this, Okonkwo will also inherit Aku-nna's bride price as a girl child is also to be inherited by him. He gives consents for her schooling only because an educated girl will bring more bride price. He is selfish in this as he wants to be get 'obi' position. It is all due to this custom of polyandry that Ma Blackie fails to give her attentions to her children who feel isolated. Not only the mother but children also fall victim to the detestable Ibuza customs. Emecheta comments, "One or two things were certain to Aku-nna. She had not only lost a father, she had also lost a mother. Ma Blackie found herself so immersed in the Okonkwo family politics, and in making ends meet, that she seldom had time to ask how the world was with her daughter" (82). Aku-nna adapts herself to the given circumstances and remains isolated and lost in her own world. In polygamy men treat women as objects and exploit them physically and mentally. And when they realise that women are not acting in a way that suits the male members of society, they very easily discard them as unwanted things. When truth dawns on Okonkwo that Aku-nna has eloped with Chike – a person from a slavish origin, all his dreams of becoming the 'obi' and that of receiving a hefty sum in the form of bride price shatter. His anger knows no bounds and he shows his bare posterior towards Ma Blackie (156) symbolising divorce. Unfortunately, Aku-nna's step-father shuns his fourth wife, Ma Blackie. The journey of Ma Blackie from Lagos as the single possession of a good husband and then to become the fourth wife of her husband's brother to finally being discarded as an unwanted objected is poignant and excruciating.

Thus, as a feminist writer, Emecheta exposes dehumanising social framework that allows male superiority and insincerity. She censures and disapproves the customs that play havoc with the life of women. She lashes her whip on those who hypocritically disvirgine young girls and crave and insist on their wives being virgins. There are men who marry young girls old enough to be their daughters. All these gruesome customs prove patriarchal environment where women are seen as incidental as opposed to the essential. (Beauvoir 16)

Marriage is of great significance in the traditional patriarchal custom of Africa – the custom that permits the bride and the bridegroom live merrily and to procreate. Unfortunately, the custom of bride price is a stigma on the African culture that equates women to mere commodities that can be bought and sold in the marriage market. As per the custom of marriage the groom has to pay bride price in terms of money or properties to the bride's family. This is one of the widely practiced customs in Africa. The bride price is either paid in the form of cash or sometimes also in the form of other material such as cowries, yams, farmlands, palm wines or animals like goats and cows. What causes fear psychosis among brides is the belief that the bride dies in childbirth, if her parents fail to pay the bride price to the family of the bridegroom. This custom is still prevalent in modern societies of Africa.

The title of the novel *The Bride Price* holds importance as the whole story revolves around the custom of bride price and the repercussions if one fails to pay the bride price. The bride price is obligatory as the husband can only claim the children born by his wife as his own if he has paid the bride price to the bride's parents. The name "Aku-nna" literally means "Father's wealth." This name suggests hypocrisy on the part of patriarchal society that sees daughters as means of earning money. Aku-nna is father's wealth as she will procure money to her father at the time of her marriage. Emecheta feels that various forms of male oppression which have been sanctioned by the patriarchal society need to be scrutinised and readdressed (Rathika 208). It is after the death of Aku-nna's father that she is adopted along with her mother and brother by Okonkwo, her step-father. He expects huge bride price out of Aku-nna's marriage for his own good, i.e., to use the money in his attaining the title of an Obi – the chief. Okonkwo is not against Nna-nndo, Aku-nna's brother, continuing his studies in Ibuza only because Aku-nna's father has "left over one hundred pounds in savings and had joined a progressive Ibuza group called the Pioneer Association, whose aim was to ensure that on the death of any member the first son of that family would be educated to grammar school level" (74).

After her father's death in cosmopolitan city Lagos, Aku-nna, too, continues her studies here in Ibuza. Okonkwo's son, Iloba, objects against her study, "Yes, I know you can do nothing about the boy. But what of that thing – what do they call her? – Aku-nna? Why waste money on her?"(74) Okonkwo's selfishness and hypocrisy is exposed in the following lines:

> You cannot see beyond your noses. You are too young. Don't you know I hope to become an Obi and take the title one day? In order to become an Obi and receive the respected *Eze* title, a man must make a big and expensive sacrifice to the gods…. Aku-nna and Ogugua will get married at about the same time. Their bride prices will come to me. You see the trend today, that the educated girls fetch more money. (75)

It is now clear that Aku-nna might after all really live up to her name and be a "father's wealth."

Whatever is repressive and humiliating in the Igbo culture and customs is earmarked for women. How bizarre customs of Igbo culture reduce women to the level of sufferers and victims of fate is highlighted in the novel by Emecheta. In Ibuza nobody ever dare defy the Igbo customs because

> In Ibuza a young girl must be prepared for anything to happen. Some youth who had no money to pay for a bride might sneak out of the bush to cut a curl from a girl's head so that she would belong to him for life and never be able to return to her parents; because he had given her the

> everlasting haircut, he would be able to treat her as he liked, and no other man would ever touch her. (103)

Here it is observed that custom is used against women in a way that they have no will of their own and they have even no right to decide who can own them. If ever they dare oppose the heinous move, their move is equated to challenge against Igbo values that deserve severe punishment. Such customs as that of cutting of hair by penniless youth cause insecurity and fear among young girls so much so that they dare not go out all alone. "It was to safeguard themselves against this that many girls cropped their hair very close; those who wanted long hair wore a headscarf most of the time" (103). In this way the freedom of young girls to move about in a carefree mood is infringed owing to Igbo customs.

Emecheta candidly attacks in the novel African culture and customs that undermine women to the level of beasts. She depicts these cultural aspects from the point of view of a woman as she herself admits, "When I write, I look for a problem in a certain society from a woman's point of view" (Emenyonu 131). One such custom that shakes the complete whole of women, particularly young girls, and demeans them obnoxiously finds mention in the narrative. That is the custom of night game. Emecheta narrates,

> Their custom allowed this, Boys would come into your mother's hut and play at squeezing a girl's breasts until they hurt; the girl was supposed to try as much as possible to ward them off and not be bad-tempered about it. So long as it was done inside the hut where an adult was near, and so long as the girl did not let the boy too far, it was not frowned on. (97)

The customs like night games suggest that young girls are treated in a very embarrassing way and what is more humiliating and painful is that these dirty games are played in the presence of their elders who passively endorse these heinous customs subjecting girls to the worst kind of trauma. The day when Aku-nna attains womanhood, Okoboshi – a boy with a limp – visits her house as a suitor for her. He frowns the presence of Chike – *osu* slave – whom Aku-nna loves. He wants to see Chike out of the hut. It is in anger that "without warning, Okoboshi walked up to Aku-nna and seized her roughly at the back of her shoulder; he grabbed at both her breasts and started to squeeze and hurt her" (120). This is not only embarrassing for Aku-nna but also hurting and painful to her body and soul. She begs, "Mother, please don't say anything. Okoboshi was hurting me, he was…Mother, look at my new blouse! He has torn it, he was so rough. He was wicked – oh, Mother, please listen…" (121). Woman has no right to object to such dreadful and detestable customs. They have to act accordingly. Since women are trained to bear these insults and pains, Ma Blackie, keeping in mind the strict code of custom, waves aside Aku-nna's pleas saying,

> You mean you have nice breasts and don't want men to touch? Girls like you tend to end up having babies in their father's houses, because they cannot endure open play, so they go to secret places and have themselves disvirgined. Is that type of person you are turning out to be? I will kill you if you bring shame and dishonour on us. How can he hurt you with all these others watching? (121)

Consequently a girl is not allowed by the custom even to oppose the violent acts on her body. Her likings in this matter are ignored point blank. These customs lower women's status to inferior and slavish existence.

The concept of 'virtue', 'purity', 'honour' or 'virginity' is held dear in almost all the patriarchal societies across the world. The concept of 'virginity' is one another custom that is used to perpetuate subjugation of women in Igbo culture. Male members of society are free to forge any illicit relationship within or outside marriage. Their virginity is not a matter of concern as they are free to enjoy their life as they wish. In patriarchy they are not asked to prove their virginity. On the contrary, women have no choice of their own as they are bound to obey the customs that, it seems, are in vogue to inflict violence of all kinds – physical, mental, emotional and spiritual – on women. As far as the concept of virginity is concerned, it is a woman who has to prove her chastity because in patriarchy men have kept themselves above moral indictments of any kind by making the concept of 'purity' and 'honour' rest entirely in women (Chopra 41). Since the concept of purity or chastity is central to men's definition of women, responses to its violence under any circumstances are problematic. The notion of virginity is so deep rooted in African culture that the virginity of African woman is valued much at the time of her marriage as it guarantees higher bride price and women who violate this custom are not only castigated but charged with committing an odious crime against tradition, law and custom. According to the Ibuza custom, a white towel is placed on the bed of the bride on the first night. It must show stains of blood as she is disvirgined and the same towel is gifted to the bride's mother next morning as a proof of the bride's virginity. This strict code of conduct and custom imposed by patriarchal system is nothing but an instrument to wreak violence on the psyche of women. If a woman fails to prove her virginity, the patriarchal system humiliates her and at the same time prohibits her opportunity to live a respectable life.

This happens in *The Bride Price.* Aku-nna who loves Chike – a slave – is not allowed to continue her relationship with him with a warning from her step-father, "Aku-nna, Chike Ofule is only a friend. You must remember that. Now that you have grown, that friendship must gradually die. But die it must!" (116) Aku-nna is prohibited by Ibuza customs to materialise her love. Okoboshi whom Aku dislikes wants to own her by hook or crook. When he fails to win her love he kidnaps her and brings her home. Emecheta poignantly describes Aku-nna's trauma, "What was a girl to do in a predicament of this sort? There was no use of struggling. There must be at least twelve of these men, all running, running and breathing hard. So this was to be the end of her dreams. After everything, she was nothing but a common native girl kidnapped into being a bride" (126). Marriage is solemnised forcefully against her desire. Love or no love hardly matters because she is a woman and a woman must submit to the custom of which she is a part. She has no right to express her desire in matter of her marriage. She is bound to offer, against her will, her body to her kidnapper and if she opposes, the custom has a way to it as Emecheta asserts,

> All the man responsible had to do was cut a curl of her hair – *isi nmo* – and she would belong to him for life. Or he could force her into sleeping with him, and if she refused his people would assist him by holding her down until she was disvirgined. And when that had been done, no other person would want to take her anymore. (132)

In this way Igbo culture endorses the act of rape to subdue the pride of woman. No doubt, one of the most common forms of violence which is all together physical and mental is rape – a patriarchal weapon to threat woman. Rape is simply one of the tools of oppression (Abdulali 201). Realising that Aku-nna is not ready to surrender herself to Okoboshi, he is ready to rape her. "The next minute he was upon her, pulling her roughly by the arm, twisting the arm so much that she screamed in pain. He forced her onto the bed, still holding on to her arm, which she felt going numb" (137). Okoboshi is almost ready to devastate her virginity, when Aku-nna tactfully declares that she is not a virgin. When the African dominant patriarchy is threatened by a woman, it is inevitable for her to face an oppressive punishment (Kharbe 5) Emecheta discloses the inhuman and beastly treatment of Okoboshi towards Aku-nna after she relates her relationship with Chike. He insults her saying,

> I was not too keen on you anyway. My father wanted you simply to get even with his old enemy Ofulue, your slave lover's father. So you are not a virgin! That will be the greatest fun of it all. You will remain my wife in name, but in a few months I shall marry the girl of my choice and you will have to fetch and carry for her and for my subsequent wives, Get out of my bed, you public bitch!(139)

He spits in her face and hits her so hard in the eye that she is sent reeling onto the mud couch. Here, it is clear that if male ego hurts men become aggressive and punish women in their own ways. In a cultural set-up where patriarchy dominates, a woman is not allowed to express even her legitimate feelings.

Taboos and customs do not let Aku-nna live happily till she breathes her last. She does not surrender herself to the advances made by Okoboshi who wants to rape her. She elopes with Chike to a neighbouring town, Ugheli, where Chike secures a job and accommodation. He looks after Aku-nna with love and care. But her predicament intensifies a lot as the custom of bride price keeps haunting her time and again and what is more disturbing and painful for her is that Okonkwo, her step-father, is not ready to accept the bride price from Chike's father who tries hard to persuade Okonkwo. Unfortunately, as the custom has it the marriage remains traditionally unrecognised. Aku-nna is all the time engrossed with the fear of consequences of going against the customs. Although Aku-nna and Chike get married happily and settle down, she is unable to defy the limitations of Ibo tradition against which she has protested. Her health deteriorates as she reels under the psychological fear that if a groom's family fails to pay the bride price to the bride's family at the time of marriage, the bride dies in childbirth. This fear haunts her so much so that she loses interest in life and inches towards death. Her trauma and depressed state of mind is laid bare before the readers when she speaks to Chike's father, "I hope I shall see you again, Father. You see, I know my uncle does not want ever to accept the bride price. He calls me back in the wind, when I am alone. But I shall never answer. I don't want to die, Father" (163). Here Aku-nna makes reference to one more ghastly custom of black magic which is done by her step-father to destroy her. He makes a look-alike doll of Aku-nna pierced with a sharp object and places it in front of his *chi* – the personal god. Whether the black magic has any bad effect on a person or not but it is clear that it does make a psychological impact to intimidate the targeted person. Consequently, due to malnutrition and young age, Aku-nna dies in childbirth fulfilling the prophecy. Thus, her fear and hallucinations about the magnitude and outcomes of the unpaid bride price become real enough. Though Chike loves her too much and tries his best to save her life at the time of child birth, horrifying traditional values become so entrenched in Aku-nna's mind and the fear of acrimonious consequences of violating the customs haunt her so much so that she is finally devastated by fear and the psychological torture. So it is that Chike and Aku-nna validate the traditional superstition they have unknowingly set out to exterminate. Emecheta, vociferously, delivers a message that the consequences of violating the law of the society are always catastrophic. Emecheta writes,

> Every girl born in Ibuza after Aku-nna's death was told her story, to reinforce the old taboos of the land. If a girl wished to live long and see her children's children, she must accept the husband chosen for her by people, and the pride price must be paid. If the bride price was not paid, she would never survive the birth of her first child. It was a psychological hold over every young girl that would continue to exist, even in the face of every modernisation, until the present day. (168)

Thus, to read Emecheta's *The Bride Price* in accordance with the cultural context of Africa shows that a woman is subject to male oppression and harassment caused in the name of Igbo culture and values. The story of Aku-nna is reiterated to the girls just to reinforce the fear of Igbo values that demand strict compliance on the part of women otherwise they will have to bear the brunt of defiance. The novel, thus, becomes Emecheta's weapon to attack values that target women to inflict violence on them. Emecheta who herself was a victim of custom of bride price does not seem endorsing this custom. Akku-nna dies due to unavailability of medical help. She dies not because her husband fails to pay the bride price to her step father but because she is ill-nourished, weak and under never-ending stress and fear of the repercussions and curse that may befall on her in the wake of non-payment of bride price.

Work Cited

Abdulali, Sohaila. "Rape in India: An Emprical Picture." *Women in Indian Society,* edited by Rehana Ghadially, Sage Publications, 1988.

Beauvoir, Simone de. *The Second Sex.* Transated and edited by M.M.Parshley.1953, rpt.Penguin,1983.

Bhusan, Vidya and D.R. Sachdeva. *An Introduction to Sociology.* Kitab Mahal, 1994.

Chopra, Vinod K. *Partition Stories: Mapping Community, Communalism and Gender.* Anamika, 2009.

Chukwu,Christian Chima et. al. *Violence against Women in Igboland, South-east, Nigeria: A Critical Quest of Change.* http://www.academicjournals.org/IJSA. Vol:6 (2), Feb. 2014.

Emecheta, Buchi. *The Bride Price.* George Braziller, 2017.

Emenyonu. "Pre-Colonial/ Colonial African Women in *The Bride Price.*" http://shodhganga.inflibnet.ac.in

Frank, Ketherin. *Death of the Slave Girl.* "Pre-Colonial/ Colonial African Woman in *The Bride Price* and *The Joys Of Motherhood.*" https://shodganga.inflibnet.ac.in

Odimegwu, C and C.N. Okemybo. *Influence of Widowhood Practices on the Psycho-Social and Physical Health of Widows in Selected States of South Eastern, Nigeria.* https://www.idpublications.org.

Kharbe, Ambreen. "Representation of Nigerian Women in Buchi Emecheta *The Bride Price* and *The Joys of Motherhood.* http://www.epitomejournals.com. vol.3, no. 1. November 2017.

Rathika, E. Autocratic Study of Buchi Emecheta's *The Bride Price.* http://www.ijelr.in

Umeh, marie Linton. "Introduction". *The Bride Price.* Buchi Emecheta. George Braziller, 2017, i-ix.

CHAPTER 7

Decoding the Politics of Denial of Female Identity: An Analysis of Beryl Subia Awuor's *Black Moon*

Roshan Lal Sharma and Prakash Kumar Meher

"Is there hope, to dream, to dare, to live
and just be me?" (Awuor 14)

This chapter undertakes textual analysis of Beryl Subia Awuor's debut collection of poems titled *Black Moon* from the viewpoint of issues concerning female identity, its denial and politics involved therein. Awuor, who is a powerful and young poetic voice from Kenya, currently teaches in Dubai. She is a graduate in Journalism and Mass Communication from the University of Nairobi (Awuor, "Committed"). The poetic universe of her debut collection is poignantly nuanced, layered, daring and challenging, evidencing denial of female identity in a deeply patriarchal society wherein "to dream" and "to dare" seems to be an impossibility. The chapter has been divided into three parts: the first briefly theorises the notions of identity, identity politics, and female identity; the second part examines Awuor's poetry from the viewpoint of decoding politics behind denial of female identity; and the third and final part offers summation of insights based on problematising female Kenyan identity as a genderised construct in Kenyan context through textual examination.

I

Whereas at one level the term 'identity' signifies distinctive personality and character of a person; at another, it includes her/his thoughts, beliefs, mindset and individuality which distinguish her/him from others. Gender identity refers to "an individual's personal sense of identity as masculine or feminine, or some combination thereof" (Morrow and Messinger 8). In this sense, gender identity is characterised by a sense of individuality, distinctiveness and uniqueness. If viewed historically, identity alludes to certain traits in a person that make her/him realise and understand as to who s/he is and how s/he is viewed/perceived by others. This implication of the notion of identity dates back to the eighteenth century. Thereafter, it has been rife in the literary discourse to discuss one's role in the society vis-a-vis issues concerning gender and sexual identity ('Identity,' *Dictionary.com*). It also points toward the "condition of being a certain person or thing" and an "awareness that an individual... has of being a distinct, persisting entity" ('Identity', www.thefreedictionary.com). However, the word 'identity' has its root in Latin *idem* signifying "the same", but the term 'identity crisis' was first recorded in 1954 ('Identity,' *Online Etymology Dictionary*).

According to Christine Coupland, as far as some fields of study like sociology and social psychology are concerned, 'identity' begins to appear therein after 1940 (2210). However, it has been a buzzword in every discipline and particularly in humanities and social sciences, after the advent of literary and cultural theories like feminism, Marxism, psychoanalytic criticism, structuralism, poststructuralism, postmodernism and postcolonialism. These modes of interpreting and examining literature have helped establish certain methods to analyse identity as a conceptual construct in various ways and thus underscore its significance. Richard Jenkins defines 'identity' as

> the human capacity – rooted in language – to know 'who's who' (and hence 'what's what'). This involves knowing who we are, knowing who others are, them knowing who we are, us knowing who they think we are, and so on: a multi-dimensional classification or mapping of human world and our places in it, as individuals and members of collectivities. (5)

Coupland examines contemporary definitions of 'identity' and observes that it is "always in flux, and that it is a perception that each person develops about who he or she is in relation to others" (2211). Thus, a person realises her/ his identity through interaction with other people. The above definition and viewpoint speak of identity in a gender-neutral manner, but the moment we see it through the lens of gender, two distinctly important constructs come to light called masculinity and femininity. Both differ from each other in terms of their definition and social construction. The primary distinction is made in terms of biological difference and thus femininity encompasses "motherhood, being nurturing, a desire of pretty clothes and exhibitions of emotions" (Ritzer and Ryan 221). On the other hand, masculinity may include "fatherhood, acting 'tough,' a desire for sports and competition and hiding emotions" (221).

This biological distinction may lend men a higher status; however, Simone de Beauvoir in *The Second Sex* writes about the social construction of identity rather than its biological formation when she writes: "One is not born, rather becomes, a woman." The role of patriarchal society thus becomes critically decisive in the formation of a subjugated identity of a woman. According to bell hooks, patriarchy is a politico-social system which insists that "males are inherently dominating, superior to everything and everyone deemed weak, especially females, and endowed with the right to dominate and rule over the weak and to maintain that dominance through various forms of psychological terrorism and violence" (18). In a patriarchal hegemonic and oppressive socio-cultural setup, a woman is forced to be submissive and obey the diktats of male members. Patriarchy, in fact, affects the existence of a woman adversely in familial, social, socio-cultural and political spheres. Her existence is either ignored, denigrated or undermined to an extent that she starts denying her own identity as a woman.

Identity Politics

The phrase 'identity politics', coined in 1973, has profound political implications and has been defined as a "political activity based on or catering to the cultural, ethnic, gender, racial, religious, or social interests that characterise a group identity" (*Dictionary.com*). It is extensively used in social sciences and humanities as a means to formulate specific viewpoints, take certain stances, and advocate particular ideologies and thus assert power with a view to have recognition and acknowledgement. Moreover, it also has the potential to provoke social and political action vis-à-vis prevailing injustice and inequality in a society. Identity politics, in fact, shot into prominence during the second half of the twentieth century in political anthropology due to the emergence of various movements such as feminist movement, civil rights movement, nationalist and postcolonial movements across the world (Neofotistos).

When we think about women's identity vis-a-vis African literature, we observe that female writings have not been gained critical attention. The portrayal of women's experience in male writings seems to be either neglected or underrepresented. This leads to the formation of a male identity discourse to dominate and check women's voices in literary arena. The traditional patriarchal culture and mindset are reflected in writings too and thus women writers struggle to get their due identities.

Judith Kegan Gardiner reviews the work of Erik Erikson, Heinz Lichtenstein and Norman Holland (male identity theorists) who have influenced literary criticism in a conspicuous manner. Gardiner discovers that none of the theorists has talked about female identity separately and views it as a male model. They assumed "stability" and "constancy" as the desirable factors for the male identity. As a counterpoint, Gardiner deliberately analyses feminist Nancy Chadorow's viewpoint who views female identity "as relational and fluidly defined, starting with infancy and continuing throughout womanhood" (352).

Female Identity

Across continents, female identity has been manipulated since time immemorial. Feminist movement that has been theorised in terms of waves and their evolution into post-feminist theory may be viewed as an attempt to assert female presence in different first world nations. Some remarkable and path breaking texts that have influenced views about female identity are Mary Wollstonecraft's *A Vindication of the Rights of Woman* (1792), Simone de Beauvoir's *The Second Sex* (1949), Betty Friedan's *The Feminine Mystique* (1963), and Kate Millett's *Sexual Politics* (1970). These texts have changed the way we think about gender identity and the position of women in a patriarchal world.

However, the third world nations in Latin America, Africa and Asia could not see such healthy developments in the arena of awareness about women and their rights. We cannot claim that the first world nations have completely overcome issues concerning gender inequality/discrimination by developing a sane and balanced understanding about female identity; nevertheless, if we take into account their educational advancement along with socio-cultural and political awareness, they have been able to at least negotiate gender politics to an extent that it may serve as a beacon light for women living in other climes and cultures of the world. Likewise, there is a whole range of female poets from the first world nations such as Emily Dickinson, Sylvia Plath, Adrienne Rich, Elizabeth Barrett Browning and Amy Levy who have created awareness and enhanced our understanding about issues concerning women. Dickinson, Plath and Rich hail from America whose poetry has pronounced a feminist slant. Of late, similarly, in Europe, poets like Browning and Levy have raised issues related to female identity. Interestingly, of late, even the underdeveloped societies/countries in African and Asian continents also seem to have come off age regarding poetic representation of female identity. In Indian context too, poets like Kamala Das and Meena Kandasamy have powerfully used poetry to give female identity a distinctly unique space.

African Female Identity

Despite the fact that the Kenyan constitution which came into effect in 2010, the women belonging to minority, ethnic and indigenous communities have been facing challenges of diverse sorts. Laura A. Young in her report on "Challenges at the intersection of gender and ethnic identity in Kenya" lucidly elucidates the issues that are common to women from diverse communities. "Poverty and lack of economic opportunities" have been identified as the biggest challenges that have been impeding the growth of women from diverse communities of the society. Young further observes thus:

> While these development challenges affect many women and men in Kenya, minority and indigenous women experience these challenges as inextricably related to their identity and the marginalisation that their communities have experienced. They are discriminated against on multiple levels; they are targeted because of their identification with a minority or indigenous group, and as women – both by cultural practices within their own community and because of gender discrimination more widely. (3)

Amidst such a scenario, the publication of Beryl Subia Awuor's collection of poetry namely *Black Moon* may be viewed as an attempt to highlight and underscore issues concerning female identity particularly in Kenyan context, which scarcely provides equal opportunities to women leave aside working committedly to empower them or allow them space to be determiners of their lives.

In fact, female identity in African literary representation has by and large been relegated to an inferior position. While situating African female identity in earlier times, Omotayo Oloruntoba-Oju and Taiwo Oloruntoba-Oju argue that its construction in both colonial and postcolonial times has been based on essentialism, which implies that women have either been portrayed in a negative light or in an essentialist manner. Taking purview of the Nigerian literature authored by male writers, they point out that the portrayal of women was underrepresented and neglected in three ways. Firstly, the presence of male representation in literary works deliberately silenced the female voices; secondly, women characters are confined only to domestic settings and motherhood; and finally, during pre-colonial and post-colonial times women were viewed in a negative way (8). Further, they cite Asha Sen and Florence Stratton and say that whereas the former views the male centric literature as "the immobilisation of the female in male imposed traditionally-convened roles", the latter notes it as "the defining feature" of Nigerian literature (8).

In African poetic scenario we have several female poets who have been making their voices heard. We cannot ignore African American poets like Maya Angelou and Alice Walker who had to wage a double war to fight for their black identity on the one hand and female identity on the other. In Africa, the poetic scenario has been dominated by men until very recently but of late there are a host of female poetic voices who have been trying to make themselves heard in a thoroughly male-dominated poetic space. Poets like Phillis Wheatley and Frances Ellen Watkins Harper have been very influential in voicing their concerns against slavery. Likewise, Audre Lorde is a poet who is quite radical in her stance in favour of women's rights and declares herself as a black lesbian feminist warrior poet. Keith D. Leonard has rightly observed: "Empowered by poetry's association with emotion and intuition that patriarchal societies often devalue, African American women poets 'adopted, adapted and transformed' the definitions of motherhood, sexual identity, love, beauty and spirituality in order to liberate themselves" (169).

Moreover, along with the above-mentioned poets and the contemporary female poets such as Harriet Anena and Ijeoma Umebinyuo, African female poetic voices have reached every part of the world. Born in West Africa, Phillis Wheatley is known for *Poems on Various Subjects Religious and Moral* (1773), which is the first volume of poetry by a woman of an African descent (Leonard 170). Africa is now witnessing the poetry of young female poets like Anena and Umebinyuo. Anena's poetry collection titled *A Nation in Labour* made her win the Wole Soyinka Prize for Literature in 2018. Thus, we see an emergence of female voices in the genre of poetry in English language. They want, nay, deserve critical attention. It is thus necessary to view afresh the representation of African female identity represented through women's poetry, which, as stated above, has been deplorably ignored on account of the dominance of the history of African literature by male poets/ writers.

Literature in its earliest form has been oral. As far as African oral literature is concerned, we do find the role of women in a significant way. In fact, women's presence in the oral literary arena is evident, as Obioma Nnaemeka writes: "In African oral tradition, women were very visible not only as performers but as producers of knowledge, especially in view of oral literature's didactic relevance, moral(izing) imperatives and pedagogical foundations" (138). They had the privilege of being at the centre due to their multiple roles of being performers, preservers and composers of oral literature. Nnaemeka writes more about their rich legacy thus: "Women were not only performers and disseminators of beliefs, cultural ideals, and personal/collective history, but also composers who, sometimes, transformed and re-created an existing body of oral traditions in order to incorporate woman-centered perspectives" (138).

However, when it comes to the literary expression by female authors in written literature, it has largely been ignored by their male counterparts. The literary oeuvres of women writers have been pushed aside or ignored by a patriarchal writing culture and this was the reason that women's voice in a community, group, and race remained unheard. Nnaemeka views this shift from speaking objects of women turning into written objects and validates "knowledge of the colonisers' languages" like English, French, German, Italian, Spanish, and Portuguese as an important responsible factor (139). The edge of having the privilege of any of the above languages established a strong male literary tradition in Africa. This may be viewed as one of the reasons behind the absence of female writers/poets in African literary canon in the early years of literary engagement.

In this backdrop the voices that try to emerge to counter the feelings of 'anxiety of authorship' à la Sandra Gilbert and Susan Gubar. This chapter critically engages with female identity and its politics as represented in Beryl Subia Awuor's poetry collection namely *Black Moon*. Through powerful imagery and penetrating poetic idiom, Awuor portrays how the female existence is rarely acknowledged and how women are subdued in a regressive socio-cultural setup dominated by patriarchal mindset. It remarkably reflects the transition from being oppressive objects to speaking subjects as the poet in Awuor starts to write. Her effort to denounce the oppressive conditions in which women somehow survive and the politics of their identity crisis will be decoded through textual analysis of some of the poems from *Black Moon.*

African and African American male writers have been able to carve a niche for themselves through their writings amid Apartheid, colonialism and slavery. They used writing as a medium to express the dehumanisation and atrocities done to them through different literary genres. In other words, they dominated the African literary canon in an androcentric manner. However, when it comes to female writers, we find that they had to fight against a regressive and patriarchal culture to articulate their struggle, trials and tribulations. As mentioned above, writers like Phillis Wheatley, Alice Walker, Maya Angelou and Toni Morrison viewed women's sufferings and their relentless struggle in a male-dominated world from female perspective, and thus offered a counternarrative to the established facts concerning female writers. Moreover, there are other prominent female authors as well whose journey to be writers has not been a cakewalk. It is a well-known fact how female writers like Mary Ann Evans used the male name George Eliot to thrive against a dominant culture and to be endorsed by male authors. Likewise, the Bronte Sisters too had to write under masculine pseudonyms to avoid public attention.

Thus, to be a woman writer has never been easy. In African context too, the women writers were forced to occupy subordinate and insignificant positions. Ama Ata Aidoo also writes that they were haunted by the question whether their literary works would be worthy of attention by the male writers. She discusses the problems of writers and views the women writers' suffering thus:

> All writers are plagued by fears, real and imaginary, by all sorts of uncertainties and some very solid problems. After all, we are also human. The truth though, is that some of us suffer a little more, simply because we are women, and our positions are nearly hopeless because we are African women. (164)

Aidoo clearly points out the disadvantaged status of an African woman aspiring to be a writer and believes that the identities of women writers are rarely acknowledged. She thinks that suffering is part of any poetic literary creation and asserts that "all art is subsidised by artists with their lives" (163). Aidoo in her influential essay "To Be an African Woman Writer – an Overview and a Detail" highlights two pertinent issues. Firstly, she puts forth the fact that

African women are not incompetent to produce any worthy kind of literary works. She justifies it by mentioning various women writers and their works across Africa. Secondly, she emphasises the need for attention to the significance of the oeuvres produced by those writers. She craves for scholarly attention to evaluate any piece of writing and thus speaks of a dearth of audience for African women's writings. In this background, this paper closely looks at some of the poems by Beryl Subia Awuor which powerfully portray issues concerning female identity particularly in Kenyan socio-cultural context. As one focuses hard, the subjugated female identity of the Kenyan woman metaphorises the plight of the larger African female identity.

II

A collection of fifty poems, Beryl Subia Awuor's *Black Moon* has been dedicated to two women who have played pivotal role in the formation of her creative consciousness, namely Beatrice Achieng (her mother's sister) and Roseline Mboya (her mother). She writes about her mother in her dedication: "I am yet to see any as strong as you, mamma" – a testimony to the fact that the very kelson/spine of her poetic endeavour has her mother as its core alongside her deep and diverse range of her personal experience as she tries to come to terms with her identity in an oppressive patriarchal familial and social set-up. The title poem "Black Moon" lends force to the central argument of this chapter concerning lack of identity of an African woman represented as "African black moon" and "[e]clipsed moon" metaphorically. Despite the fact that the poet knows her "…worth" but she writes that "somehow, it seems/ useless to be me/ With no one caring, with the earth/ Perpetually standing in my light" (14). The clouds scoff at her plight as the black moon "gets her light from the sun" (13), and so do the planets as they mock her for reflecting "only the sun's light" (14) having none of hers. The sun and moon have been portrayed as male and female respectively. Whereas the sun is all powerful, the moon has been depicted as being at the receiving end. The clouds and planets seem to look down upon her inherent potentiality to perform her duties in the world and thus jeopardising her self-belief. Excessively aware about herself, the poet-protagonist knows that her "duties surpass warming beds at night" (14). Moreover, she has to toil hard to "illumine the earth by night" (13) despite her "pain and sorrow" (14).

The female identity of the poet has never been allowed to blossom and take root in the African clime as she has been rendered a "prisoner, a weakling, a helpless thing" (13). She has tried repeatedly to be her own self and thus "produce my own light and glitter the universe" (13), but the patriarchal forces would seldom let her occupy the desired space. Moreover, she questions as well as exposes the powers that be to suggest as to how these are conspiring to impede her identity that may blossom and take rightful shape in the socio-cultural clime which has hitherto denied her due. She says: "How do I get the courage, or even/ Warmth, and in strength illumine, shine/ On?" (14). The answer is simple that she deserves a space of her own without male intervention at any point in time. Toward the end of the poem, Awuor raises yet another pertinent query: "Is there hope, to dream, to dare, to live/ And just be me?" (14), and thereby leaves it to echo in callously indifferent patriarchal world as a constant reminder of the lack of sensitivity and understanding toward women.

Whereas the sun is the source of light for the moon, the latter finds herself to be a "prisoner, a weakling, a helpless thing" (13) having tremendous capacity to see the wrong being done to her and question the same in a subdued but firm tone. Whereas the "black" symbolises the African, "moon" symbolises female identity. Like the moon, the African woman is a lone wanderer in the male dominated universe. She keeps on shining and thus knows her worth of being a guiding light. However, her shining too is linked with the man. It implies that the poet-protagonist's socio-cultural clime which makes her believe that a woman's identity is a sheer naught without a man. Her endeavour to be bright amid darkness is soon abandoned. She finds no cooperation from her male counterparts to persist any further and thus her identity seems to be in crisis. She realises her identity as nothing as it is evident when she says that it is "useless to me" (15). Moreover, she analyses her existence and questions whether she can dream and hope by just being a woman in the oppressive society which prevents her pursuit to shine on. Whether she can hope or dream or dare to be just herself remains a question which can be answered only if the males of the species will stop jeering, mocking and scoffing at her female identity/ existence/ being, and be sensitive, accommodating and understanding.

Another poem which has a radical thematic core is "Clarity" wherein a would-be mother is caught at the crossroads full of doubts, fears and dread as to whether she should go for abortion or not. The poet terms the process of "sad" grappling with her indecisiveness as the one that enables her to delve into "meditation" (39). The "haze" and unclarity, however, disappears and all doubts are dispelled as "[c]larity stands bold and bright/ Smiling down at me" (39). She is firm in her mind that she has to keep the baby as "Somehow I know now/ We will survive this/ Abortion will not do, not for me" (40). Such an inner assurance, self-belief and confidence to "survive" in times to come, howsoever tough and trying, brings to the fore the assertion of her female identity steeped in deep resilience against all odds.

The first poem, "Twenty and Crippled", is centred on a young African woman who is homeless and nameless. She finds her identity/existence lost somewhere in the hustle and bustle of Kenyan streets. Though young, she is abandoned by people around her who do not even notice, leave aside acknowledge, her existence. Awuor writes: "People see you/ But they don't notice you" (2), and thus draws our attention to inhuman indifference on the part of the people around. Moreover, a twenty-year-old woman, crippled, homeless, and left so cruelly to fend for herself is yet another worrisome aspect of this society wherein a woman is subdued, ignored, ill-treated and even orphaned. The poet's concern does not lie in food only; it is, more importantly, the abandoned woman's desire to find a respectable place in the society: "Food is not all/ Important is living well/ A place to sleep/ A friend to greet" (3). Homelessness here may be construed as a marker of loss of identity/self in a setup wherein a woman is relegated as well as ignored; however, Awuor keenly observes and underscores a desire in the orphaned woman's mind – the desire to be recognised first as a person and an individual, and then, more importantly, as a woman in African society: "I see a longing in her eyes/ A desire to be held/ A need for male warmth next to her" (4). It is not fulfilled and she just survives as a redundant presence.

In African continent, women become victims of violence (be that domestic, sexual or psychological) quite often and one of the reasons that can be attributed to this is gender inequality. The African Gender Index Report, 2019 (in association with UNICEF State of the World Children Report) indicates about domestic violence done to young African women and reveals that one third women in the age group (15-34 years) have been victims of domestic violence over the last 12 years ("African Gender Index," 25). This clearly shows gender inequality and precarious condition of women in African context. Interestingly, gender inequality appears to be a motif in Awuor's poetic world. She articulates her pain through some of the poems that portray helpless and pathetic condition of women as discarded entities totally devoid of any sense of identity.

Sexual violence on women and girls are clearly evident in many poems like "Innocent Little Anyango" and "Men on the Streets." A little girl namely Anyango becomes a victim of sexual assault and the poet is quick and perceptive enough to underline the power of the perpetrator to indulge in similar kind of sexual violence with other girls and women too. It is evident when the man says: "I will do it again to Beryl/ I will do it again to Cheryl/ I will do it again to Sheryl" (36). It speaks volumes as to how blatantly fearless and motivated this "stranger" of a man is who clearly announces his intention to sexually abuse other girls as well. Jennie Ruby outlines various characteristics of the patriarchal culture and in particular, the "[c]onstant threat of rape and harassment of women by men" and "[m]en controlling women's bodies and lives" (38) rightly corroborate what is powerfully depicted in Awuor's poetry as it uncovers the fact how female identity and self-respect are constantly in jeopardy.

The opening remarks of the unrepentant audacious stranger in "Innocent Little Anyango" also reflect the privileged position of men in Kenyan society wherein they control/dominate women and thus deny females their identity through persistent coercion, constant torture, and sexual abuse. The women are reduced to sheer objects devoid of any sense of self, identity or individuality. Such an objectification of women gains legitimacy due to the patriarchal socio-cultural, familial, and political setup which is in cahoots with the perpetrators like the stranger in the poem who knows that the society will scarcely take notice of the wrong being done do the likes of Anyango, Beryl, or Sheryl. Awuor thus shocks as well as jolts us out of our complacence by lucidly portraying the perpetrator bent on and pre-decided about committing rape because of a deeper systemic malaise, and that is lack of will and the requisite legal mechanism to nab the wrong doer and punish him adequately. The message is loud and clear to the patriarchal powers that be that they stand implicated, nay, are the equal partners in the crime committed against innocent Anyango. The poetic idiom of Awuor is thus gentle, persuasive, evocatively suggestive and profoundly radical that can trigger instant transformation in the mind of the reader to firmly stand with the wronged, the exploited and the weak.

When Awuor articulates about the subject position of the man, she brings attention to the fact that he appears to be invincible and enjoys the privilege of being a male. The wrongdoer even proclaims that nobody can punish him in a court of law because the society is blind towards any atrocities committed against women. It is the sad reality of African society in general and Kenyan in particular, and the poet powerfully conveys the perpetrator's/ stranger-rapist's belief thus: "No one will ever find me out/ Because they are all blind/ Blind to the care of such young as you" (36).

The streak of intended sexual abuse is also visible in the poem "Men on the Streets." The men here refer to the people of diverse age groups who turn out to be the molesters. However, unlike the "Innocent Little Anyango", this poem expresses a sharp disapproval of the act of molestation. Here, the intended victim strongly resists and maintains her dignity under all circumstances. In case of a molester, she "[l]anded a stinging slap on his back/ Blocked tears in her eyes/ Let loose her lips/ And rained abuses on him"; in another's case, "She clenched her fists/ He apologised/ But winked as he walked away" (49). In both the cases, female resistance shines forth as Awuor seems to suggest that after a point, women cannot afford to remain passive recipients of the wrongs being done to them. They do have to stand for themselves. The man winking and walking away in the second instance is remarkably suggestive of male complacence about things that they can do to women anytime at will. Whether he will/ won't indulge in the same indecent behaviour in times to come remains a perpetual point of consideration. As far as the female protagonist in the poem is concerned, Awuor assigns her a task, even though she realises its habitual curve, by writing: "She still has things to do/ Errands on the streets/ Even if it means slapping them/ She must walk on the streets" (49).

The attempt to show defiance in a male society can be observed as a black woman's fight against the darkness to embrace light. This has been further beautifully signified in the poem "Clarity." We hear an African pregnant mother's dilemma regarding whether to live or not to live. She thinks of her "forbidden" child and visualises the grim future. The place of women in the society makes her apprehensive vis-à-vis nurturing a child. To her future seems, "foggy and misty/ hazy, unclear", and her heart "hopes/ Dreads at same/

Doubts…" (40). However, she clings to hope despite all odds/ haze that overpowers her mind, and decisively declares about the survival of both (mother and her child in the offing), and thus abandons the idea of going for abortion: "I decide to keep the baby" (40) as she is sure to survive somehow. At one level it is defiance, at the other, it is assertion of her female identity and acknowledgement of the fact that she *can* make a choice and be *herself* even in the face of oppressive patriarchal forces.

The female identity is denied in a love relationship as she is through and through subjugated through male/patriarchal dictates. She experiences fake love which is thrust on her when she looks for truthfulness on the part of her partner. The poem titled "I Don't Think You Love Me" represents it cogently when the beloved says: "You say you love me/ Ha/ Will you prove it?" (74). However, she knows that it is futile to expect an answer since man would either evade it or ignore. In fact, Awuor's diagnosis of the basic problem with men is so accurate and profound that she, in fact, seems to give two hoots for an answer. She knows it will never come on expected lines. Hence, she states her case in a rather matter of fact manner and thereby sharing the naked truth of her being as a woman in most sensuously evocative terms: "When you look at me/ My breasts tingle/ When you shake my hand/ My lips quiver/ When you hold me to you/ I burn, I blaze" (74). The lover's promise to some other woman is no big deal to the beloved as she just wants him to "[u]npromise" the former. However, she is no fool as she knows deep down that her lover cannot give her any hope despite the fact that she excruciatingly longs to be his: "I die to be with you/ It kills me-/ This longing/To be yours" (75). This poem, in fact, offers a deep and stark realisation to the beloved that her lover is not hers any more as the title vividly states despite a little sense of incertitude. In a sense the whole poems may also be seen as an attempt to break the chain of suffering on account of her profound longing for her lover who is into a different relationship. This typical male trait of moving on at will without caring a wee bit for the former beloved needs to be denounced as it wounds female psyche and jeopardises/ impedes her future trajectory/ growth as a woman. She wants to go away from such regressive society where love is manipulated to the advantage of men only. She no longer believes in the fake promises and seeks a detachment. She wants to carve her own identity by choosing to living in her own way. It is clearly evident in the poem "Freedom" wherein the female-protagonist strongly spells her desire to be free: "To grow wings and fly/ Detached from this muddle/ Free from this mess/ Of lies/ Of half-truths/ Of 'I love you'" (72).

Awuor portrays the crisis of female identity in most of the poems. We see considerable textual evidence of the woman's voice being forcefully subdued. She cannot speak because her physical condition does not allow it as her lips are cracked and tongue is stuck. She is no longer a human being as male dominance has reduced her and forced her into servitude befitting a servant. The poet questions it forcefully: "Must it be always/ That a goddess be turned to a servant?" (86) The lost female identity is further evident female protagonist in the poem "Goddesses and Gods": "Me, once human, a child of God/ Today something else" (86). Thus, the poem presents a sharp disapproval of gender inequality and discrimination to an extent that a woman is more often than not deprived of her due in relation to her male counterparts.

Awuor depicts how men's position in the society is similar to that of gods. In fact, men have declared themselves as gods. It is a position which is superior to that of women and hence men degrade them as servants, as less than them. Describing about the male-character in the poem, Awuor writes: "He thinks that all men are gods/ He bites into my flesh with his words/ He undresses me with his comments/ He strips me of my being/ Me, once human, a child of God/ Today something else,/ A creation of some god indeed" (86). At one level, it is a satire on male-idiom which can be sharp-edged, ripping and also vulgar to the point of striping one's "being." Despite such an oppressive and disheartening state of affairs, the female-protagonist in the poem wants to reclaim her strength which has been lost owing to patriarchal politics. She raises her voice of concern vis-à-vis African woman to remind men with patriarchal mindset by saying that she had heard about the stronger stature of goddesses compared to gods at one point in time, and that she wants a reassurance, a confirmation regarding the same. Awuor writes thus: "Once, I thought that goddesses were stronger than gods/ Reassure me/ Confirm to me/ Please tell me/ That yes, goddesses are still stronger than gods" (86). She is seeking solace so that she can fight back against the established repressive tradition with the help of her male counterparts be that lovers, friends, husbands, fathers, brothers, and others. Will her plea be heard/ heeded? This question may be hard to answer but since it has been raised it deserves critical attention. It is through lucid, relentless, probing and unsettling questioning that we may disrupt hegemonic discourses. The politics of denial of female identity in Kenya/ Africa also needs to be decoded through disrupting its patriarchal core which tends to perpetuate itself at all costs simply because 'female identity' both as a theoretical construct as well as prevalence (howsoever subdued) remains a threat for the powers that be. Awuor's strategy of poetically and textually evidencing profound awareness of the wrongs done to women in diverse familial, interpersonal, socio-political and other contexts in Kenya is a weapon enough to topple hegemonic patriarchal discourses/ authority/ power centres.

Awuor's also highlights the practice of social evil like polygamy through her poetry and it reinforces the denial of woman's identity. In the process, she loses her right to be loved by her choicest partner and it results in the denial of her right to both her corporeal self/ body and existence/ individuality. She denounces the men who possess "the highest brain power", simply because they cheat on their wives or marry several women. She finds animals and birds ("dogs" and "doves") as better lovers than men as they do not practice polygamy. Awuor writes in the poem "Dogs are better Lovers" thus: "But if a man/ With the highest brain power/ Will cheat on his wife/ Or marry many others/ When she is alive still/ Then,/ Even dogs,/ So despised by men/ Are better lovers" (103). This is strong denunciation and condemnation of male privilege of cheating on their wives – a patriarchal prerogative which men exercise more often than not. Awuor, besides questioning it, also undermines the same to put forth her firm authorial stance which enables and empowers her to consider men worse even than dogs. The poet thus is extremely direct and forthright in her perception of men and makes corrective inputs as well even though suggestively and obliquely.

We do come across the practice of polygamy in African novels also. Major female writers like Buchi Emecheta, Mariama Ba, Ama Ata Aidoo and male authors like Chinua Achebe have engaged with the issue of polygamy in their fiction. Vuyiswa Ndabayakhe and Catherine Addison observe that the representation of African female identity in novels by male and female authors is markedly distinct. While male authors like Achebe in *Things Fall Apart* and Onuora Nzekwu in *Highlife for Lizards* treat polygamy as a system which is beneficial for women; its representation by female authors like Emecheta in *The Joys of Motherhood* and *Kehinde*, Aidoo in *Changes*, and

Ba in her *Une si longue lettre* (*So Long a Letter*) and *Un chant ecarlate* (*Scarlet Song*) expose the "female suffering and oppression" at the hands of male-centred traditional practices like polygamy (90). Thus, Awuor as a poet joins hands with above novelists to raise issues concerning African female identity vis-à-vis polygamy.

The poem "In the Memory of Athela" is yet another powerful poetic narrative of the subjugated identity of the female-protagonist, who has mothered six children. Her five children died before their birth and she mourns the death of all including Athela who dies after being born. The reason of Athela's death is not natural as it is instead an outright murder by her husband while he was beating her physically. This poem exemplifies male brutality in its cruellest form. The mother fails to understand the reason as to why her husband, Jomo, had to be so ruthlessly inhuman with herself and her children: "Why did Jomo have to kick all the children out of my womb? / What wrong did I ever do/ To deserve five dead children,/ All born with nothing more than scattered hair, blood mucus/ Not even with toes or fingers/ Children too young to be born – he just/ Kicked them out of my womb" (107). Such brutality has become a norm in her life. Jomo, in connivance with his mother, brings a "skinny woman with no bottoms" to live with him and her arrival aggravates things further for the mother and worsens her situation by demeaning her and hurting her self-respect as the "first wife." Articulating her deep sense of humiliation, the female protagonist says: "Someone called it the plight of being a/ first wife/ I insist, it is the death of bearing the 'first/ Wife' title" (110).

After Athela's murder by Jomo, when the women from the vicinity come to mourn Athela's death, the female protagonist undergoes a strange transformation as her "womb stretches over" and her "body is on fire" (116) as she finds it hard to reconcile with her daughter's death. She has been perforce deprived of her motherhood achieved after such inhuman trials and tribulations. She now prays that her daughter be accorded an opportunity to benefit from maternal solicitude, and get educated so that unlike her, she can go to "places" (117). She also wanted to grow, evolve but could not; but after Athela's death, and after this "pain has melted away," she also wants to go and "seek the book/ I flee from ghosts of Jomo and his mother/ I go in the hail stones" (117). Her inner turmoil and wrath are elemental as she wants to "Walk in the thunder/ I choose the lightening /A path travelled by few" (117). Having laid her Athela to rest, she wants to relax and go into a forest "[f]ar from this madness/ In the bosom of a new mother/ In the breast of many books" to eventually seek "Freedom/ Liberation/Womanhood" (118). Thus, towards the end of the poem, the female protagonist breaks all shackles to seek freedom and liberation to realise her identity as a woman – an identity that has been denied to her thus far.

III

Summing up, we can thus aver that Awuor's *Black Moon* is a path-breaking text dealing with the female-protagonist's/ poet's excruciating struggle to first realise and then reclaim her female identity in a deeply patriarchal world characterised by patriarchal dominance, violence of diverse sorts, unimaginable brutality against women, and gross sense of injustice. The poet is sharp enough not to be prescriptive in her depiction of such an abysmally depressing and profoundly perturbing world. She powerfully evokes and unravels the Kenyan socio-cultural, familial and political context having bearing on the African reality at large particularly from the viewpoint of mutilation, bruising, and rupturing of female identity. She does not mention about any law or court of law to deal with basic human rights violation and crimes against African women; she rather chooses to sensitise and create awareness regarding fundamental rights of women through several poems compiled in *Black Moon.*

Awuor certainly represents a society where justice is not only denied, it is also distorted through male point-of-view. In a Kenyan society, a woman cannot have her voice; she cannot be herself; she cannot articulate her actual experience; she can neither resist nor stage a protest; and she cannot think of actualising her potential both as a woman and an individual. She thus happens to be just there like that twenty-year-old orphan portrayed in the poem titled "Twenty and Crippled" who is not even noticed by the passersby and whose existence is ignored as well as relegated. The Kenyan woman also happens to be the victim of unwanted and unlawful sexual assault, resistance against which at times seems futile in a male-dominated world.

However, all is not lost as Awuor's poems powerfully expose the politics of the denial of female identity to women as its realisation may cause problems for their hitherto hegemonic patriarchal status prevalent since time immemorial. *Black Moon* can also be read as a forceful counternarrative to the oppressive powers as it systematically questions as well as exposes the patriarchal socio-cultural setup which has been depriving women their space in every sphere of human activity for long. The clarion call in the last poem to accomplish and experience "Freedom/ Liberation/Womanhood" (118) is strategic enough to explode the politics of denial of female identity and thereby underscore the importance of reclaiming the space that has been denied to women by the patriarchal forces in familial, societal, cultural, political and psychological arenas.

Works Cited

Africa Gender Index Report 2019. *African Development Bank and United Nations Economic Commission for Africa*, 2020, www.afdb.org/en/documents/africa-gender-index-report-2019-analytical-report. PDF download.

Aidoo, Ama Ata. "To Be an African Woman Writer – an Overview and a Detail." *Criticism and Ideology: Second African Writers' Conference Stockholm 1986*, edited by Kirsten Holst Petersen, Scandinavian Institute of African Studies, 1988, pp. 155-72.

Awuor, Beryl Subia. *Black Moon.* Kindle ed., 2012. Cited as *BM.*

---. *Black Moon.* Academia, www.uonbi.academia.edu/BerylSubia/Book. PDF download.

---. "Committed and Consistent (Why I Love Being a Seventh-day Adventist, #6)," *The Compass Magazine*, 9 Oct, 2015, thecompassmagazine.com/blog/committed-and-consistent-why-i-love-being-a-seventh-day-adventist-6.

Beauvoir, Simone de. *The Second Sex.* Vintage Books, 1973, p. 301.

Coupland, Christine. "Identity: The Management of Meaning." *The Blackwell Encyclopedia of Sociology*, edited by George Ritzer, Blackwell, 2007, pp. 2210-11.

Gardiner, Judith Kegan. "On Female Identity and Writing by Women." *Critical Inquiry*, vol. 8, no. 2, 1981, pp. 347-61. *JSTOR*, www.jstor.org/stable/1343167.

Hooks, Bell. *The Will to Change: Men, Masculinity, and Love.* Atria, 2004.

"Identity." *American Heritage Dictionary of the English Language*, Fifth Edition. 2011. Accessed 26 Nov. 2021, www.thefreedictionary.com/identity.

---. *Dictionary.Com*, www.dictionary.com/browse/identity. Accessed 23 May 2021.

---. *Online Etymology Dictionary.* www.etymonline.com/search?q=identity&ref=searchbar_searchhint. Accessed 23 May 2021.

Jenkins, Richard. *Social Identity.* Routledge, 2008.

Leonard. Keith D. "African American Women Poets and the Power of the Word." *The Cambridge Companion to African American Women's Literature*, edited by Angelyn Mitchell and Danille K. Taylor, Cambridge UP, 2009, pp. 168-86.

Morrow, Deana F., and Lori Messinger. *Sexual Orientation and Gender Expression in Social Work Practice*, edited by Deana F. Morrow and Lori Messinger, Columbia UP, 2006, p. 8.

Ndabayakhe, Vuyiswa, and Catherine Addison. "Polygamy in African Fiction." *Current Writing*, vol. 20, no. 1, 2008, pp.89-104.

Neofotistos, Vasiliki. "Identity Politics." *Oxford Bibliographies*, doi: 10.1093/OBO/9780199766567-0106.

Nnaemeka, Obioma. "From Orality to Writing: African Women Writers and the (Re)Inscription of Womanhood." *Research in African Literatures*, vol. 25, no. 4, 1994, pp. 137-57. *JSTOR*, www.jstor.org/stable/3819872.

Oloruntoba-Oju, Omotayo, and Taiwo Oloruntoba-Oju. "Models in the Construction of Female Identity in Nigerian Postcolonial Literature." *Tydskrif Vir Letterkunde*, vol. 50, no. 2, 2013, pp. 5-18, doi: 10.4314/tvl.v50i2.1.

Ritzer, George, and J. Michael Ryan, editors. *The Concise Encyclopedia of Sociology*, Wiley Blackwell, 2011.

Ruby, Jennie. "Resistance to Patriarchy." *Off Our Backs*, vol. 33, no.3/4, 2003, pp. 38-40. *JSTOR*, www.jstor.org/stable/20837789.

Young, Laura A. "Challenges at the Intersection of Gender and Ethnic Identity in Kenya." https://minorityrights.org/wp-content/uploads/old-site-downloads/download-1164-Challenges-at-the-intersection-of-gender-and-ethnic-identity-in-Kenya.pdf

CHAPTER 8

The Reconstruction of Myth, Memory, History and the Element of Resistant Aesthetics in the Postcolonial Women Poets of Africa

Pallavi Mishra

Memory that played a vital role in the rare oral tradition of Africa acts as an equally important practice in the African literature of Postcolonial times. The restorative powers of memory through required manipulation is used as a tool for creative ends. The simple act of recollection becomes a complex process of self-questioning. Association of ideas leads to reconstruction of ideas; the retelling of an old story embedded in the mind becomes a revision. The Postcolonial African poetry sees myth and memory, revolt and rebellion, land, man and woman in a newer light. The poetry depicting truth also reflects a process of feeling which is a testimony to prove that poetry is not a simple, linear movement. In this paper, I propose a reading into the poems of African women poets, viz., Noemia de Sousa, Otymeyin Agbajoh-Laoye, Ifi Amadiume and Abena P. A. Busia.

Postcolonial interrogation calls attention to the "historical fact of European colonialism and its aftermath, focusing more profoundly on issues of representation, otherness, diaspora, hybridity and voice. It offers a more objective view by bringing to focus the contemporary ramifications in terms of borders, multiple identities, independent economies and hybrid cultures. In areas pertaining to agency, representation and voice, it calls for a self-representation that acknowledges the highly diverse, changing and shifting nature of marginalised and dominant forms of identity, highlighting the saliency of constantly shifting difference in terms of past histories, current situations, and individual worldviews. The poetry of postcolonial women poets mirrors the change posing a demand before their readers for the creation of a balanced, accommodative world. Unlike Dalit Poetry, that reveals a world of deprivations, hopelessness, anguish, pain, anger, where darkness inhabits physical, material, mental spaces; despair is the order and habit of life; where liberation is possible only through death; the poems by the African poets have a sense of control, a resistant will to set things right and emerge victorious despite the rupture, despair, frustration and anxiety. The African poetry functions as a testimony to a profound faith in the human spirit, the courage to withstand all and the joy of togetherness.

It has been the contention of many artists and poets around the world that the entire history of poetry could be seen as an index of the expanding human awareness but this does not imply that there has been a logical and linear expansion as the nature of poetry does not allow anything like that. There is an obvious, deep felt link between a poet and the people. Czeslaw Miloz puts it rightly that poetry has always followed "the mysterious movements of the great soul of the people" (8). In some societies in Africa, many indigenous cultures and oral literatures were banned in order to give a free course to European models of literature. In other instances, even post-independence African governments preferred European-styled literature ahead of those by indigenous African writers. As Anthonia C. Kalu in her Introduction to *The Reinner Anthology of African Literature* writes:

> Earlier, the African Poets writing in European languages learned their craft in European languages which is reflected in the subject matter and poetic techniques employed but this approach began to change when negritude poets like Leopold S. Senghor, started to address the question of Africa and black identity. Whereas topics range from traditional to present-day African experience and life, contemporary African Poetry most closely reflects the artist's efforts to 'sing' Africa back to its feet. (14)

In response to the colonial imposition on literature which was enormous and acute, African writers both men and women re-invented old rituals and myths with new functionality. *The Rienner Anthology of African Literature* records the African postcolonial period from 1957 to the present.

The European occupation of most African nations lasted less than eighty years with Ghana attaining the first political independence in 1957, yet many western-educated Africans, as Anthonia C. Kalu remarks, did not know that the continent had not always been occupied by European powers, and most non-western educated Africans did not understand the extent of Africa's identity crisis or loss of power. This rupture affected its political leadership, making it difficult for the newly independent nations to present a unified front both domestically and internationally. That dissonance is evident in postcolonial literature. In the face of such crises, contemporary African literature played its self-assigned practical role, urging western-educated Africans to take the lead in redirecting all Africans to their birthright and true freedom. (12). Colonialism 'infantilizes' the native, rendering him/her helpless, vulnerable, and dependent on the white master. The resistance to colonial domination, seeking self-expression and basic freedoms, made the idea of a united, homogenous, and well-defined 'nation' or 'culture' attractive and even feasible. The main purpose was to raise the 'national consciousness' by constructing images of a tribe/region's history, glorifying its pasts, reviving myths, and rejuvenating pride in its cultural forms. "History", Mahasweta Devi also endorses "cannot be visualised without the statements of protest by the common-men" (205).

Abena P. A. Busia's poem "Achimota: From the Story My Mother Taught Me" introduces the readers to a landscape and its history that has suffered distortions due to colonial intervention. Achimota, a place that lies between Accra and the Legon hills has a school in it which has become its sole identity. Everyone thinks of the school first whenever Achimota is mentioned. The new school that took the name of the place never bothered to discover the meaning of the name associated with the place. The poet emphatically says that the name is *A-chee-mo-ta* meaning a forest that occupied the landscape since ancient times; long before the school or the roads or the railways or street side markets came up. Every feature of the land has a name and names have specific meanings. The names of the places, in many indigenous cultures, tell what the place is/was used for, who used it, or what historical events occurred there. Toponymy, which is an important example of the sources of indigenous history helps in linking space with collective memory. The forest is primitive, the first locator of the place and yet its name is never spoken of. The new school, new people and expanding market are indifferent to the spirit of the place and its exact nature, "The trees still stand, /but they do not speak the history they have seen. / A-chee-mo-ta-no, not at all./And only the name remains the reminder/ of who we are, what we have been,/and what we have been through" (600). The poem exposes the social and political control of the natives by the colonial powers. The poet further concedes, "Sometimes it seems we are forgetting/ but so long as there are people alive who remember, we will remember the meaning" (601). These lines indicate an effort towards a re-assertion of 'native' cultural identity through memory. For the natives, westernisation leads to incompleteness just as the name of the place lost its meaning just to become a label. Between the memory of an old identity and the concreteness of a new one lie the crises and the attempt towards negotiation continues.

However, the retrieval of history has its other side too. The forest is a stoic reminder of the trauma of slavery as the inhabitants hid themselves in its darkness as they fled from the chains of servitude. "Here we came, fleeing/ To a place of shelter/Escaping the chains and lash/ We would not submit to/ And these trees hid us" (600). Retrieving histories invariably means dredging through some horrific memories and an intense awareness that native history without colonial contamination is simply not possible. The accumulated insults by the white 'master', the continued negation of native culture and the prolonged indoctrination in western culture result in an unstable condition for individuals. The poet laments that the 'underground railroad' had its precursor that nobody ever mentions. Bakhtin emphasised the interconnectedness of the life-forms in a specific locale. He suggested that the folkloric and vernacular elements of a place provide an alternative to the constructed or imposed "official" landscape or culture. J. B. Jackson extends Bakhtin's idea of the chronotope when he speaks of the vernacular landscape. The official landscape rarely accounts for local differences and seeks, rather, to unify and homogenise land/culture/people into a controllable cartographic panoptican. Jackson's landscape is postcolonial for it is fragmented and embodies the conflicting traditions of the community. Unlike the official landscape which is constructed in order to impose political unity (or perhaps development programmes), the vernacular landscape is scattered, mobile and changing (78).

The theme of memory figures prominently in postcolonial writings as reclaiming history entails reclamation of memory. Layers of memory are searched by the writers and poets and since memories are always collective, ethnic and racial; local histories are intimately linked to the specific topos of a tribe or clan as Achimota is the connecting link between space and racial memory. The lines, "We are being taught forgetting/ But some remember still/Achimota and its history/A forest, and its meaning-/ The place, and its silence" (601); gives the message that when the evidence of trauma survives in a certain space, there is always the possibility that future generations will retrieve its history for multiple re-readings. The landscape of Achimota is a reminder of the colonial expansion, its stereotype and the violence associated making it simultaneously into a site of traumatic slave history of bondage, suffering and death. Certain things are never mentioned, remembered and are forcibly forgotten, rather the successors are taught to forget every piece of memory that causes despair and meaninglessness. The pasts are forgotten as recovering from their traumatic effect is much needed. The negotiation helps to achieve an identity different from the one imposed by the coloniser; as the name of the forest and the role that it played in the past lend historical identity to it. The retrieval of buried histories and stories reconstructs cultural and national histories and identities. In her book *Fashioning a Self in the Contemporary World: Notes Toward a Personal Meditation on Memory, History and the Aesthetics of Origin,* Abena Busia writes, "The tension we live with in Africa today is often that we have many conflicting myths, in particular those of social origins. To the contemporary world, that sense of self is dependent on memories which are both personal and collective, and a history which is both personal and national" (22). The question of origins, mythical and personal remains a driving force in both the contemporary art and the contemporary literature of Africa, of Africa of the New World, desperately in need of sustaining roots.

In her "Poem of a Distant Childhood", Noemia de Sousa, demonstrates that nostalgia and memory constitute an attempt to understand the violence of cultural-national 'severance.' The lines, "Ah, but for the outside world/ my tears died in the fire of revolt/ And the Sun has never shone on me as in the first days/ Of my existence/" show the effect of exile and dislocation on individual lives that desperately make effort to retain 'original' culture. The restorative power of memory is fully explored in the poem as the poet describes various adventures that the poet-narrator and her companions shared, from raiding the cashew trees, to hunting for lizards and listening to stories of terror being told by an old black man. The essence of solidarity made it possible to imagine and create a future free of oppression. Solidarities built on a common history of suffering or battles against oppression, and fought at various levels and in multiple locations constitute a postcolonial, hybridised and transnational ethic (210). As a function of history, home is the reservoir of public myths and private memories. Community having its relatedness with home, exercises tremendous influence on the lives of people living in it and history gets a proper shape in the processes that occur within it. The empathy of the community with the individual and vice-versa causes the necessary evolution in both; the personality of the individual and the history of the community as the lines in the poem reflect,

> If today the Sun doesn't shine like the day
> In which I was born, in the large house
> Beside the Indian Ocean.? I don't let myself sleep in darkness.
> My companions are my steadfast guides/on my way through life
> They proved to me that "brotherhood" is not merely a pretty word
> Written in black in the dictionary in the bookcase:
> They taught me that "brotherhood' is a beautiful sensation, and
> Possible
> Even when the skins and the surrounding landscape
> Are so different. (909)

The poet emphasises on the awakening and sustenance of the African qualities of brotherhood that can be the potent "life-force" that can define and shape the life-processes. Biddy Martin and Chandra Talpade Mohanty suggest that "community as the product of work, of struggle is inherently unstable; contextual it has to be constantly reevaluated in relation to critical political priorities: and it is the product of interpretation, interpretation based on an attention to history" (20). Reclaiming the past/history and retaining certain memories is important for the postcolonial condition. History, as retained in the memories of the people, contains symbolic power as they become the symbolic projections of peoples' hopes, values, fears and aspirations.

In the poem, "Let My People Go", the poet is agitated and restless after listening to the Negro Spirituals from Harlem sung by Robeson and Marian that resound inside her. She says that as long as these lamentations from Harlem reach her and she is haunted by the familiar faces of her mother having rough hands and tired face with rebellions, pains and humiliations, she would not sleep and continue to write. The lines, "And you my friend with the gentle blue look/ Holding my hand and making me write/ With gall flowing from our rebellion" (911) show the psychological protest witnessing an upsurge in everything that reminds her of her home and people. A psychological protest gets reflected in the works of writers and poets with deep thought and comprehensibility, having finer sensibilities, ones which are humane, compassionate and reactionary at times; trying to instill a little emotion and understanding in the people who are otherwise insensitive or complacent towards the problems of "Others". The readiness of the 'native woman' to speak and to write is the empowerment and agency that any struggle requires. She does not want to be 'ventriloquised' or spoken for by the voice of America and thus, the resurrection of voice happens on her own. Voice and consciousness are linked in confusing and inconsistent ways. Some texts see the woman's lack of consciousness of rights which should be hers as preventing her from acting on her own behalf. Consciousness, therefore, comes from outside, when women "are encouraged to voice their resentment, to identify their oppressors and to struggle to improve their condition" (97). The unresolved paradox here is that consciousness relies on voice to be recognised and generated yet there can be no voice without consciousness.

According to Noemia De Sousa, the 'voices of lamentation' from Harlem have same ancestral source; and singing here becomes an act of trans-continental, mythical solidarity. The word 'Harlem' signifies black America, the place where Africa is returned to her. In all fairness, 'Negro Spirituals' did not originate in Harlem, but in the slave plantations of the South. The word 'Harlem' is not the exact space but emerges as a locus around which are the signifiers to poverty, squalor, the idea of 'black ghetto' and also a place of black achievements and music. Her poems delineate political equality and social emancipation, literature as a source of courage, strength and an agent of social change; re-working old identities and identity-markers; and the erosion of stereotypes and myth. The words of Walter Benjamin definitely sum up the essence of these poems:

> Politics and production are inseparable. The rigid, isolated object (work, novel and book) is valueless for dialectical analysis unless 'inserted into the context of living social relations.' Such relations involve political commitment. But the political tendency of a literary work will be 'correct' only if the literary tendency itself, its aesthetics, is correct. Only those literary tendencies which are 'implicitly or explicitly included in every

> correct political tendency, this and nothing else makes the quality of a work. (86-87)

Black maternity has culturally and historically been mythologised and black mothers stereotyped as Barbara Christian also asserts that, "such idealised images have served as content for some other major dilemma or problem that society cannot solve" (2). These myths delineate black mothers as matriarchal figures, superbly strong and protective, and at the same time, selfless, all embracing, demanding nothing or little, and totally self-sacrificing creatures whose identities are inseparable from their nurturing services. An emphatic protest is registered by Noema De Sousa in her poem, "If You Want to Know Me" where she equates her own state with tattered Africa and vice-versa. She translates the land of Africa into a body, its cultural conditions and material factors where Africa becomes an iconic space of exploitation. She identifies her body as one tattooed with wounds apparent or hidden from the harsh whip strokes of slavery. She describes herself and simultaneously the condition of Africa thus, "This is what I am/ Empty sockets despairing of possessing of life... " The poem captures the worst aspects of colonial rule: the destruction of identity, bodily pain, and the complete rejection of a culture. Images of nations and cultures are constructed in metaphors that situate women in marking the identity of the nation. The powerful image of "proud and mysterious Africa" that is broken and "tattooed" with injuries interrogating the economic, political and cultural basis of colonialism simultaneously suggests the condition of her women who suffer oppression at the hands of not just colonial masters, but also patriarchy and their strategies at escaping/negotiating power-relations between genders. The hardest criticism of African situation undoubtedly originates from Africans themselves.

In a powerful critique, which is also a manifesto, novelist Mariama Ba says:

> The woman writer in Africa has a special task. She has to present the position of women in Africa in all its aspects. There is still so much injustice... In the family, in the institutions, in society, in the street, in political organisations, discriminations reign supreme. We no longer accept the nostalgic praise the African Mother, who, in his anxiety, man confuses with Mother Africa. Within African Literature room must be made for women. (117)

The relative status of women across communities is still used to assess the progress of culture.

Motherism is an attempt to re-work two kinds of representation of women: the image of Mother Africa and images of African femaleness. Motherhood is central to women's lives in many African countries; yet the postcolonial women poets reject the measurement of social worth and standing entirely in terms of motherhood. Ifi Amadiume made tremendous contributions to new ways of thinking about sex and gender, the question of power, and women's place in history and culture. Developing the 'motherist' model of African feminism, she argued that a shift to the 'motherhood paradigm' is required to allow for a shift of focus from man at the centre and in control, to the primacy of the role of mother/sister in the economic, social, political and religious institutions. (152). In her poem "Nok Lady in Terracotta", she brings forth the position of women in Africa placing a demand for more justice, equality and social emancipation. Her poem stands as a critique of strategies of representation where the issue of motherhood, the role of 'mothers', and the intimate linkage between motherhood and motherland is raised that deprive women of their individual rights. She stands in solidarity with the women of her race, "And sad-eyed sisters I see daily,/I know by your looks,/Though recorded in no books,/we too travelled the same road,/carried the same load,/and sipped of the same sorrow" (595). The way the sisters and mothers have been controlled is stated in the lines:

Your sons in vengeance
Did they not desert you?
Appropriate your daughters?
Take control of the lands?
Seek alliances exchanging sisters?
Mother You were thus left neglected, those sons left you unprotected,
Then the rape began: You see sister, The beginning of our anguish.
They too cunningly control lands, mindlessly exchange sisters,
Purposely pass on knowledge
Controlling your minds. (596)

Both the stereotyping and exploitation is condemned as men partake in control and oppression of their women in the same vein as the colonisers. In all cultures, woman is identified with the reproductive or copulative body; mothering assumes the form of work that ignores the mother as a subject or a human being. In reality, she is a slave-woman or slave-mother who collapsed under the burden of immense expectations of both Nature and Culture, though the society she lived in glorified her till she had a 'utility'. The abstract, homogenised maternal figure, as inscribed and promoted by the nationalist patriarchal/paternalistic discourse is punctured by her. The issue of motherhood is a gendered construct which is based on the existing master-definition of mothers fashioned on the binaries of "male-female, mind-body nature-culture, reason-emotion, public-private and labor-love" (Glen etl.13). While women's fiction in the postcolonial context foregrounds issues of female identity and its constructions, one should not immediately assume that such writing ignores social and political problems in favour of psychological explorations of the "woman condition."

Otymeyin Agbajoh Laoye dedicates her poem "Motherhood Cut Short For Igra, Mother to the End" wherein Igra is a single mother whose identity for her children is that of a phone call made to/from some distant land. A wireless and seamless phone call made by a single mother suggests the disconnectedness in her life. She is the one who is keen on departing; the sound of bell echoes the pain of her waning life; a reminder of her solitude, one who arranges for her own funeral living an exile within the society she lives in. Here, a single mother emerges as independent, strong, determined and self-seeking. Essentially, the aura of black maternity, born out of the system of slavery, developed as a result of inevitable separation of fathers (black slaves or white owners) from their children. In the absence or unavailability of fathers, mothers become the only link which identifies the black slave's parental heritage. The lines, "Your repose/Seamless and wide/ Linking forgotten homesteads left behind/ Remembered ancestral resting place/Motherhood all encompassing" (637) signifies the link that mothers preserve for their children who would be in need of a familiar ancestor for themselves. The ideology defining black matriarchy, rooted in the slavery system and subsequently a cultural fixture in the black communities, has peculiar properties. One such property as Judith Wilt has put it "is the myth of the black earth mother, indestructible under the heaviest load" (135). The poet addresses Igra as a warrior woman; she mentions her seamless motherhood yet bares the wounds that she has received in her long and tiring struggle of rearing her sons resulting in her premature death that would destroy every simple joy of parenting:

Warrior woman
Before death's door and beyond
To the end you fight the battle left you alone
Your first and last thought/are to your sons

Deprived of children's debt to mother struggle
But still thankful to have known this seamless motherhood
Reaching from beyond through the seeds of time
Exiled completely by death's premature call. (637)

She laments for her motherhood as she suffers as an exile all through her life; first by the society for being a single mother and then death causes her separation from her children as the poet writes, "I will not see my sons/ from college graduate/ Walk up the aisle of time/ Rock grandchildren on my knees/ Sing quiet re-remembered lullabies" (636). As death stands at the door, the poet asks the anxious question, "How will you ensure your children connect?/With our source of life" (636) and suggests that "to ensure your children's return/ you must return home" (636). Homesteads have a connecting link to mother's love, emotions and memories for which "passports rushed/ Visa's secured for home never visited" (636). So, dislocation can be dealt with by re-locating with the collectivity, with memories and customs enabling a return to a space that is not quite forgotten and in the process a community moves through a cultural nationalist stage into a political one. It is an act not just of committing to memory, but a way of making 'real' their connections to home. Exiles tend to hold on to their traditions in an almost desperate effort to retain/ reclaim their 'original' culture. Caught up in an alien culture in whose cultural life the migrant/slave community may have little or no role to play, the community clings to its own customs and cultural codes seeking a cultural citizenship within his/her community while also seeking legal citizenship within the nation. The fusing of gender with culture and tradition continues when the space of the "home" and practices within it provide an oasis of secure identity for communities experiencing dislocation or subordination. The poem moving around the struggles of a single black mother depicts broader aspects of diaspora, migration and exile that happen in the lives of first generation immigrant communities.

Most postcolonial women writers/poets see cultural identity as evolving rather than fixed, plural rather than singular, adapted rather than inherited. Cultural identities, as Stuart Hall writes, "have histories... But, like everything which is historical, they undergo constant transformation... are subject to the continuous "play" of history, culture and power" (2). Women writers and poets generally focus on the transformative aspect of tradition and cultural identity. To understand creativity is like attempting to grasp the ocean by gazing at the water held in the palm." Mallika Ghanti, a feminist poet, expects a different duty from poetry; she says: "Whatever the world approves, poetry rejects it outright/ Whatever the world denounces, poetry accepts with zeal" (23). In the same vein, in her poem "Yanga Woman" Otymeyin Agbajoh depicts a Street Sex-Worker as an empowered woman for whom her work is for survival. There is a sense of liberation as the poem is written in glowing, exultant terms. The Yanga woman readies herself before going to work, throws a last glance in the mirror, her Eyes dollied and ready-to-roll, hips well-girthed and battle ready/ The comforting knot around her still slim waist/Market bag in hand battle ready/Yanga Woman weaves her knowing way" (638). She exercises a power and control over her clients, "Completely mesmerised/ austere alien to pulsing life/Caught in the web of her design/Transports Baba to bedroom of his raging yout" (638). Her work is done as the price is fixed: "The weight of basket/ To drown rumbling stomachs" (638). To nurture is intrinsically spiritual and maternal and the Yanga woman is an individual in her own right. Here, the Yanga woman is a gendered subaltern suffering deprivations and economic constraints but trying to create a socially desirable feminine role which is more in control of her situation. The lines of Octavio Paz regarding poetry in his "The Bow and the Lyre" stand true and relevant in regard to the African poets and their poetry, as he writes:

> Poetry is knowledge, salvation, power, abandonment. An operation capable of changing the world, poetic activity is revolutionary in nature; a spiritual exercise, it is means of interior liberation. Poetry reveals this world; it creates another. Bread of the chosen; accursed food. It isolates, it unites. Invitation to the journey; return to the homeland. Inspiration, respiration, muscular exercise, Prayer to the void, dialogue with absence; tedium, anguish and despair nourish it. Prayer, Litany, epiphany, presence. Exorcism, conjuration, magic, sublimation, compensation, condensation of the unconscious. Historic expression of races, nations, classes. It denies history... Madness, ecstasy, logos. Return to childhood, coitus, nostalgia for paradise, for hell, for limbo. Play, work, ascetic activity. Confession. Inmate experience, Vision, music, Symbol. (3)

Postcolonial women's writing/poetry can no longer be relegated to the margins as 'domestic' writing. The past, present and future are harnessed in postcolonial texts where trauma (colonial), pride (nationalism) and hope (postcolonial) merge. The poems by African Women Poets bear the force and energy that can 'stir' the mind of the readers and emphatically support the notion that a literary text not only reflects an age, it shapes those contexts by persuading people to accept/change their popular beliefs and opinions. Unlike Dalit Poetry, that reveals a world of deprivations, nihilism, disillusionment, hopelessness, anguish, pain, anger, where darkness inhabits physical, material, mental spaces; despair is the order and habit of life; where liberation is possible only through death; the poems by the African poets have a sense of control, a resistant will to set things right and emerge victorious despite the rupture, despair, frustration and anxiety. When Dalit Literature works on the paradigm of "You", the African Literature shows the energy and verve of "We" and "Our."

The African history is replete with examples of resistance, social tensions, conflicts and obstacles that some individuals or races faced in the process of transformation. Myths and memory integrated the individual into the history that led to the rise of nationalist consciousness. In their oral narratives, writings, stories and poems, African women writers/poets have woven it all and preserved the spirit of their tribes. Despite the literary tradition's non-inclusive tendency towards women's texts and writings; relegating them to a less-privileged space and ensuring that their political opinions are not taken seriously, the postcolonial African women poets have raised their voice, energised the social space, through their poetry with strength and assertion.

Works Cited

Amadiume Ifi. *Re-Inventing Africa: Matriarchy, Religion and Culture.* Zed London, 1997, p. 152.

Asgharzadeh Alireza, "The Return of the Subaltern: International Education and Politics of Voice". *Journal of Studies in International Education,* 2008; originally published online Feb 15, 2008. http://jsi.sagepub.com/cgi/content/abstract/12/4/334.

Barbara, Christian. *Black Women Novelists: The Development of a Tradition.* Greenwood Press, 1980.

Benjamin Walter, *Understanding Brecht.* New Left Books, 1973.

Choube, Kripashankar, ed. *Mahasweta Samvad.* Vani Prakashan, 2001.

Ghasemi Parvin, and Hajizadeh Rasool. "Demystifying the Myth of Motherhood: Toni Morrison's Revision of African-American Mother Stereotypes." *International Journal of Social Science and Humanity,* vol.2, no.6, Nov.2012, p. 477. accessed on 20 July 2020.

Glenn, Everlyn Nakano, Grace Chang, and Linda Rennie Forcey, *Mothering, Ideology, Experience and Agency.* Routeledge, 1994.

Hall, Stuart. "Cultural Identity and Diaspora." *Post-Colonial Theory: A Reader,* edited by Patrick Williams and Laura Chrisman. Columbia University Press, 1994, p. 394.

http://english.rutgers.edu/images/documents/faculty/busia-ja-2004.pdfttps://www.academia.edu/5307409/Harlem_and_Ancestral_Blood_Chapter_3_https://pdfs.semanticscholar.org/8372/f133e8c9e843a0d2504ab5e595c28c69ec20.pdf

Idoko, Frank Emman. "Morountodun and the Politics of Liberation in Nigeria." *The Literary Criterion: A Dhavanyalika Quarterly Mysore,* vol.39, 2004.

Jefferson Antonette, "The Rhetoric of Revolution: The Black Consciousness Movement and the Dalit Panther Movement." *The Journal of Pan African Studies*, vol. 2, no.5, July 2008.

Kalu. C. Anthonia, *The Rienner Anthology of African Literature.* Lynne Rienner Publishers, Inc. 2008.

Miloz Czeslaw, "The Witness of Poetry" Harvard University Press, 1983. quotd in Murali S. In a Season Our Discontent: Modernism and Malayalam Poetry in *The Literary Criterion* A Dhavanyaloka Quarterly Mysore, vol.40. p. 8.

Nayar, Pramod K. *Frantz Fanon.* Routledge Critical Thinkers, 2013.

---. "Hybridity, Cosmopolitanism, Diaspora." *Contemporary Literary and Cultural Theory from Structuralism to Ecocriticism*, Pearson, 2012,

---. "Postecolonial Theory: A New Ontopology and Radical Politics." *Journal of Contemporary Thought*, vol.9, Summer 1999, p.78.

---. *Postcolonial Literature: An Introduction*, Pearson, 2012.

Okoro, Dike "Healing Mother Africa: Contemporary African Poets Explore New Rhythms and Themes." *Black Issues: Book Review*, vol. 5, no. 5, 2003, pp.32-33

Paz Octavio, *The Bow and the Lyre*, University of Texas, 1973, p. 3.

Rath, Sura P. "Home(s) Abroad: Diasporic Identities in Third Spaces." *Journal of Contemporary Thought,* vol.9, Summer 1999, p.20.

Senghor Leopold, "Negritude and Modernity or Negritude as a Humanism for the Twentieth Century" *Race* edited by Robert Bernasconi. Blackwell Publishers, p.144.

Stephens, Julie "Feminist Fictions: A Critique of the Category 'Non-Western Woman' Feminist Writings on India", in Ranjit Guha ed. *Subaltern Studies VI,* Oxford University Press, 2010.

Ugbabe Kanchana, "Revision or Reconstruction? Memory and Artistic Creativity in Nuruddin Farah's Maps and Tayeb Salih's Season of Migration to the North in *The Literary Criterion," A Dhavanyalika Quarterly Mysore,* vol.39, 2004, p. 162.

W. Judith, *Abortion, Choice, and Contemporary Fiction.* University of Chicago Press, 1990.

CHAPTER 9

Post-Apartheid Effort to Repatriate: Dis(re)memberment, Violence and Betrayal in Zoë Wicomb's *David's Story*

Subhash Verma

Women's role in the history of South Africa has gained some recognition, belatedly, only in the last three decades. A long history of women's struggle for community rights and gender equality was largely ignored. Likewise, men often occupied most of the leadership positions in the fight against Apartheid and an equally significant role played by women was overlooked. Though women's involvement and their struggles in the anti-Apartheid movement have not been recognised at the same level as the men's, there are ample historical and literary evidences that illustrate their active participation in the struggle. Black women had to struggle more as they faced three forms of oppression in South Africa during Apartheid – racial, social and sexual.

Many South African writers like Lauretta Ngcobo, Kagiso Molope, Njabulo Ndebele and Zoë Wicomb responded to Apartheid and its effects on women in one way or the other. Susan Arndt opines that the Apartheid literature "captured a vivid sense of the emotional and psychological toll that Apartheid exerted on its victims" (251). The novels of Zoë Wicomb, the most influential female novelist of South Africa, focus on the portrayal of women's struggle against Apartheid in South Africa. They explore the different ways in which Apartheid oppressed women and how women responded to the forces of oppression. Central to her work is the contention that the anti-Apartheid movement was shaped as much by women as it was by men like Nelson Mandela and Walter Sisulu. Her novels appreciate and recognise the efforts and sacrifices that were made by women towards the cause for liberation in South Africa.

The present paper explores the portrayal of women's activism in Zoë Wicomb's *David's Story*. The text reveals the plight of Black South African women during the (post)Apartheid era and explores the theme of oppression in all its ramifications, which include racial prejudice, exploitation and brutality. The novel also highlights the twofold struggles of women in (post)Apartheid South Africa; on the one hand women suffer as a result of the oppressive policies of the Apartheid government, and on the other hand women struggle as a consequence of domestic issues revolving around patriarchy which promote men to unearned positions of dominance. Further the novel also delineates women's bravery in confronting the oppressive forces which worked against them. *David's Story* blends history and fiction to depict what women in South Africa actually did to survive and resist Apartheid and African patriarchy.

Just as her first novel *You Can't Get Lost in Cape Town* (1987), Zoë Wicomb's second novel *David's Story* deals with the experiences of coloured South Africans during the Apartheid years. Exploring the world of the liberation movements, a world filled with betrayal and danger, the novel is set in 1991, a time when new South Africa burgeoned. The protagonist David Dirkse hires an amanuensis to write down his story as he is struggling with the consequences of his involvement in the fight for freedom. Eventually it becomes pellucid that his story spins around his fellow comrade Dulcie Oliphant, otherwise known as 'the beloved', who was tortured and possibly even killed. David, the former guerrilla fighter; Sally his wife; the enigmatic and physically powerful Dulcie, his comrade and suspected lover are central to the novel.

Dulcie's own voice remains absent and she is only presented in the silences of the text. David is unable to talk about her so the narrator invents a story for her based on a few inferences from the conversations with David. Dulcie's absence exemplifies the other absences in the novel and in all South African discourse, such as the struggle of the women before, during and after Apartheid. The novel is not about the male guerrilla, as it is about the coloured women who were directly and indirectly engaged in the struggle against Apartheid. All the women characters in the novel – Dulcie, Sally, Sarie, the unknown narrator – possess characteristics that can be traced back to author herself or women she might have met. As Hein

Willemse observes, "A good third of *David's Story* is based on Wicomb's childhood experiences. People she has known, people she has spoken to" (151).

The presence of historical figures like Sarah Baartman and Eva/Krotoa in the novel draws attention to how women are always represented through stereotypes in a patriarchal society and the contemporary women are victims of the violent responses to these stereotypes. The novel highlights the fact that stereotypical representations of women lead to violence on their bodies and violate their true nature. Any attempt at an accurate representation, paradoxically, will lead to violence as well, especially to violence through language.

Zoë Wicomb's representation of the women in the novel is influenced by her background. She was born in Namaqualand in 1948 – David comes from the same region. She belonged to a poor family and was categorised as 'Coloured' under Apartheid legislation. The people of South Africa were divided in four racial categories: White, Coloured, Indian and African by the Population Registration Act of 1950. The Whites had absolute control over the state as they were considered 'civilised' and the state was not obliged to provide equal facilities for the subordinate races. The segregation inevitably diminished people's chances to rise to their full potential. In Wicomb's life this disadvantage was compensated by her education. Being a coloured woman, she is particularly sensitive to the experiences of women like her. The foremost aim of this novel is to make African women's voices heard. It is also about accepting one's heritage and one's colouredness. Through this novel, Wicomb helps to make history, culture and the traumatic experiences of South African women known to a broader public. *David's Story* is not so much about, a male guerrilla, as it is about those colourd women who stood against and were actively engaged in the struggle against Apartheid. Being a coloured woman Wicomb also suffered a lot under the Apartheid regime as well. The characteristics of all the female characters, Dulcie, Sally, Sarie and the unknown narrator, can be traced back to the author herself.

Writing back to colonial discourse is an omnipresent phenomenon in postcolonial literature. Writers question centuries-old discourses that misrepresented them and they change the representation of their people in order to proclaim their value as a unified nation. In order to prove their worth, the postcolonial writers use literature as a powerful tool. Though in the novel this phenomenon is touched upon, Wicomb seems to criticise it. The novel is not simply an act of writing back to colonial discourse, but to postcolonial discourse as well. When Apartheid was abolished in 1991, the people of South Africa started constructing a South African nation because the coloured people of the country had been subjugated since Jan Van Riebeeck reached at the Cape in 1657.

The nation-building project during the transition period is a major theme in *David's Story* but the novel criticizes the consequences, especially in regard to women. The criticism is highlighted in the novel through the references of two historical figures, whose bodies were used in both imperial and in nationalist projects: Sarah Baartman and Eva/Krotoa. Eva is mentioned briefly in the novel, she is nonetheless important since she is a woman whose image was often changed. She was seen as an ally of the Dutch and traitor of the Khoisan and vice-versa and then finally represented as "Mother of the Nation." Similarly, Sarah Baartman was portrayed as a sexualised savage by the colonisers and later turned into a symbol of the 'new' South Africa by the South Africans. In building their new nation, South Africans violated these women's bodies in the same way as the colonisers did and the author exposes this in the novel. The two women have always been represented by others. Their bodies have been used to convey certain meanings. Meg Samuelson rightly wonders whether "the project of remembering nation, dismembers women" (2). Sarah and Eva's influence can be seen everywhere in the novel. They are incarnated women like Dulcie, the narrator and Sally. Baartman's steatopygia is a physical characteristic of every female in the nation. The novel depicts the way the representation of women constantly alters to fit in a particular project.

In an attempt to write back to the racist colonial discourse, the nationalistic discourse in the post-Apartheid era was constructed around two historical figures of South African history: Sarah Baartman and Eva. The narrative constructed for these two women is an example of how the past is changed to suit the present interests. Their stories are completely invented by both the colonisers and their own people as there are only few facts known about them.

Sarah Baartman belonged to Griqua tribe, a part of the Khoi-Khoi people who lived on the Eastern Cape of South Africa, and she worked as a field hand on a Dutch colonial farm. When she was nineteen she attracted the attention of William Dunlop, a medical officer in the British Army. Dunlop convinced her that she could make money by going to England with him and exhibiting herself as an oddity. "With stars in her eyes, she accepted his offer" (Tobias 214). In 1810 she appeared in Piccadilly on a "stage two feet high, along which she was led by her keeper and exhibited like a wild beast, being obliged to walk, stand or sit as he ordered" (Tobias 214). Here 'Hottentot Venus' was the name given to her. Hottentot refers to the African tribe and Venus is a reference to the Roman goddess of love. Naked, she was paraded in London at different areas over the next four years. The young woman was prostituted as she was also exhibited in private sessions.

Then she was sold to an animal trainer in 1814 and was taken to France where she continued to appear as an oddity on display for both private and public consumption. Later she attracted the attention of George Cuvier, Napoleon's surgeon who experimented with her body and she died within a year. Eventually he dissected her – preserving her genitals and brain in a glass jar – and reassembled her skeleton. Till today, the actual cause of her death remains unknown. She was accorded neither funeral services nor burial. The physical remains of Baartman's body were shipped to Paris and placed on display until the middle of the twentieth century. Her body was always reduced to her sexual parts even after her death. In 1994, when democracy dawned in South Africa and Nelson Mandela became the President, attempts were made to repatriate Baartman's remains. It took several years and finally in 2002, the cast, skeleton and the jarred remains were returned to her native South Africa, 187 years after she first left.

Eva, a Khoisan girl who acted as a translator for the Dutch colonisers "served respectively as a youth goodwill apprentice, interpreter, trading agent, ambassador for a high-ranking chief and peace negotiator in the time of war" (Wells 418). At first she was trusted by both the Dutch and her own people as she was close to a Dutch Commander and she could acquire information about the Khoena too. Later, it seemed as if she favoured the Dutch people above her own and therefore, her people broke off with her. After she married a Danish surgeon, she converted completely to the Dutch way of life. The cause of her death is unknown, though rumours indicate that she could never fully adapt to the Dutch society. The colonisers and even her own people ruined her name and turned her image into a disloyal alcoholic.

During colonial times Baartman was represented as an icon for the sexualised savage, whereas Eva was associated with treachery and alcoholism. A lot of time and effort was needed to change their colonial image into a more positive one. As a result of domestication of their images by the South Africans, who felt ashamed for their inferior status, they were turned into national symbols: 'Mothers of South Africa.' A project of domestication was put into motion as being a mother could not be associated with wild sexuality and alcohol abuse. They decided to change their image into a more proper one in order to boost their self-esteem. They adopted the European point of view and perceived themselves and these two icons as inferior to white people. In *David's Story,* Zoë Wicomb refers several times to the violence that was done to their images. In the novel, the nationalist project – with Baartman and Eva as icons is often questioned. The lives of women characters in the novel contain striking similarities, no matter what period they live in. The novel illustrates not only the author's problems with nationalism as a whole, but her concerns with the use of women's bodies as icons. First of all, South Africans used the same discourse as the colonisers: they domesticated the women and then turned them into mothers of the nation.

The second concern of the author is that an individual's suffering is compared to the suffering of a large group of people. So the South Africans completely ignored the real, personal pain Baartman and Eva suffered. David perceives that Baartman represents every single one of them and every South African associates himself / herself with Sarah Baartman including the Griquas, who are prominently figured in the novel. Baartman is used by every group for their own means to represent certain aspects that suit their group and that was not what she was about. In *David's Story,* though the writer is also writing back to imperial discourse but not by covering up the truth about these two historical figures. Similar things are experienced by all the women in the novel.

In *David's Story* the presence of Baartman is noticeable in the women who carry her name: Saartjie – who later changed her name to Sarah and Sally – and her mother Sarie Meintijes. Sally changed her name so that it would sound more European. Sally met David because she was an active ANC member but when Apartheid ended, she was forced by her fellow comrades to accept her role as a housewife. The male members of the movement reclaimed their superiority in the country and severely punished women who did not comply – Dulcie, for instance, ends up on a hit list. Rachael, the wife of Andrew Lefleur, was also pushed into a subordinate role and it is an act of domesticating powerful women which is a phenomenon of all times. She was a modern girl before her marriage, influenced by European customs; but afterwards, she handed over her power to her husband and for the rest of her life "she resolved to obey" (48). People gave her a name, "Mother of the Volk" and this domestication brings Sarah Baartman and Eva/Krotoa to mind.

Dulcie's life is invented by the narrator of *David's Story* based on a few facts David had provided her with. The narrator herself admits, "since there is little to go by other than disconnected images, snippets of Dulcie, I must put things together as best as I can, invent, and hope that David's response will reveal something" (80). The story created by the narrator may or may not do justice to what Dulcie actually went through. Though Dulcie is one of those women who were supposed to be domesticated in post-Apartheid times, she refused and remained in her strong position. Not only was she working as a negotiator between civilians and the United Democratic Front but also a military leader within the Movement. David is mesmerised by "her boldness" (122) and he is inspired by her strong character and her power of speech. Her role as a negotiator between two groups of people reminds us of Eva's middle position between the Khoisan people and the Dutch colonisers. The narrator of the story, like Eva, is a learned woman who constantly oscillates between her European education and her African roots. Just like Eva her value as a writer is accepted but her distance from her own background is often criticised. David often accuses her of not being able to understand what happened to Dulcie because her world is altogether different.

The steatopygia of Sarah Baartman is illustrated as a condition that many women possess in South Africa and the theme of steatopygia is redefined by the author in the novel as she wanted to write back to negative colonial descriptions. The sexuality associated with it is seen as good thing. In the novel, Sally is proud of the shape of her body and demonstrates how it can be very appealing to men. It is linked with power as Rachael's physical appearance also saves her life, when she ties a package of important documents on her back:

"the package setting in the curve of her back, in the generous space shaped by stealtopygia, where it would never be found" (55). The novel substantiates that since steatopygia is a perfectly natural condition that has nothing to do with lasciviousness or savagery and that there is no reason for women to feel ashamed of their bodies.

The true protagonist of the story is Dulcie Oliphant, though the novel maybe called *David's Story*. She is an embodiment of unrepresentable trauma. Like David Dirkse, she is a guerrilla fighter for 'Unkhonto we Sizwe', the armed wing of the African National Congress (ANC) and little is known about her, except that she fills an important position in the Movement. She is an extraordinary politician "who wins the trust of the conservative Griquas of Kliprand by knowing their hymns and praising their sense of community" (Gane 106) and her military actions are legendary. Drastic sexual violence is inflected on her and other women because of their increasingly active involvement in the struggle. Living in a patriarchal society, South African women are supposed to play the role of a mother and a wife effectively. Inevitable punishments by torture and rape were given to several women – including Dulcie and Sally – during the struggle if they gained the same power as men. They were forced to accept what men did to them and were constantly reminded of their subordinate status. In the novel, Dulcie and Sally never speak up about the cruelties done to them and the violations of their bodies.

These atrocities have a traumatic impact on David's mind as they are committed in the name of freedom and his beloved is one of the victims. That's why he feels compelled to talk about his life and the things that are bothering him. He finds himself unable to do that, so he hires an amanuensis to write his story. That way he could distance himself from it. In the end, he chooses suicide over dealing with the reality of the events as he never seems to get over his traumatic experiences. The narrator herself is traumatised but she seeks closure and that's why cshe ontinues to write the story. Though she invents a storyline for Dulcie, she is unable to get any definitive answers about what happened.

Dulcie is the silent voice in the story but paradoxically, seems to speak through this silence. Her absence draws attention to the other absences in South African history, such as the experiences of all those female ANC members. The trauma that she experienced is a constant element throughout the story. The novel also challenges our understanding of language as a means to represent reality. Language ultimately fails as Dulcie and the trauma that she suffered, can never be expressed in language.

One can assume that Dulcie was traumatised by the treatment she received as a female member of the ANC. This treatment is meant to teach her a lesson. It is impossible to accept women who do not fit into the stereotypical roles in a patriarchal society like South Africa. The female activist, a new type of woman, emerged as a result of Apartheid and the resistance to it. These female ANC members, especially the guerrillas played an important role in the movement. Both Sally and Dulcie went to other countries for training camps where they were prepared for their tasks as guerrillas. Later Sally became a passive member of the ANC. The camps were supposed to empower the members but they were also used to show the women their right and real place in the society. For the Movement, women had to put aside their female sexuality and appearance and they had to behave as men. Though Sally never went this far and remained very feminine, being a true guerrilla, Dulcie had the appearance of a man. To keep her in place and to keep the stereotypical roles of men and women intact, the men violated her body and reduced her to a helpless victim. Gillian Gane opines that physical violence and rape are the best ways of showing women their place because it is, "always a political act – the exertion of male power over a female body" (104).

Men did not approve of female activism during the struggle but since they needed as many fighters as possible, they accepted them and kept showing them their place by raping them. Sally leaves the Movement and accepts the traditional roles but Dulcie, on the other hand remains active in the Movement and therefore, has to suffer the consequences. Both Sally and Dulcie remain silent and decide to conceal their scars. They seem to accept it as something completely natural and refuse to speak about their rape. Sally painfully calls it as "the unspoken part of a girl's training" (123). Both grow up in patriarchal society and realise that there is nothing they can do about it. The novel depicts that strong women do not deserve to be physically and psychologically tortured, since they are not subordinate to men.

David's Story also illustrates how impossible it is to represent trauma in literature. Dulcie, the true protagonist of the novel, is the embodiment of severe trauma and this is the trauma David wants to narrate but is not able to. He is not able to talk about Dulcie at all and wants the story to be written by an amanuensis. When the narrator agrees to write Dulcie's story – instead of trying to talk to her – he comes up with a page which the narrator describes as "a mess of scribbles and scoring out and doodling of peculiar figures that cannot be reproduced here" (135). The novel is an attempt to depict the difficulty or even impossibility of representing violence through language. In the novel, many postmodern techniques are used by Wicomb to make the reader to consider the (im)possibility of representing the truth.

David remains constantly scared that he will betray the Movement if he provides too much information to the narrator but he is not aware of the fact that meaning can be found in silences and in-between the lines. After David's death, the narrator continues to write the novel and it proves that she is either very interested in the story or has taken over part of the trauma and therefore, doing closure herself. She is also traumatised by the violence done to Dulcie and it can be seen in the form of hallucinations and the surreal vision of Dulcie, in her dreams. She has never seen Dulcie before and has no way of knowing or even assuming that the woman in her garden was Dulcie. "Only when I turn to go back to work do I see her sturdy steatopygious form on the central patch of grass, where she has come to sunbathe in private… She yawns and stretches in the warm sun. Is this no longer my property? I ask myself. I have never thought of Dulcie as a visitor in my garden" (212). The narrator in her vision sees Dulcie's body being violated by insects, while she does nothing to stop them. It also reflects her silence and acceptance of the violations she suffered in real life.

In conclusion *David's Story* is a tale of violence and betrayal, political commitment, love, writing and representation of truth. The novel deals with the struggle against Apartheid and the suffering of women who were/are directly involved in it. Saarah Baartman and Eva/Krotoa's transformation into 'Mothers of the Nation' highlights a substantial aspect of the South African patriarchal society. Some strong and powerful women like Dulcie disturb the balance in such a society and therefore, they are punished in the most violent and humiliating way. The domestic stereotypical representation of women always leads to some sort of violence. David's representation of Dulcie leads to the post-structuralist realisation that language always fails. The violence done to Dulcie can never be adequately represented in language. The only possible way to represent Dulcie is by not representing her. Therefore, her presence can be found in the silences or the gaps in the novel. The women in the novel resist all forms of representation because it always leads to violence in one way or the other, so Wicomb chooses silence over speech.

Works Cited

Gane, Gillian. "Unspeakable Injuries in *Disgrace* and *David's Story*." *Kunapipi*, vol. 24, no 1-2, 2002, pp. 101-113.

Samuelson, Meg. *Remembering the Nation, Dismembering Women? Stories of the South African Translation.* University of KwaZulu-Natal Press, 2007.

Susan, Arndt. *The Dynamics of African Feminism: Defining and Classifying African Feminist Literatures.* Africa World Press, 2002.

Tobias, Philip. *Images of Humanity.* Ashanti Publishing, 1991.

Wells, Julia C. "Eva's Men: Gender and Power in the Establishment of the Cape of Good Hope, 1652-1674." *The Journal of African History* Cambridge UP, 1998, pp.417-437.

Wicomb, Zoë. *David's Story.* The Feminist Press, 2001.

Willemse, Hein. "Zoë Wicomb in Conversation with Hein Willemse." *Research in African Literatures,* vol. 33, no. 1, 2002, pp. 144-152.

CHAPTER 10

Reading Buchi Emecheta: Invalidating the Myth of 'Complete Woman' in *The Joys of Motherhood*

Archana Thakur and Hem Raj Bansal

Abstract

Motherhood is an exalted concept all over the world. Caring and compassionate image of a mother is venerated as that of a goddess. Narratives glorifying motherhood reinforce the importance and values of a self-sacrificing mother. In Africa, where motherhood defines a woman, a mother of many children is held in high esteem and is hailed as a complete woman. But Nigerian writer Buchi Emecheta contests this notion of glorified motherhood in her novel *The Joys of Motherhood* (1979). Set in early 20th century Lagos, the novel delineates the unprecedented suffering a mother has to undergo in the name of motherhood. The objective of the present article is to study the notion of African motherhood and to uncover the underlying politics of patriarchal idealisation of motherhood. The paper also aims to uncover the myth behind popular African notion of complete woman.

Keywords: Suffering, Motherhood, Africa, Complete Woman, Children.

Nigerian female writer Buchi Emecheta (1944-2017) is a champion of women's cause. With a plethora of her writings, she inveighs against wrongs done to women and fights for full-fledged female rights. Right to education, gender bias, marriage, motherhood, economic independence of women are some of the central issues in her works. Through her writings, she confronts the archaic assumptions about women that accord them a second class rank. Being a native of traditional Igbo society of Nigeria, where she lived all through her childhood, Emecheta had closely observed the injustices meted out to females both in society and in literary world, discord between tradition and modernity, African superstitions, and the severity of British colonialism. Deeply hurt by the second class status given to women, she used her pen to write about this inequality and at the same time challenged it. In her novels, Emecheta inscribes her resentment against the tyranny of cultural traditions and myths; gender bias, slavery and compulsory motherhood that oppress African women and enslave them, thereby denying them any identity outside domestic sphere. Her novels are a powerful critique of sexist nature of her community.

Like numerous other societies, the concept of motherhood has been of utmost importance to African societies. A woman with a large number of children is held in great respect because "African motherhood is all about children" (533) to quote Lauretta Ngcobo, a South African novelist. Popular assumption says that motherhood is an important part of a woman's life and her identity. It is believed that she attains fulfillment and becomes a complete woman only after becoming a mother. This is the reason why most of the girls are expected to seek womanhood by becoming mothers. Young girls in every society are seen as potential mothers for future and they are usually conditioned in such a way that they start believing in marriage and procreation as their ultimate destiny. They are encouraged to marry early and produce a large number of children, mainly sons. A childless woman is seen as the "dead end of human life" (qtd. in Akujobi 3), whereas a woman with numerous children is seen as a complete woman. The reason for the African obsession with high fertility rate is that they value kinship for "human capital" and "social security" (534). Talking about African culture, Toyin Falola posits that "children are necessary to sustain kinship and the economy" (255). This fixation for a large number of children is what Lauretta Ngcobo holds responsible for "institutionalising of motherhood" (534) which is controlled by patriarchy and reduces a woman to the level of a mere reproducing vessel. Patriarchy thrives on the notion that women should remain subordinate to men, stay at home, take care of children, and discipline them. It expects women to give birth to sons who will carry forward the family name. Under patriarchy, most women have embraced motherhood without choice and motherhood, in Adrienne Rich's opinion "without autonomy is one of the quickest roads to a sense of having lost control" (245).

Emecheta derides the myth of glorified motherhood in her novel *The Joys of Motherhood* (1979) and condemns the popular notion that motherhood is the only way to achieve womanhood. In this novel, the protagonist mother Nnu Ego, an illiterate woman faces every ordeal bravely and silently for upbringing her sons and daughters, affirming her faith in the age-old African saying that a mother of many children, especially sons is an accomplished woman and is well-looked-after in her old age. American feminist writer Barbara Christian (1943-2000) fittingly remarks that, "... the role of mother, with all it implies, is universally imposed upon women as their sole identity, their proper identity, above all others. The primacy of motherhood for women is the one value that societies, whatever their differences, share" (212). The chapters of the novel such as "The Mother," "The Mother's Mother," "The Mother's Early Life," "A Mother's Investment," "A Mother of Clever Children" and "The Canonised Mother" highlight the importance placed on the idea of motherhood in Nigerian Ibo society.

Nnu Ego is a loving daughter of a rich village chief who gets married to a local boy at the age of sixteen but soon her husband deserts her and remarries because of her inability to produce a child. Her husband sends her back to her father's home calling her 'infertile,' 'dry,' 'jumpy,' 'a nervy female' and 'as barren as a desert' (*TJOM* 39) thus causing her great distress and making her believe that a childless woman is a failed woman, an incomplete person. Terms like 'infertile', 'childless' or 'barren woman' are social constructs. Every married woman is expected to be a mother and if she fails to bear children, she is ill-treated in society and labeled as a barren woman.

Nnu Ego herself feels that "she is failing everybody" (31) and the fault must be within her because nobody dares question a man's potency and also because "The term 'nonfather' does not exist in any realm of social category" (Rich 12). Being a woman, that too childless, she has no right to stay in her husband's home as Toyin Falola observes:

> ... Men are regarded as the heads of households while a woman has relevance as a mother and wife. She keeps traditions and kinship alive by bearing children and socialising them. As a bearer of children, she acquires respect within the household; as bearers of male children, she acquires prestige and ensures the stability of her marriage and the continuity of kinship and its traditions. (252)

A woman incapable of producing children loses her dignity and status within the family and community just as Nnu Ego did. Nnu longs to get married again because she wants to become a mother believing in the dominant ideology that a woman's life is complete only on becoming a mother. She gets married to Nnaife who works as a washerman in Lagos. She travels four days to reach Lagos from Ibuza and is crestfallen on seeing her ugly husband but tolerates him for the sake of becoming a mother. She soon gets pregnant and gives birth to a baby boy. She even starts loving her husband for he made her a woman and declares, "He has made me into a real woman – all I want to be, a woman and mother. So why should I hate him now?" (53). Nnu Ego's happiness knows no bounds on the birth of her boy as now she has proved her fertility and worth to society. But her boy dies within a month. Society judges mothers on the basis of their performance as mothers, that is, how their children behave, how they adjust on social level and what they become in the future. Mothers are often blamed for any problem that arises with their children. This is the reason for Nnu Ego's suicide attempt after losing her first child. On being questioned and thrashed by the crowd, she cries in pain, "But I am not a woman anymore! I am not a mother any more. The child is there, dead on the mat" (62). Her confession makes the crowd sympathetic towards her and they all agree that "... a woman without a child for her husband was a failed woman" (62) highlighting the futility of life for a childless woman in a society that boasts of compulsory maternity. Once again, the sense of being incomplete envelops Nnu Ego in darkness for a couple of months. She is considered a barren though she had given birth to a son.

Emecheta here attacks the social or patriarchal construction of motherhood which, American feminist writer Adriene Rich (1929-2012) in her book *Woman Born: Motherhood as Experience and Institution* (1976) refers to as "institutional motherhood" (13) something that makes it obligatory for every woman to bear and rear children, most preferably sons. Rich differentiates between two meanings of motherhood: "the *potential relationship* of any woman to her power of reproduction and to children; and the *institution* which aims at ensuring that the potential – and all women – shall remain under male control" (13). Along with this, she explicates that motherhood gives pleasure if it is a matter of choice, rather than compulsion.

It is surmised that women's ability to give birth makes them the natural caregivers and nurturers. But feminist critics like Simone de Beauvoir (1908-86), Adrienne Rich (1929-2012), Nancy Chodrow (1944), and Andre O' Reilly (b.1961) challenge this notion of motherhood as being innate. Rather they view it as a "social construction of motherhood" (*Encyclopedia of Motherhood* 1133) and "an unconscious response to pressure" (Alizade 18) from family and society. Rejecting the naturalness of maternal instinct in a woman, Simone de Beauvoir in her book *The Second Sex* (1949) explains that a girl child is usually given a doll to play with and she looks up to her mother as a role model, and imitates her, "identifies with her" and starts playing the doll's mother. She loves, breastfeeds, scolds, beats, and tortures her doll. She does everything for it just like her mother would do for her. She makes sure that "the care of children falls upon the mother. She is so taught; stories heard, books read, all her little experiences confirm the idea" (287). This is how a girl child is ushered into being a future mother and thus "her vocation is powerfully impressed upon her (287). So, Beauvoir asserts that there is no "'maternal instinct' innate and mysterious" (287). Similarly, Adrienne Rich refutes claims of motherhood as being innate or natural, she writes, "Motherhood is earned, first through an intense physical and psychic rites of passage – pregnancy and childbirth – then through learning to nurture, which does not come by instinct" (31).

After months of mournful state of mind, Nnu Ego once again gives birth to a son and names him Oshia. She now engages herself rigorously in taking care of her child. She learns to be satisfied with whatever little her husband earns. She stops going out to earn money and devotes full time for rearing her son, as now she is well aware of the old saying that "money and children don't go together: if you spent all your time making money and getting rich, the gods wouldn't give you any children, if you wanted children, you had to forget money, and be content to be poor" (80). She realises that her wish to be a modern working woman cost the life of her first son. She is now contended with being poor and having just one outfit as long as her baby is safe. Most mothers like her make sacrifices for their sons because they are always told "never mind, he will grow soon and clothe you and farm for you, so that your old age will be sweet" (80). Like Nnu Ego, women are often under pressure to live up to the expectations of the society. Fear of being labeled a selfish / bad mother compels many a woman to engage in 'intensive mothering', a term coined by Sharon Hayes in her book *The Cultural Contradictions of Motherhood* (1996). Intensive mothering foregrounds such beliefs:

> Children need and require constant and ongoing nurturing by their biological mothers, who are primarily responsible for meeting their needs; mothers must rely on experts to guide them in meeting their children's needs; mothers must spend large amounts of time and energy on their

> children; mothers must regard mothering as more important than paid work. (573)

Thereafter, Nnu Ego gives birth to seven children, one after another and six of them survive. Nnu Ego tries her level best to fit in the role of a good mother all the while ignoring herself. According to the popular assumption, the term 'good mother' refers to a mother who raises her children in the best possible manner, devotes her full time for childcare, neglects her own needs, never gets angry, loves unconditionally, leaves her job, takes care of the whole household affairs, and also gives time to her husband. She is the embodiment of forgiveness, humility, patience, and kindness.

She struggles with poverty and hunger for her children and sells cigarettes and matchboxes to make both ends meet as her husband Nnaife does not earn enough. Nnu Ego faces destitution and humiliation for sake of her children all the time believing that her children will take good care of her in her old age. Ironically, this dream later turns out to be false, illusory as her both sons live far off in other countries and she dies alone. The birth of her every child adds more to their poverty. For a family already having limited resources, every new child brings additional burden and responsibilities. When her eldest son is on the verge of death due to malnutrition, she even sells all her clothes believing that "... if her sons should live and grow, they would be all the clothes she would ever need" (104). Nnu Ego does not like to be pitied and "if you made the mistake of pitying her, she would tell you what her two sons were going to be when they grew up" (105) but compromising with her self-respect, she accepts food from her neighbour to save her son's life.

When her husband Nnaife takes one wife after another, Nnu Ego is tormented but she comes to terms with her husband's polygamous nature for the sake of her children. There is constant struggle and quarrel in the household to make both ends meet with ever growing family. Emecheta here exposes the obnoxious practice of polygamy which existed in Africa from ancient times. This practice of polygamy has adverse effect on women. Having several wives may add to a man's prestige but it surely traumatises a woman to share her husband with other women. In polygamous marriages women often compete for their husband's love and favours. There is often a competition of producing large number of children in order to secure a greater share of property. Women often suffer sexual neglect which affects their mental and physical health and moreover, there are frequent quarrels in the household.

Miriam Koktvedgaard Zeitzen defines polygamy as "... a practice whereby a person is married to more than one spouse at the same time, as opposed to monogamy, where a person has only one spouse at a time" (3). There are several reasons for polygamy to flourish among common masses. Need of large labour force on farms, desire for social status, sexual gratification, and veneration for ancestors are some of the reasons cited for the continued adoption of this practice. Large family and numerous children is a status symbol in most of the African societies and is also a way to immortalise one's name.

Never ending quarrels, jealousies, troubles and lack of money to fulfill basic needs makes Nnu Ego realise that "... she was a prisoner, imprisoned by her love for her children" (137). With every birth in the house, house becomes stuffier; there is scarcity of food, water, clothes and money. The family receives a blow when Nniafe is taken away by the soldiers to serve in the British Army. There is no help from anywhere yet the mother relentlessly strives to bring up her children. She has no friends due to lack of social movement and time. She stops attending family meetings and paying visits to her acquaintances, fearing that they would think she has come to ask for food or money. Moreover, she does not have proper clothes to attend meetings and in addition to that she has several small children who need constant attention. She starts selling firewood which does not require much money but energy. Her children also help her in selling firewood and roasting groundnuts. Her own misery and her co-wife Adaku's prosperity makes Nnu Ego more jealous and miserable. She even starts hating people who are rich and well-dressed because she herself is rotting in poverty. She yearns to go back to her native place Ibuza but she knows that she cannot afford doing this as she will then lose her husband, her status of senior wife and will be labeled as ungrateful.

Although Nnu Ego is dispirited, society commends her for being an accomplished woman, i.e. having a lot of children. Her own father dies with complete contentment to see his daughter as a complete woman. Ironically everyone fails to see her miserable condition. A complete woman is considered to be a satisfied and happy woman. However, Betty Friedan (1921-2006) in her seminal work *The Feminine Mystique* (1963) is highly critical of the popular notion of her time, that is, "Motherhood, a fulfillment held sacred down the ages, is defined as a total way of life" (80). She defines 'feminine mystique' as "the problem that had no name" (15). Friedan discusses the lives of many unhappy housewives and mothers in the US who were suffering from this problem with no name despite having all the luxuries and a comfortable life. Even after living up to the standards set up for an ideal woman in the US, they were in distress. Friedan believes that the reason for this distress and dissatisfaction was that women had no identity outside of domestic sphere and the only identity they had was in relation to "man's wife, sex object, mother, housewife – and never as persons defining themselves by their own actions in society" (15). She goes on to argue that radical feminists of her own time have broken free of this feminine mystique by declaring "war on marriage, motherhood and family" (22).

Adaku, Nnu Ego's co-wife, being a mother of daughters is considered to be similar to a childless woman and there is no place for a childless woman in a society which places high value on sons. For every little quarrel in the family, she is reminded again and again that she is to be quiet and grateful because she has only two daughters. Many a times Nnu Ego pities her but also draws comfort from the fact that she herself is the mother of sons. Emechata writes, "Yet all because she was the mother of three sons, she was supposed to be happy in her poverty, in her nail-biting agony, in her churning stomach, in her rags, in her cramped room" (167). Knowing very well that Nnaife too prefers Nnu Ego over her and she herself can never get any significant position in her family, Adaku decides to become a prostitute and live her life on her own terms. Neglect and disrespect by family and society for being a mother of daughters only forces Adaku to take up this desperate step.

Due to abject poverty and no sign of Nnaife coming back from war for a very long time, Nnu Ego's two sons Oshia and Adim have to give up their school for lack of fees, and they along with their twin sisters start hawking and selling wares with their mother. Still there are pangs of hunger. Girls are especially trained to do more work whereas Oshia and Adim continue going for private lessons. Nnu Ego passes her own patriarchal conditioning to her daughters and nurtures them likewise, "But you are girls! They are boys. You have to sell to put them in a good position in life, so that they will be able to look after the family. When your husbands are nasty to you, they will defend you" (176). She has huge expectations from her boys and teaches her daughters to serve them but her hopes in her sons shatter eventually.

Nnu Ego becomes quiet and breaks down when her eldest son accuses her for his failure to win scholarship for higher studies and also for giving him a disturbing childhood and keeping him engaged in numerous works. He now sees her as a "nagging and worrying woman" (185). For Oshia, his father is a hero, who after his return from war brings some money and promises to pay for his education. According to him, it is due to Nnu Ego's greed that Oshia fails to win the scholarship because she kept him busy in her own business. Her second son Adim is disappointed due to lack of funds to support his education. She realizes that "her love and duty for her children were like her chain of slavery" (186). She wonders "God when will you create a woman who will be fulfilled in herself, a full human being, not anybody's appendage?" (186).

She now reaches a stage where she knows that she has not gained anything through her motherhood. Motherhood might have elevated her status in front of others but deep inside she realizes that all her efforts bore no fruit. Lamenting the pointlessness of her pains, she says:

> What have I gained from all this? Yes, I have many children, but what do I have to feed them on? On my life. I have to work myself to the bone to look after them, I have to give them my all. And if I am lucky enough to die in peace, I even have to give them my soul. They will worship my dead spirit to provide for them.... When will I be free? (186-187)

She also knows the answer as well that she will never be free, not in this life and even not after death. Years ago too when her first son had died she had suffered from such pain and feeling of helplessness. She further laments her vulnerability thus: "I am a prisoner of my own flesh and blood. The men make it look as if we must aspire for children or die. That's why when I lost my first son, I wanted to die, because I failed to live up to the standard expected of me by the males in my life, my father and my husband – and now I have to include my sons" (187).

Multiple pregnancies rather than bringing joy to her become a burden which Simone de Beauvoir calls "burdens of maternity" and "... they are crushing if the woman is obliged to undergo frequent pregnancies and if she is compelled to nurse and raise the children without assistance" (80). Beauvoir is of the view that a woman's biological condition is responsible for whatever position she is in the world. Her reproductive capacity has always been exploited by man. Life, during and after pregnancy, does not remain same for her. She loses her identity and her body in this process. Gestation, i.e., the nine-month-long period between conception and childbirth "is a fatiguing task of no individual benefit to the woman but on the contrary demanding heavy sacrifices" (57). Even after she passes childbearing age, a woman feels alienated as multiple pregnancies during her childbearing age make her "prematurely old and misshapen" (58).

Although situation has changed gradually, in some societies there is little or no knowledge about birth control. Even some literate do not use contraceptives believing them to be against nature. Also, preference for a son is a major reason for large number of children in a family. As a result women still have to undergo repeated pregnancies which are detrimental to their health. Some even lose their lives during childbirth. Motherhood rather than being a matter of joy turns out to be a burden for many women as it did for Nnu Ego. Multiple pregnancies, childbirths, hard work, hunger, lack of peace and bringing up several children in sheer poverty and adverse environment prove detrimental to her health and she becomes prematurely old. Her son Adim notices how bony she has become and her teeth are already rotten. She looks seventy at the age of forty.

Nnu Ego knows that she cannot expect any assistance from Nnaife. He has no qualms in impregnating his brother's senior wife whom Nnu Ego calls 'big mother' and again in marrying a girl of her son's age. Emecheta here questions men's role in the upbringing of their children. Men like Nnaife are satisfied as long as they can impregnate their wife / wives and play no role in child rearing. A woman who is a child bearer becomes a child rearer too. Feminist sociologist and psychoanalyst Nancy Chodrow in *The Reproduction of Mothering: Psychoanalysis and the Sociology of Gender* (1978) assert that "Being a mother... is not only bearing a child – it is being a person who socializes and nurtures. It is being a primary parent or caretaker" (11). And if that be the case, Chodrow questions the status quo: "why are mothers women?" (11). She further states that women's mothering has been taken for granted due to the "... seemingly natural connection between woman's childbearing and lactation capacities and their responsibilities for child care" (3). This has resulted in making a mother the primary parent who has to take responsibility for childcare. According to Chodrow mothering was not women's central occupation two centuries ago even though "... marriage, especially for women, was essentially synonymous with child-bearing" (4). They also carried out other outdoor responsibilities along with men. Husbands used to cooperate in child-rearing and in their training. But with the rise of capitalism and industrialization small household trades vanished as factories took them over and women lost their ways of earning. "Home and workplace" became separate. As a result of this, "women's family role became centered on child care and taking care of men" (5). And now mothering has become more "isolated and exclusive" (6) domain for women especially as the concept of nuclear families has become more prominent.

Nnu Ego outwardly seems happy as people call her "mother of very clever children" (197) because two of her sons are receiving higher education. Nnu Ego's dream of a happy family shatters when her children choose their own different paths and the blame for family dispersal is on Nnu Ego. Her eldest son Oshia, who she believes will take up family responsibility grows cold and distant to the family, refuses any financial help, leaves for United States after insulting and fighting with his father. Nnu Ego knows that Adim wants to get educated like his brother but seeing that Nnaife would not pay for his fees, the boy becomes disappointed and grows weak; she promises to pay for his fees anyhow. She regrets that she could not send her daughters to school due to lack of subsistence and strict rules. Now she does not desire anything for herself because "Her joy was to know that she had brought up her children when they had started out with nothing, and that those same children might rub shoulders one day with the great men of Nigeria. That was the reward she expected" (202). She secretly wishes that she did not have so many children but she is pregnant again. Nnu does not feel like asking for help when her time comes and she gives birth to a dead baby girl, her ninth child. She soon loses consciousness and wakes up days later only to remain guilt-ridden for days for deliberately killing her daughter. In her guilt, she curses herself for not taking help during childbirth, because she knew that she cannot afford to feed and clothe another child.

One of her twin daughters, Kehinde, now fifteen, elopes with a butcher's son. This enrages Nnaife beyond limits as the butcher is a Yoruba Muslim and he being an Ibo has low opinion of Yorubas. He heaps all kinds of abuses on Nnu Ego and her children and asks them to leave his house. Nnu Ego ponders over the fact that when the children are good, the father boasts of having them and when they are bad they belong to the mother. Nnaife, in his attempt to kill butcher, wounds a person and is jailed. In the court trail that follows, he makes a complete fool of himself. When Nnu Ego is questioned by the lawyers, she in her innocence blurts out the whole truth but not before heaping all kinds of praises on Nnaife. She tells the court that he is a perfect husband who works hard and worked all his life. Moreover, he loves his children dearly. Prosecuting lawyer cleverly makes Nnu Ego tell every detail about Nnaife and his behaviour. So, based on her statements and other witnesses, Nnaife is imprisoned for five years. Everyone blames Nnu Ego for tragic life of Nnaife and she herself wonders where she went wrong as "she had been brought up to believe that children made a woman. She had had children, nine in all, and luckily seven were alive, much more than many women of that period could boast of" (219). She realizes that time has changed and with time values and morals have changed too but "how was she to know that by the time her children grew up the values of her country, her people and her tribe would have changed so drastically, to the extent where a woman with many children would face a lonely old age, and maybe a miserable death all alone, just like a barren woman?" (219). At this stage of life, she repents that she never tried to make friends. But making friends needed time, money and good clothes and she had none of these. She spent her life bearing and rearing children but failed in everything. After the court case against Nnaife, she is certain that he would never like to see her again and her two elder sons have already chosen their path. Since she can no longer survive alone and without money in Lagos, she thinks it better to leave for Ibuza, where at least she will not have to pay the rent and where she can grow her own vegetables.

Taiwo, one of the twins too is hurriedly married to a clerk and her bride price goes to Adim for his higher education. Nnu Ego also has to leave her little daughter Obiageli in Lagos on the insistence of her daughter Taiwo and her husband. She reluctantly leaves her little daughter behind when Magnus and Adim assure her that the girl will be looked after well and will get good education. Nnu Ego's heart aches to leave the girl behind and she says, "I don't know how to be anything else but a mother. How will I talk to a mother with no children? Taking the children from me is like taking away the life I have always known, the life I am used to" (222). But she feels happy to see her children happy. This is the only joy of her life to be happy in her children's happiness and she does not want anything for herself now.

Ibuza people back home and their kinsmen at Lagos curse and blame Nnu Ego for keeping herself busy in money-making and not rearing her children properly. Nnu Ego is well aware that Nnaife and her own children blame her too. With mixed feelings of sadness and joy for her children, she leaves for Ibuza in a motor where she gets the front seat as a mark of respect for a complete woman. The driver of the motor praises her for being a mother of so many children, with one living in America and other children living happily in Lagos. Such a privileged and successful woman commands respect and the driver envies her, resenting that "life is very unfair for us men. We do all the work, you women take all the glory. You even live longer to reap the rewards.... You must be very rich" (223). Nnu Ego knows the reality of her life but she thinks it better to remain quiet rather than answering back to the ignorant man.

In Ibuza, Nnaife's family and kinsmen label Nnu Ego a bad woman and thus, she has to live in her father's compound. She knows this will happen as only "... good children belonged to the father.... " (223). Nnaife is released from jail and he too leaves Lagos and returns to Ibuza but never to Nnu Ego. He prefers his young wife Okpo over Nnu Ego. The latter suffers in loneliness as her son Adim also goes to Canada for higher education and Oshia too settles in America after marrying a white bride. They never come back to see their mother and she learns to live like this but she soon becomes absent-minded. She would tell people that she has great children who live in America and Canada. With her disillusioned mind and sorrowful heart, one night she lies down by the roadside believing that she has reached home and dies there quietly and alone despite having seven living children. They do not bother to come and see their mother once but after her death they all come home to give their mother a respectful and the greatest burial in Ibuza. Since Nnu Ego was a complete woman in the eyes of society, a shrine is also built in her name so that subsequent generations can pray to her for blessing them with children. The last chapter "The Canonised Mother" implies that Nnu Ego too becomes a *chi* (a god) but she never blesses anyone who comes to seek her blessings as after death she had realized that there was no joy in being a mother. And she is not spared even after death. Emecheta remarks:

> Stories, afterwards, however, said that Nnu Ego was a wicked woman even in death herself because, however many people appealed to her to make women fertile, she never did. Poor Nnu Ego, even in death she had no peace! Still many agreed that she had given all to her children. The joy of being a mother was the joy of giving all to your children, they said. (224)

Nnu Ego's faith in her children fades as she faces alienation and rejection. It is this realization which changes her perspective after her death. This is the reason why she never answered / answers the prayers of those seeking to bless them with children. She herself could not get joys associated with motherhood and she does not want subsequent generations of women to suffer like her.

The Joys of Motherhood breaks the myth that a woman needs many children, chiefly sons in order to be happy and to be called a complete woman. It shows a harsh reality of traditional Nigerian society which demands a woman to be a mother and sacrifice herself for the sake of her children. The title is highly ironic because Nnu Ego does not get any joy out of this compulsory motherhood, rather she suffers on account of her children and dies a sad death. Ketu H. Kartak observes: "By the conclusion of the novel one recognizes the irony of the title – the joys of motherhood are experienced by Nnu Ego as the sorrows of motherhood" (167). Orthodox society makes her aspire to become a mother, making her believe that if she has enough children, especially sons, her old age will be full of comfort and she will be acknowledged by society as a complete woman. On the contrary, she gets unparalleled suffering and lonely tragic death. All her life she keeps hoping that her children will look after her, she bears every adverse situation believing that if she tolerates now for the well-being of her children, her old age will be better. But the same children desert her to make their own lives better, never caring for their mother. Her belief that there is no joy in life without children makes her attempt suicide when her first son dies. She tolerates Nnaife only because she wants to become a mother after she fails to have children from her first marriage. There are numerous women like Nnu Ego who count on their children all their lives but still remain alone when they are of no use to those children. Old age homes around the world are the best examples to substantiate such situation which Nnu Ego and many other mothers confront. Motherhood rather than bringing joys to her makes her a slave. Marie A. Umeh in her article "The Joys of Motherhood: Myth or Reality asserts that "In *The Joys of Motherhood* Emecheta extends her metaphor of the enslaved Igbo woman, arguing that the society also programs women to be slaves of their male offspring as well as their husbands" (45).

Another ambitious mother in the novel, Adaku is made to feel low on account of her having two daughters. It is thrust on her that she has failed her husband because she is not the mother of sons. She is forced to feel the stigma of a childless woman, an incomplete woman. Earlier, she also craves to have a son but later gives up hope and makes her own way. She chooses to become a prostitute, also succeeds as a rich business woman and sends her daughters to a convent school. She is happy in her life even without sons and husband. Thus, she breaks the myth of a complete woman having sons and living a happy life. Adaku makes an important observation during her stay with Nnu Ego: "A mother's joy is only in the name. She worries over them, looks after them when they are small; but in the actual help in the farm, the upholding of the family name, all belong to the father" (122). Nnu Ego on the other hand has several children, three of them are male. She takes immense pride in being a mother of sons and dotes on them. She often tries to make Adaku jealous on this front. But she does not gain anything by being proud of them. Her sons leave home when time comes for them to look after their parents. Nnu Ego fails tragically while Adaku gives an important lesson that one can rely on daughters too and that life can be lived without sons and husband also.

Through Nnu Ego, Emecheta presents the unfortunate condition of thousands of women across Africa who lose their freedom and identity in pursuit of happiness for their children. They strive hard to make things comfortable for their children, believing that their rewards will come in the old age but in vain. Either the children are too busy with their lives or situations are such that the expected joys are never attained. Motherhood rather than being a mandatory institution should be a matter of choice which Andre O' Reilly calls "Empowered mothering" and it refers to "... any practice of mothering that seeks to challenge and change various aspects of patriarchal motherhood that cause mothering to be limiting or oppressive to women" (viii).

Works Cited

Akujobi, Remi. "Motherhood in African Literature and Culture." *Comparative Literature and Culture*, vol. 13, no.1, 2011.

Alizade, Alcira Mariam, editor. *Motherhood in the Twenty-First Century*, Karnac, 2006

Beauvoir, Simone de. *The Second Sex*, edited and translated by H. M. Parshley, Jonathan Cape, 1953.

Chodrow, Nancy. *The Reproduction of Mothering: Psychoanalysis and the Sociology of Gender.* U of California P, 1978.

Christian, Barbara. "Angle of Seeing: Motherhood in Buchi Emecheta's *The Joys of Motherhood* and Alice Walker's *Meridian*." *Feminist Criticism: Perspective on Black Women's Writers.* Pergamon, 1985.

Emecheta, Buchi. *The Joys of Motherhood.* Heinemann, 1979.

Falola, Toyin. *The Power of African Cultures.* U of Rochester P, 2003.

Friedan, Betty. *The Feminine Mystique.* W. W. Norton, 1963.

Hayes, Sharon. *The Cultural Contradictions of Motherhood.* Yale UP, 1996.

Kartak, Ketu H. *Politics of the Female Body: Postcolonial Women Writers of the Third World.* Rutgers UP, 2003.

Ngcobo, Lauretta. "African Motherhood – Myth and Reality." *African Literature: An Anthology of Criticism and Theory*, edited by Tejumola Olaniyan and Ato Quayson, Blackwell, 2007. pp. 533-541.

Reilly, Andrea Ó, editor. *Encyclopedia of Motherhood.* Sage, 2010.

CHAPTER 11

Autonomy and Agency of Women in *The Bride Price*

Kanu Priya and Sheelpa Sweety

The world has seen unprecedented progress in education, freedom, rights, opportunities, and exposure of women over the years. Yet where these existing gaps have been narrowed down to some extent, discrimination exists when it comes to the power and agency of women. Hierarchy still exists and the deprivations and constraints reveal the deteriorating side of human values and ethics where discrimination against and subjugation of women is multiplied by factors such as gender, class, caste and illiteracy.

This chapter explores the social constructs that jeopardize a woman's agency and her autonomy over her body and life in a typical Nigerian society as portrayed in the novel *The Bride Price* by Buchi Emecheta. This novel is based on the African practice of bride price. According to this norm, a groom has to pay a token money to the patriarchal head of the bride he intends to marry. The novel juxtaposes the traditional and orthodox constructs such as socio-cultural practices, imposed tradition, marriage, child birth, polygamy, and hierarchy that make women inferior to men. This chapter intends to describe the institutional, social, and cultural barriers to women's power and agency over their bodies through the poignant story of Aku-nna and Chike.

'Agency' is the ability to make decisions about one's own life and act on them to achieve a desired outcome, free of violence, retribution, or fear. The ability to make those choices is often called empowerment (World Bank 3). According to Naila Kabeer, agency is the capacity of an individual to make choices relating to one's life (qtd. in World Bank 3). In various societies, the agency of a woman is often restricted to the patriarch of the family. Many social constructs are, thus, devised to limit the autonomy of a woman. In *Seeing Like a Feminist* (2012), Nivedita Menon talks about various social rules that exist to enforce the conformity of power with a particular gender in social and cultural spaces: "The maintaining of social order is rather like that. It requires the faithful performance of prescribed rituals over and over again throughout one's lifetime" (Menon VII). Alda Facio extols the socio political mechanisms that conspire to maintain the patriarchal hegemony and calls it "Patriarchal Institutions" (1).

In many societies, the female body often is the bedrock of male surveillance constantly subjected to control and monitoring. The society utilizes many constructs that aim at continuing this dominance of female body. A whole array of social sanctions exists to prevent a woman from reclaiming the right to have agency and autonomy on her life. In most societies, woman exists as a property whose ownership is claimed by the male head of the family. She is expected to succumb and adhere to the sanctions and decrees of the institutions. Any case of deviance is always punished with alienation and abandonment. Her consent is overlooked with respect to key stances in her life such as marriage and choice of partner. Iniquitous alliances are thrust upon her in the garb of upholding the honour and sanctity of the community and social institutions. This chapter aims at throwing light on the social practice of bride price observed in many African communities, which aims at subverting the agency and autonomy of women in the society. This chapter strives to link the notions of the rights of women living in the realities of Africa and also dealing with the problems of education, marriage, hierarchy, culture, tradition, agency, procreation, polygamy and bride price.

One of the oldest rituals performed in every part of the world is marriage as the union of man and woman has been universally and socially accepted. In African countries as well, it is given high importance as reflected in African Literature but it also leads to various issues resulting in gender bias and subjugation of women wherein the worth of a girl is directly dependent on her virginity, beauty, education etc. The misnomer that the basis of a marriage is to transfer a woman's fertility to her husband's family is encouraged by African people and a woman is expected to give birth in order to express womanhood.

The dominance of practices like dowry and bride-price in marriage existed since centuries and continues to dominate many parts of the world. It is, in fact, a way of meeting the requirements of a marriage. As stated by John A. Conteh:

> Bride-price is payment to the family of the bride. Depending on the economic status of the groom, payment is typically done by the groom. However, family members of the groom can sometimes be collectively accommodating in helping the groom meet the cost of payment. Historically, bride-price is more common in subsistence economies where horticultural or pastoral farming practices exist. (1)

Marriage and bride price are intertwined and have become an indispensable part in the lives of African men and women. Many people in Africa strictly adhere to and believe in the practice of giving the bride price to the bride's family failing which the bride might doom to death while giving birth to her first child. Under such superstition no matter how modern the people might have turned, they still follow the practice to avoid death. Resultantly, women in such traditions are doubly suppressed for being females and unable to attract good bride price for themselves. The French feminist Simone de Beauvoir has historically described various stereotypical norms of beauty and conformity that assuage the position of women in the society as the "weaker or second sex" (334).

Similar kind of representation of women exists in Africa where women are mere puppets in the hands of their fathers, step-fathers and later their husbands. Before marriage, a father is the shelter of a daughter and it is her responsibility to get good bride price for herself and once she is married, the control is in the hands of her husband. The wives' roles are defined and they are supposed to work within those prescribed roles as husbands overpower the entire family. The practice of polygamy that makes women the victims of male chauvinism is highlighted by Emecheta in her novel *The Bride Price*. She has beautifully depicted traditional, orthodox culture of Africa which represents women as victims, commodities and a property to be inherited in the patriarchal setup.

Bride price which could have been great support to the family and community and motivate people to stay united and focus on their daughters' education has created hegemony where the masculine force dominates the females thereby causing gender discrimination and subordination, and thus grabbing agency and power over the females. The practice of bride price has been commercialized and commoditized in recent time, thus raising problems related to affordability and defining females as commodities. Hague, Thiara and

Turner have explained bride price as "an on-going cultural longevity, the practice has been subjected to increased scrutiny by women activists and academics concerned by its negative impacts on women and girls" (1).

Virginia Woolf in her famous essay "A Room of One's Own" has wonderfully carved the fictional character of Judith Shakespeare, the sister of William Shakespeare, and explained the plight of women in a male-dominated society. The story of Shakespeare's imaginary sister reverberates all over the world, thus ringing the awakening alarm about the status of women. History has been witnessing women's suffering since ages and fighting for their rights whether concerning education, politics or socio-economic status. In Africa also the scenario has been the same as in a traditional and poor family only the sons were allowed to educate and even if the family could manage to educate the girl child, the focus would be more on her marriage rather than education. Mercy Amba Oduyoyoe has described the stereotypical representation of African women thus: "Westerners often see the African woman as a beast of burden walking behind her husband carrying his children, one inside, one on her back and many more following in a long procession of children whom she brings forth from puberty to menopause. She is clearly an inferior creature to the western woman, a person at the bottom of the human pecking order" (2).

Responding to the double standards that exist in western academia with regard to women's issues in Africa, Obioma Naemeka mentions the same for African women: "Abuse of the female body is global and should be studied and interpreted within the context of oppressive conditions under patriarchy" (61). Motherhood in the west is considered as a hindrance towards the self-realization of a woman and an obstacle towards economic independence. But in Africa it is the motherhood that encourages women for economic productivity because it is the responsibility of the mother to provide for a child. Commenting on the experience of motherhood, Ilina Soiri explains, "... motherhood is seen, not as a silent passive domestic activity, but rather as a revered and valued position from which to fight against injustice" (qtd. in Naemeka 26). As such, motherhood is one of the most important aspects of African women.

Florence Onyebuchi Emecheta was born on 21 July 1944 in Lagos, Nigeria and died in the year 2017. She was a prominent woman writer in African literature who through her works critiqued the position of women in African society. Her novels such as *The Bride Price* (1976), *The Slave Girl* (1977), *The Joys of Motherhood* (1979) and *Destination Biafra* (1982) revolved around the social constructs inhibiting the role of a woman. She wrote about her own subjective experiences as a woman after getting married and emigrating to the UK at the young age of sixteen. Right from her childhood, she was inclined towards acquiring western education, being well aware of the patriarchal set up where male child's education was given priority. She evolved as a prolific writer and incredible narrator who braved innumerable struggles, racism, and sexism, physical and domestic abuse to attain independence. Her struggle for success had started from her childhood to get education and later abandoned by her husband and left with five children to sustain themselves. She kept striving for education overcoming the hardships thereby maintaining a balance between her career and children. Her son had rightly put forth, "Some writers write because they have to. Buchi was a compulsive writer. She once admitted half-jokingly that writing kept her sane and that this and the love of her children were what made her get up in the mornings" (Onwordi 1).

Her writings include books for children, novels, autobiography, poems, blogs, etc. on several themes like feminism, slavery, liberation, child marriage, bride price, domestic violence, womanhood and motherhood. Her major concern was the issues pertaining to womanhood which in African societies was only associated with sexuality and procreation whereas their economic status was dependent on their status as mothers. Her works stressed on marriage, responsibility, and sacrifice. Lloyd remarks, "Of all the women writers in contemporary African literature Buchi Emecheta of Nigeria has been the most sustained and vigorous voice of direct, feminist protest" (4).

Emecheta's writings expose the physical burden caused due to childbirth, widowhood, polygamy and bride price. Her novels also talk about the protagonists who are ready to fight against all odds and oppressions. Katherine Frank appropriately says, "Emecheta's novels compose the most exhaustive and moving portrayal of the extant African woman, an unparalled portrayal in African fiction and with few equals in other literatures as well" (1).

Emecheta overtly presents the structure and function of a Nigerian family. A man occupies the hierarchical position as the ceremonial head of the family. The position of the woman is in proportion to her reproductive ability. Marriage of a girl can reap dividends for the patriarch in the form of the bride price. The chief protagonist is Aku-nna, whose name signifies "father's wealth." She is seen to be an asset to her father as she is touted to fetch a huge bride price and thus, fulfil her duty as a daughter. Stella Wen speaks about the implicit patriarchy in her name which limits her existence as a tradable object within her father's possession. Such an arrangement bounds the autonomy of Aku-nna from exercising free will and agency.

Roze Ure Mezu analyses the oedipal bond of Aku-nna with her father, Ezekiel. Akunna is considered to be a prized possession based on her utility and ability to fetch a good price. The father and daughter fit into a patriarchal mould that desalinates the role of a father as the custodian of a daughter's body and agency. Aku-nna's mother, Ma Blackie, also lacks the ownership and agency over her life and body. She occupies a diminished status owing to her limited child bearing capacity. In a patriarchal society, a woman is judged based on her capacity to beget male children. Ma Blackie's history of multiple failed pregnancies relegates her to a vulnerable position. In order to achieve her worth, she takes on "the two hundred mile journey to her home town of Ibuza. There she asked the river goddess to send her a baby" (2).

"I paid double the normal bride price for you,' he told her. 'And we were married in church. But what have you given me – just one son!'" (2). The tragedy of Ma Blackie can be summed up in the above lines. She is berated for not having produced enough male children. Ma Blackie was not barren. She had mothered two children namely Aku-nna and Nna-nndo. Aku-nna, being a girl, does not contribute much to her mother's status and position in the household. Like any other patriarchal family, a girl child is not considered to be an asset to the family. Aku-nna is well-versed with this truth and hence, she resolves to prove her worth by conforming to the social dictates of marriage and fetches a reasonable bride price for her father. "'I will not leave my father's house without all the proper ceremonies,' she thought" (3).

The death of Ezekiel is a disruptive event to this arrangement which is immediately replaced by uncle Okonkwo. It can be gauged by Aku-nna's contemplations where she ruminates that the death of the father implies the absence of a protective valve. "So, not only have we lost a father, we have lost our life, our shelter" (12).

In accordance with the patriarchal setup, the possession of Ma Blackie and her children was passed on to Okonkwo, the brother of Ezekiel. Okonkwo has his heart set on to the ambition of becoming the village chief. In order to become the chief, he has to pay large sums of money which he intends to raise by the bride prices of Aku-nna and his daughter Oguguga. The girls were raised with the underlying idea of finding the highest bidder to their possession. A lot of hope is placed on Aku-nna's ability to fetch a good bride price. Such practices denigrate the agency and autonomy of a woman and reduce her position to that of an object whose ownership is controlled by a man. The range of the bride price is proportional to social constructs such as class, age, beauty and youth and 'virginity' of the bride. Virginity, another social construct, is aimed to deny the autonomy of a woman on her body. It sabotages the agency of a woman with regard to desire and sexual choices.

There were many practices that emphasize the idea of virginity of a woman. In a Nigerian society, there exists a tradition that entails that the groom's family has to bring a pot of wine as a gift to the girl's father, if she is perceived to be a virgin. In the absence of the same, the pot would be brought empty. When Aku-nna is kidnapped by Okoboshi, and Okonkwo has to negotiate her bride price with Obidis, it can be clearly seen that a lot of importance is paid to the condition of Aku-nna's virginity. Her achievements such as her education do not matter much while deciding her worth. "'After all,' the Obidis said, 'there's nothing special about her except her education, and all this modern education doesn't do women any good... it makes them too proud'" (60).

Emecheta delineates various regressive practices to limit the agency of a woman in the African society. The women in Okoboshi's family justify her kidnapping by saying that Aku-naa was kidnapped by them to save her from Chike, the slave. Aku-nna's agency to choose her partner is denied. Even when she is clearly besotted with Chike, she is prevented from exercising her agency to marry him because of Chike's social class.

The novel is replete with many instances which throw light on the lack of sexual agency among women in Nigerian society. Sexual agency can be defined as an individual's choice to participate in a sexual activity without any coercion (Psychology Today). Apart from controlling the woman's autonomy to choose her partner; it assumes that the participation of a woman in sexual intercourse is not supposed to be a pleasurable experience for the woman. When Okoboshi's mother was counselling and preparing Aku-nna for the sexual encounter with Okoboshi, she had said, "'Don't worry,' said Okoboshi's mother. 'He'll be gentle with you. You may even like it – lots of girls do!'" (62). This statement is problematic on many counts. It, not only, ignores the consent of a woman but also, spells out the idea that a woman's participation in a sexual act is to fulfil a man's desire. In the novel, it is seen that the sexual agency of a young girl like Aku-nna is conceded to the male patriarch of the family. A woman is prohibited to express her desire and she internalizes the idea of according the primacy of man's feeling over hers.

However, Aku-nna uses the social construct of virginity and purity to her advantage to prevent herself from being raped by Okoboshi. She lies about her sexual experience which makes Okoboshi reject her as his bride. Okoboshi, in turn, threatens to malign her reputation in the community. The male entitlement of owning a woman's body when challenged shall leave no stone unturned in destroying the standing of a woman. Emecheta also talks about the practice where a man who is unable to pay the bride price can simply claim his ownership to a woman by fraudulently chopping off a lock of hair. The hierarchy of men is sustained by many such practices which subdue the agency of women. When Aku-nna elopes with Chike to escape a forced marriage with Okoboshi, the latter concocts the story of having consummated the marriage with Aku-nna. He produces a lock of hair to prove his ownership over her. It is decided that Okonkwo should reject the bride price from Chike which will ensure the possession of Aku-nna by Okoboshi. It is interesting to note that Aku-nna's consent is overlooked despite having faced abduction and violence. Her kidnapper is given legitimate authority over her body and life. Another such practice is the belief that a woman whose bride price is not paid, will die during the child birth. Aku-naa's unfortunate death during the child birth reinforces this patriarchal decree. Her tragic story is taken as an example to ensure obedience and conformity among generations to come.

Despite the oppressive standards of the society, Aku-nna is able to exercise her agency and autonomy in various aspects concerning her life. She allows herself to fall in love with Chike in spite of knowing the resistance to the match. "'I'm on my own,' she thought. 'No one can help me. I must look after myself'" (63). She decides to be her own saviour by tactfully averting sexual violence by Okoboshi. Such courage in the face of adversity speaks of Aku-nna's resistance and assertion of agency over her life. In the face of alienation and social rejection, she gathers up the perseverance to continue with her life. According to an African folklore, a girl child is said to be the product of passionate love-making. Upon knowing about Aku-nna's pregnancy, Chike playfully anticipates for boy as he wants his sexual life to be private from prying eyes. However, Aku-nna remarks that she would pray for a girl as she does not mind coming across as a sexually active individual. Heren is a woman who is not afraid to wear her sexuality on her sleeves. Despite having faced a lot of trauma, she does not whole-heartedly submit to conformism that is expected of her.

In *The Bride Price*, Emecheta gives us a glimpse into the regressive practices of a patriarchal society that endeavours to limit the agency and autonomy of a woman. She speaks with a dual voice of Aku-naa and of her own experiences as an African woman. A social custom such as the bride price is clearly intended at reducing the autonomy of a woman to an object whose value is negotiated between the male patriarchs. Such customs exist to ensure conformity of women to the social order. The central theme of the novel *The Bride Price* revolves around the idea of Aku-nna's bride price. It traces the growth of a young girl who believed in proving the worth of her life by fetching a good bride price for her father to a young woman who defies the norms by marrying a person of inferior social class. Her family punishes her by not accepting her bride price and swearing her off to a life of misery and death. Her unfortunate death serves as a legacy to ensure the future generations of women for not daring to reclaim the agency and autonomy over their body and life. Aku-nna tries to break the quasi-universal barriers and somewhat challenges the patriarchal set up. Emecheta rightfully confronts the stifling social norms that enforce patriarchy in the novel by presenting a microcosm of class and gender.

Works Cited

Beauvoir, Simone de. "Introduction" to *The Second Sex*. Lowe and Brydone, 1989.

Brown, Llyod. *Women Writers in Black Africa*. Greenwood, 1938.

Conteh, John. A. "Dowry and Bride Price." *Wiley Online Library,* 21 April 2016, https://www.researchgate.net/publication/305348271_Dowry_and_Bride-Price.Accessed 24 March 2021.

Emecheta, Buchi. *The Bride Price.* George Braziller, 1976.

Frank, Katherine. "Buchi Emecheta." *Modern Women Writers,* edited by. Lillian S. Robinson, Continuum, 1996.

Klugman, Jeni et al. *Voice and Agency: Empowering Women and Girls for Shared Prosperity.* World Bank Group, 2014.

Madsen, Pamela. "On being Female and Sexual Agency." *Psychology Today,* 18 June 2014, https://www.psychologytoday.com/intl/blog/shameless-woman/201406/being-female-and-sexual-agency. Accessed 14 April 2021.

Menon, Nivedita. *Seeing like a Feminist.* Penguin, 2012.

Mezu, Rose Ure. "Buchi Emecheta's *The Bride Price* and *The Slave Girl*: A Shizonalytic Perspective." *Ariel,* vol. 28, no.1, 1997, pp. 131-46.

Naemeka, Obioma, ed. *The Politics of (M)Othering: Womanhood, Identity and Resistance in African Literature.* Routledge, 1997.

Oduyoye, Mercy Amba. *Daughters of Anowa: African Women and Patriarchy.* Orbis, 1995.

Onwordi, Sylvester. "Women and Empowerment: An Interview with Buchi Emecheta." *New Statesman,* 31 Jan 2017 Accessed 15 Aug 2017.

Wen, Stella. "Radical Feminism: Patriarchy in *The Bride Price* by Buchi Emecheta." 14 June 2014. Accessed 15 April 2021.

Facio, Alda. "What is Patriarchy?" 22 March 2021, <http://learnwhr.org/wp-content/uploads/D-Facio-What-is-Patriarchy.pdf>

CHAPTER 12

Violent Times, Vexed Lives: Surfacing of the Innate African 'Female' in Jennifer Nansubuga Makumbi's *The First Woman*

Khem Raj Sharma

Since the earliest days of European expansionism, Africa has been predicted as a space of futurelessness projecting it as an uncivilized society. But, the root cause may be otherwise, wherein the white futurities were dependent on its exploitation. Following the years after the independence of Uganda from the British Empire, the country was regarded as the literary pride of Africa. This certainly was due to the reliance of its writers on their culture, traditions, history and mythology; and with a view to make Ugandan audience "feel like this is their world and they have a stake in it and they have something to say about it" (Kyomuhendo 41). Drawing on the historical, mythological and literary texts, the researcher in this treatise seeks to demonstrate the surfacing of the innate African 'female' self in Jennifer Nansubuga Makumbi's *The First Woman*, (2020) even during the times when Uganda was reeling under the dictatorial regime of Idi Amin.

Through oral story-telling, mythologies and folklore, Makumbi's latest novel is a powerful feminist narrative of a young African girl, who, attempts to discover who she is in an African patriarchal society, throughout varied chronicles of time. Further, she comes to know how being a woman can take different forms; and who women are and can be for each other. Such a discourse in the text then follows the last stage of feminism by Elaine Showalter wherein the reader focuses on the women's texts about women thereby uncovering everything that concerns a 'female.' It would propagate Showalter's advocacy for the 'female' phase as the genuine experience evidenced by themes, the language, the style and the culture which are distinctly woman.

Makumbi's maiden novel, *Kintu*, has focused on the multifarious consequences of masculinity; and the mythicality involved in various familial relationships, and historical chronicles of modern day Uganda. The tale involves the generational saga of the cursed Kintu clan that has inundated the family and the nation for centuries. Her second novel, *The First Woman* furthers the ideas from myths, oral tales and history but from the females' perspective. Initially titled *A Girl is a Body of Water*, and later republished as *The First Woman* in 2020, the novel brings to fore the surfacing of the subversive resistance capacities in women for resilience and endurance within the complexities of patriarchal dominance. While the former title presages a woman's shaping herself according to the prevailing circumstances like water; the latter directs her to mythmaking. Alex Clark aptly describes the novel as centering

> … on the original myths of motherhood, the contested ground of women's sexuality and the intersection between personal, public and political power, in a style that is frank, funny and direct. Beginning in 1975, in the middle of Idi Amin's dictatorship, the story captures the surrealism of living in unpredictable and violent times, folding awareness of vast events into the minutiae of daily life. (n.pag.)

Amidst the brutalities prevailing in Uganda during this dictatorial regime, Makumbi's story prepares the women for resistance, resilience and survival in the face of patriarchy and political anarchy.

The novel is set in Uganda, mostly in the early 1970s when Idi Amin was the country's president. Considered as one of the cruelest dictator in world history, his portrait hangs on the wall of a shop within the chronicle. However, Kirabo and her story has not much been affected by his regulations, but the echoes of his brutalities keep on haunting the lives of characters. Women in the country cannot wear trousers; and when Aunt Abi asks her to try one, she couldn't muster the courage. While she tries it indoors, Aunt Abi exclaimed and cursed the despot: "I knew it; you were built for trousers; may Idi Amin die a horrible death for banning them" (138). After Idi Amin expelled whites and Asians back in 1972 from Uganda, it had hit Jinja's status as an industrial city harder than anywhere else: "Buildings were crumbling. Boutiques sold bananas and fruit. Grocery stores had gossipy women twisting hair" (372). Kirabo reflects, "Uganda was that woman who bleached just the face and imagined the rest of her body light-skinned too" (372). No one could buy or sell their land even if people were impoverished. But the situation changed after his regime, and the Ganda's started selling it if need be.

The book is divided into five distinct chapters namely – "The Witch," "The Bitch," "Utopia," "When the Villages Were Young," and "Why Penned Hens Peck Each Other" with inconsistent number of parts. From the small Ugandan rural village of Nattetta, young Kirabo recounts her captivating story. In 1975, the adolescent Kirabo is undergoing through the pre-pubescent phase of her life. As the story progresses, "each part shows an older and more mature Kirabo, a Uganda of decades past and all the nuances and revelations of growing up" (Review n. pag.). She has questions about everything she sees and hears around her. During this time, one query that keeps haunting her throughout her entire life is the absence of her mother, as she had been raised by her grand-parents. The want of her mother gives rise to the "emergence of a mysterious second self, a headstrong and confusing force inside her at odds with her sweet and obedient nature" (Norton n. pag.). The opening lines of the story place Kirabo at a point from where her bildungsroman begins:

> Until that night, Kirabo had not cared about her. She was curious on occasion (*Where is she? What does she look like? How does it feel to have a mother?* …), but whenever she asked about her, and family said *No one knows about her,* in that never-mind way of large families, she dropped it. After all, she was with family and she was loved. But then recently her second self, the one who did mad things, had started to fly out of her body and she had linked the two. (3)

Thus, Kirabo certainly comes to know that she has two selves: one is of an ordinary girl, while the other one keeps flying out of her body and is an evil self. She seeks advice from an old woman, Nsuuta, whom the villagers deem as the 'witch'; and who was her grandmother, Alikisa's foe as well. Kirabo asks her to solve two biggest problems of her life. Her first problem relates to the stopping of her flight while the second is to find her mother. Therefore, begins a

> … sweeping tale that encompasses fundamental issues affecting women in Ugandan society, including god-making, skin bleaching, the clan system, trafficking, polygamy, colonialism, and superstitions around women. Because stories, as Nsuuta explains to Kirabo, have great power, the ancients controlled women with the myth of their originating from and

> belonging to the sea – leaving the land as the province of men. (Newson-Horst n. pag.)

She adds, "Since then, women have been rootless – moved not just across places but clans, tribes, nations, even races" (55) – and they have become migrants on the land.

Mythology has the power to reify, reshape, challenge and subvert the traditional discourses prevalent in the contemporary literary scenario. Makumbi weaves her narrative around various myths to portray the condition of the Ugandan women living under the shadows of horrific political conditions and patriarchy. Kirabo exposes the stark realities of patriarchy in telling the tale of one tortured woman who had to hide the female child in an anthill hole despite giving birth to a male twin as well to remain in the marriage. This is analogous to the situation prevalent in different parts of the world where a girl child is not preferred; and had given rise to the cases of female foeticide and infanticide. Moreover, the daughter strategizes "to make the darkness bearable" (7) by singing "sweet but sad song": "We were born multiple like twins – Wasswa/ But father had dropped a weighty word – Wasswa/ You bear a girl, don't bother bringing her home – Wasswa/ But a boy, bring the boy home – Wasswa" (7). This girl's situation finds semblance with Kirabo's story too when she slumped into self-pity while explaining her situation to the teenagers in the house: "My mother does not want me. … because I am a witch. … *Perhaps she found out her baby had a split self and abandoned me. Perhaps I started flying out of my body as soon as I was born*" (11-12). This quest for finding the answers to these recurring questions makes Kirabo to elope from her house and keep meeting with Nsuuta. The witch not only keeps on telling her numerous tales about the African people but could also convince her about her existence as the "first woman" – a streak of the original, independent and ultimate state which is missing in the other women of the world.

The First Woman narrates two contrastingly coming of age stories of women in friendship. While the first talks about Kirabo and Giibwa placed during the 1970s and 80s; the second relates to Alikisa and Nsuuta living in the 1930s and 40s. The narrative being mainly the story of Kirabo, takes the reader in flashback to the time of colonial Uganda of her grandparents. Both stories ask the same fundamental question: "What does it mean to fly out of the body?" (14) It is perceived that women suffering due to patriarchy often find solace in connecting and nurturing in friendship. Alikisa and Nsuuta are best friends in their youth, so close were they that they resolve to marry the same man so that their friendship could persist. However, when Nasuuta couldn't achieve the same, she spends her life all alone except some occasional nurturance of Alikisa's son, Tom; and at times, in the company of Kirabo's grandfather. If Kirabo has that innate 'female' self-inherent in her, Nsuuta is the original prototype. She is an empowered woman, who accepts the realities of life without resorting to manipulations. When Kirabo questions her perverse nature, she explicitly accepts and counter argues: "Everyone says that …you make men do things for you. I do. Nsuuta was shameless. "Tell me, how do you know you are a witch?" (22) She instructs Kirabo about the dynamics of the two selves wherein the flying self being a bad one takes the inside one along many a times. This flying self-had made Nsuuta a sexual perverse through which she could show her resilience and resistance to her society.

After completing her education, Nsuuta wants to be a nurse, like all those proud Asian nurses whom she met during her youth. She believes, "Hang on to your books, the pen never lies" (355). Although a child of privilege, intelligence, and beauty, the society doesn't give her the freedom which males of her times have been enjoying. Her perceptions about life and career perturb Nasetta's rural society because it has the spirit of radicalism inherent in them. Her choices while in school scandalize her pastoral community. After the homecoming, she settles on to satisfy her sexual desires by taking on lovers, instead of waiting incessantly for the occasional visit of her married lover. In this context, Muzenda aptly avers, "Sexual pleasure continues to exist in relation to taboo and shame, and remains stigmatized and silenced within public discourses and private discussions" (Marais 87). Owing to such misrepresentations, Mukambi reframes and constructs the contemporary African sexualities by challenging and unsilencing women's sexualities through the character of Nasuuta. For her, sexual pleasure outside the institution of marriage is a liberating act that breaks the cultural silences. Talking about her sexual encounters with Kirabo's grandfather and other unknown men, Nsuuta tells her: "You know why you are shocked, …? Because women are brought up to treat sex as sacred while men treat it as a snack" (396-97). Furthermore, by examining women's lived sexual experiences through Nasuuta, the writer has paved the way for women to unsilence themselves by reclaiming their sexual pleasure and power.

Kirabo's 'female' voicing too stands articulated in her freaking out independently. She remains oblivious of the excruciating patriarchal dynamics and expresses her free will and choices. Like her mentor, she pursues higher studies to become a veterinarian. Her eventual confrontation with her unpalatable stepmother Nnambi and her biological mother, Nnakku makes her more sensible towards the sad plight of many women in her community and the world around. Even her attempts to settle things with her best friend, Giibwa, for her betrayal somewhere show her temperament and about the choices of being in the world. However, her being a privileged girl like Nsuuta causes problems in her relationship with Giibwa, who is the daughter of laborers working for Kirabo's family. Despite being the best friends as children, their friendship ends bitterly. Here, it becomes pertinent to illustrate that friendships have duly been tested by men and the patriarchal intuitions in the narrative. In such pressing situations and societal pressures, is there a possibility of true friendship? This account vividly portrays that even though females can be best friends and support to each other, they can prove to be the bitterest enemies as well. Whereas, Alikisa and Nsuuta realized their friendship in the most congenial and coexisting manner, Giibwa exposes their relationship as uneven, a class issue. When Kirabo tries to make her understand by exemplifying the change in Grandmother and Nsuuta's relationship after the death of Tom, Giibwa remains unconvinced. She proclaims: "Nsuuta and your grandmother made up because they are the same. One was a Muluka's daughter, the other a daughter of a reverend. …They understand each other. Me and you, our relationship is lopsided" (422). Kirabo tries hard to reconcile but Giibwa remains unconvinced and asserts: "But for me the problem is not that a male finger rules the hand; it is the fact that the four female ones are not equal. … 'Got tired of being the little finger; tired of you people having power over us" (422). It is the feudal position of her family as laborers who live on Kirabo's family's land that disturbs her most. Moreover, this significantly explains the title "Why Penned Hens Peck Each Other", wherein Makumbi brings the discord amongst women to its culmination.

Finally, in this entire ciphering of females' relationships, what matters the most to Kirabo is her search for the mother and understanding of motherhood. Though, many women including the Grandmother, Nsuuta, Aunt Abi, Nnambi have made her to experience varied facets of motherhood, but its ultimate discernment possibly stays with her biological mother whom she had been trying to locate from the very beginning of the narrative. When she reaches the Jinja road and was almost to meet Nnakku, her mother, she accentuates:

> All her life, from the first time she asked about her mother, the first night she shot into the night sky and saw that light germinate, to consulting Nsuuta, to Tom's house in Bugoloobi, to moving in with Aunt Abi, all those posters at St. Theresa's, Tom's dying, down to this moment, and that was her. (374)

At this moment, she almost demonstrates waging a war with herself, her mother and the society. The mythic reality of a girl buried into an anthill aggravates her challenge, and she stopped: "I, Kirabo Nnamiiro, refuse to be stuffed into an anthill. I have a mother. Her name is Lovinca Nnakku. I did not come out of nowhere" (403). On reaching Nnakku's office of "Save the Children", Kirabo encounters her husband Mr. Luninze and narrated the entire story. She hands over the birth certificate to him, which he furthers towards his wife. To her utter surprise, "Nnakku took it, looked at it and tore it into pieces" (412). The reader as well as the Ugandan society would never have expected such a culmination of the physical and psychological journey of a daughter craving for her biological mother's love. The African societies where families "sacrifice whatever is necessary so children can have a mother and a father" (365), this was an unwelcome and perplexing response. Even for the headstrong and smart Kirabo, who has throughout the narrative been overshadowed by the absence of the mother she has never known, it was a bolt from the blue. Utterly frustrated and appalled by Nnakku's impulsivity, she insists that "if she had to choose between Nnakku alive and Nnakku dead, she would opt for a dead one: A dead mother gives you options. You can imagine and create and give yourself the perfect mother" (413). However, Sio, her boyfriend, understands it differently and tells Kirabo that in the process of evolution, parents, at times, let us down to make us mature. He affirms that this experience will make her "the best mother ever" (413).

In conclusion, it can be reiterated that Jenniffer Nansubuga Makumbi's *The First Woman* surfaces the innate and the ultimate 'female' self to counter various 'ism's prevailing in the world. Blended with folklore, this unforgettable account explores family, feminism and history. In the novel, Kirabo has a streak of 'the first woman' who couldn't be marginalized, subjugated, and suppressed on the basis of patriarchal mindsets, because she can fly out of her body that makes her remain in the independent and original state, which has been lost in all women folk of the world. It is that 'evil' and innate self that characterizes her as 'the first woman' who would be the ancestor of all women folk. Nsuutu recognizes her as the matrilineal "Mitochondrial Eve" not of all human beings, but especially of the 'Female' in all women. She is a strange and independent girl, who on the surface, accepts her role in life, but regularly exercises her independence. Her two-dimensional character tries to resolve the ambiguities prevailing between traditions and modernity, family life and education, and most of all, the role of women. Therefore, Kirabo's story being mythical and epical in nature brilliantly portrays the condition to which females of the world in different families, communities and countries have to resort in order to voice their concerns in the face of patriarchy. Steeped in the rich folklore of Uganda but with an eye firmly on the future, Makumbi has presented an assorted range of female characters to highlight their apathy; in addition to providing remedies to counter those institutions determined to silence them in the twentieth-century.

Works Cited

Clark, Alex. "*The First Woman* by Jennifer Nansubuga Makumbi Review – Coming of Age in Uganda." *The Guardian,* 30 October 2020, https://www.theguardian.com/books/ 2020/oct/30/the-first-woman-by-jennifer-nansubuga-makumbi-review-coming-of-age-in-uganda.

Kyomuhendo, Goretti. "Goretti Kyomuhendo in Conversation with Jennifer Nansubuga Makumbi." *Wasafiri*, vol. 33, no. 3, September 2018, pp. 39-42. Taylor & Francis Online, https://doi.org/10.1080/02690055.2018.1468403

Makumbi, Jennifer Nansbuga. *The First Woman.* One World, 2020.

Marais, Kylie. "Calls for Pleasure: How African Feminists are Challenging and Unsilencing Women's Sexualities." *Agenda*, vol. 33, no. 3, 2019, pp. 87-95, Taylor & Francis Online,

https://www.tandfonline.com/doi/abs/10.1080/10130950.2019. 1644960

Newson-Horst, Adele. "*A Girl is a Body of Water* by Jennifer Nansbuga Makumbi." *World Literature Today,* Summer 2021, https://www.worldliteraturetoday.org/2021/ summer/girl-body-water-jennifer-nansubuga-makumbi.

Norton, WW. "*A Girl is a Body of Water.*" https://mtl.drawnandquarterly.com/books/2716/ quick_view.

"Review: *The First Woman* by Jennifer Makumbi." *NewAfrican,* 22 September 2021, https://newafricanmagazine.com/26929/.

CHAPTER 13

Representation of Women Suffering under Regressive Traditions in African Literature: A Reading of Buchi Emecheta's *The Bride Price*

Priti Paul Verma and Roshan Lal Sharma

The word 'tradition' means an indigenous heritage, foundational, unwritten beliefs and customs handed down from distant past to be used in present and carried forward in times to come endlessly. We all knowingly/unknowingly give acquiescence as well as acceptability without much grumble or grouse and adhere to them in our day-to-day lives. It is the emotional fabric, which binds us to our forefathers and makes us distinct from one another. It enjoys the privilege of being followed blindly. The *Mariam-Webster* describes 'tradition' as "cultural continuity in social attitudes, customs, and institutions" (Merriam-webster.com). In fact, some of the finest memories in our lives comprise moments when we uphold the traditions of our family, clan or country. Men have laid down their lives for upholding noble traditions and have become immortal and great like patriotic warriors who can do anything and even die to uphold their traditions. Tradition is a stimulus to progress and it lays down guidelines for simple and complex decision-making and leaves us free to live our life, obeying those set customs and rules.

Every country has its distinct set of culture and tradition that suits it best according to its geographical location and instills a discrete quality in its social relations and practices. South Africa is famously referred to as the rainbow nation due to its diverse and synchronized cultural tradition and religion that on close scrutiny seem to be deeply rooted with their sacredness. Myriad of tribes with their unique tradition live in South Africa making it spellbindingly colourful. Along with indigenous religions, Christianity and Islam are the main religions followed in the entire African continent and in the endeavor of adaptation to both these Abrahamic religions, a slow and continuous modification has been taking place in the traditional belief systems of the continent. It is beneficial for the growth of the society as all traditions are not free from dust of many a flaw that might have crept into it without people ever realizing or resisting them. It does not mean we need to abandon all traditions altogether. We need to distinguish between progressive and regressive traditions. There are some regressive traditions that have no place in modern society as they hold us back and are a stigma to our society. Therefore, there is a dire need to reconcile and of weeding out such regressive traditions. Sustainable development is possible only when everyone gets a seat at the table. It will be apt to quote Raphael's view on tradition here: "To be tied to tradition is to be locked into a Janus-faced posture, condemned to falter between two worlds, in which any fleeting vision of the future is persistently challenged by dogma from the past" (9).

As one of the best-known Ibo writers, Buchi Emecheta's literary accomplishment reveals the existence of umpteen traditional beliefs prevalent in the society among which regressive tradition related to women and their ancillary status like patriarchy, polygamy, child marriage and bride price will be scrutinized closely in this chapter. She overtly highlights all such problems faced by women in African society in her writings. Extolling domesticity and servility of women in the name of tradition as done by male writers is just a hidden way of forcing women to cheerfully accept their exploitation and subordinate status in society. This cheerful and contended female complacency in the literature of male writers is replaced by fights on the part of Emecheta's female protagonists for equality and dignity in the society. Victimization of women and their forced servitude by men in her community remains the major strand that Buchi Emecheta thematically weaves in her writings. Male writers generally marginalize women and present them stereotypically in bad light in literature that they produce as observed by Kolawole who says "male writers in the early phase of African literature encouraged the women's marginalization" (79). Reinforcing Kolawole's point, Fonchingong states thus: "African Literature is replete with write-ups that project male dominance and inadequately pleads the case of African women" (135). Emecheta, by voicing her own point of view, changed rather than subverted the male-defined representation of women in literature. Male writers used to present women as submissive, benign and a weaker subject but Emecheta's female characters show defiance to this subsidiary status and also question the validation of such traditions and their brunt on their lives. It will not be wrong to quote Elleke Boehmer here who believes: "To write is not only to speak for one's place in the world. It is also to *make* one's own place or narrative, to tell the story of oneself, to create an identity" (94). Thus, Emecheta as a spokeswoman voices the story of women, their suppression and their persistent desire for independence.

Emecheta unravels the complexities of lives of women with remarkable subtlety, sophistication and feministic sensibility. Realistic and distressing portrayal of the plight of women in literary imagination of this prolific writer can be attributed to her first-hand encounter with those experiences in her own life while living in that culture for most part of her life. The protagonist of *The Bride Price*, Aku-nna's life and her tragic death while giving birth to her first baby has a glimpse of Emecheta's own life as she was also a weak, frail and an unwanted girl like Aku-nna. Emecheta confesses thus, "Aku-nna died the death I ought to have died. In real life, due to malnutrition and anemia, I had a very bad time with my first daughter, Chiedu" (Mezu n.pag.).

Buchi Emecheta has given a new voice to her female characters who dare to challenge their fate without accepting defeat and emerge as strong women, heralding the new era of emancipation. It is the magic of her emotive power that a real picture of tribulations of African women is conveyed to the readers. Other renowned women writers who bring forth plight of women in patriarchal society are Ama Ata Aidoo, Mariama Ba, Assia Djebar, Bessie Head, Flora Nwapa and Chimamanda Ngozi Adichie. Actually, Africa is a strictly traditional and patriarchal society treating women as secondary subjects, or rather vessels of motherhood and womanhood. Whereas Adichie leans more towards challenging and usurping patriarchy, Emecheta valorizes traditional patriarchal society in her works. She is more aggressive in questioning, criticizing and subverting patriarchal authority compared to Emecheta. Kate Millett aptly observes: "Our society... is a patriarchy. The fact is evident if one recalls that the military, industry, technology, universities, science, political offices and finance in short, every avenue of power within the society, including the coercive force of the police, is empty in male hands" (25). Thus, each arena of human activity is patriarchal and remains under male control, and the same is true of the society Emecheta hails from, and which she represents in her fictional universe.

Men are regarded as natural leaders who are superior and they are believed to have been born to rule over women and treat them as inferior humans. They fully control the life of females and children directly and indirectly in domestic as well as social arena. The women are considered weaker vessels and according to the society, they are subsidiary to male. Such is the plight of these women that they are not only subjected to social, economic and political discrimination and thus marginalized, but are also abused physically and sexually. Their inner acceptance of self-enslavement is a big reason behind this perpetual exploitation.

Actually, patriarchy uses different lenses to see and treat men and women of society where women are left with no choice than to accept patriarchy and its associated problems that weigh them down socially, economically, psychologically, and physically. Moreover, going against set social norms of the dominant discourse for being coined as abnormal in society is not everybody's cup of tea especially for diminished courage of African women attributed to unrestrained blow of life. Preference for male child is the main repercussion of patriarchy which does not end with single son as a number of sons are needed to boost/ satisfy the male ego. In the novel, *The Bride Price*, Aku-nna's father had a single son and expects more sons as he had "paid double the normal bride price" and was also "married in church" (2). In some communities in Africa, it is said that every married woman stands with one leg in her husband's house until she gives birth to a male child. The gravity of this custom of lending importance to male child in a patriarchal society is evident because of the fact that in its absence virility of father is questioned. According to Wentworth, this patriarchal system makes a daughter "a liability since it requires that she be married, a status that normally affords her in long-term possibility of economically benefitting her family of origin. Male privilege also means that a son stands little chance of having his life snuffed out at birth" (). Therefore, most of the issues reflected in African society are related to the social practice of marriage in one way or the other.

Marriage comes with other traditional and indispensable customs in the African society. One of them is bride price which is a widely practiced social custom in Africa wherein the prospective groom has to pay in terms of money or property to the bride's family. There is a belief in African society that if the bride price is not paid, the bride dies in the first childbirth. The African men and women strongly hold this belief irrespective of the level of their modernity and allow a mother the joy of bringing up her child. Therefore, the institution of marriage is the real test of a woman's fighting spirit, endurance and individuality and it decides her destiny. The unfortunate fact, however, is that almost all traditions are anti-women and conspire to make them obedient as well as submissive. It is outrageous though that society does not only accept such regressive traditions but also propagates them.

The paradox of this blissful curse ceremony namely marriage lies in the fact that it is both sublimating and subsuming. Through it, on the one hand, a woman attains a status acclaimed and adored by society as she fulfils her biological need of procreation and companionship; on the other, she is made to take up the path to a world of anonymity for the sake of family as a second-class citizen. The novel, *The Bride Price* embodies the economic issue of the bride price along with other problems related to female subjugation in the sacred institution of marriage. Buchi Emecheta exposes the malpractices in African society which is deeply patriarchal in an unhesitant manner and exposes the inhuman treatment of women therein. Moreover, she also portrays the role of women in Nigerian society, the influence of the Ibo customs on its members, and the clash of these customs with the modern ideas, consequent upon educational awareness in the society.

Emecheta portrays her female protagonists carefully and lends them a place of centrality in the narrative. They might be weak, fragile and meek in the beginning of the story but exhibit a clear transformation and growth with every situation they encounter and eventually turn out to be strong characters capable of articulating their viewpoint and thus taking decisions to manage their lives accordingly. Their unique way of encountering stifling situations makes them individuals, and not merely types in reader's mind as they gain appreciation for the strength of their character. Emecheta thus delineates characters whose "outrageous, courageous or willful behaviour" (McEmrysm 2) makes them stand apart from the rest.

The story of the novel begins in Lagos, a port city in Nigeria, Africa. In Ibo society, marriage has an economic basis and like a business deal, the highest bidder cracks the deal. Here, love or will of the girl has no consideration as girl is father's wealth, a source of income to her parents and hence, their decision by and large remains final. In the novel, "Aku-nna was determined not to disappoint her father. She planned to marry a wealthy man who could afford an expensive bride price" (3). The lives of Aku-nna, her mother, Ma Blackie and her brother, Nna-nndo take drastic turns due to tragic incidents that took place at the onset of the novel. They lost the head of the family, Ezekiel and were forced to shift to traditional, agrarian society of their ancestral village from modern and urban setting of industrial town, Lagos. In their culture, a woman without a husband is unable to take care of herself and her children as "*father is the shelter*" (3). In Nigerian culture, "the mother is only a woman" (3), a boneless creature; and a "fatherless family is a family without a head" (3), which means a non-existent family. This shift affects both children deeply. Aku-nna's ambiguity at every point in life can be attributed to her oscillation between modern and native culture of Lagos and Ibuza respectively.

The subordination of women in marriage is the leitmotif in *The Bride Price*. Patriarchy, as evident, is all about domination of women by men, and Emecheta has delineated this gender-based subsidiary status of women in her fictional world holistically including domestic, social, political, economic and cultural spheres of life. Women have to make sacrifices and lose their individuality and autonomy in order to keep their marriage intact. Out of numerous ways of direct/oblique ways of dominating women, discrimination, indifference, insult, control, exploitation, subjugation and forceful imposition stand out. Needless to think of equality as a girl is denied her very existence in the family. For instance, Aku-nna's father used to complain to her mother saying "'what have you given me – just one son!' He did not speak of Aku-nna. She was only a girl" (2).

Thus, women are non-existent in the family and are treated as commodities who during marriage would fetch financial gain to her father and pass from father to her husband. If unfortunately, she would lose her husband, she would then be "inherited" (23) by the brother of the deceased along with other items of property. But, before she would be passed on to her brother-in-law, she would lead a deplorable life by living "for nine full moons and mourn for her dead husband" in "a special mourning hut" from where "she was not allowed to leave" or "have a bath, or cut or comb her hair" and had to wear "an old, torn dress" (26).Thus, being victimized in the name of tradition would mean to demean her by depriving her of any sense of identity.

In this novel, the issue of bride price, a social stigma is accentuated right at the beginning of the novel through the life of the protagonist, Aku-nna – a name that literally signifies "*father's wealth*" (3). Her name thus refers to the bride price that her father will receive upon her marriage. Referring to her father, the narrator says: "To him that was something to look forward to" (27). Aku-nna too, at the age of thirteen, is well aware of the meaning of her name as well as her role in the society she lives in. She would not let her father down, and therefore marry a wealthy man. This is Aku-nna's assigned role. In fact, it is the role of every woman in her society. She would bring in wealth to her family in the form of a good bride price and will fulfill her role of being a daughter. Thereafter she has to bring wealth to her husband's family as well, even though metaphorically, in the form of male children preferably as the birth of a female child would anyway remain inconsequential.

Aku-nna like all other girls in her patriarchal community is insignificant and the only benefit she is expected to bring to her family is bride money at the time of marriage. In their native culture, wasting money on girl education is not preferred. Aku-nna is sent to school for the simple reason that educated brides can fetch good bride price. It is for this reason that Okonkwo expresses his attitude in response to his son's query as to "why waste money on her?" (28), by saying that "these days, people pay more for educated girls" (30).

The unequal treatment of a man and a woman in marriage had long meant a certain imbalance as well as a degree of hypocrisy in this institution. The so-called two halves are never equal. Males, the bread earners, are given supreme position and treated as heads of the family, the decision-makers and the owners of the house. The women, who are the home-makers, are relegated to secondary position with negligible role in important family decisions as Bernard pertinently argues:

> It is not so much the specific kinds of work men and women do – they have always varied from time to time and place to place – but the simple fact that the sexes do different kinds of work, whatever it is, which is in and of itself important. The division of labour by sex means that the work group becomes also a sex group. The very nature of maleness and femaleness becomes embedded in the sexual division of labour. One's sex

and one's work are part of one another. One's work defines one's gender. (3)

Which, of course, is unfortunate and thus, despicable, and requires clearer understanding and greater degree of maturity on the part of patriarchal mindset.

Emecheta has a much nuanced understanding of traditions and customs prevalent in her society and therefore, captures every minute detail of how the prevailing socio-cultural setup marginalizes and victimizes womankind. Polygamy is one such tradition that represents male hegemony in traditional society of Africa and "it is natural for a man to have as many wives as he wishes; only economic reasons put limits on polygamy; the husband can disown his wives at whim, and society barely accords them any guarantees" (Beauvoir 118). Okonkwo, the second husband of Ma Blackie in *The Bride Price* is the embodiment of this system. He already had three wives and also inherited his brother's widow, Ma Blackie along with his children who are left with no voice of their own. Cutting a woman's lock of hair and forcing her to marry is another social evil and a tool for female subjugation as it outrightly rejects her right to decide about her own life and thus, relegating her to a mere commodity with no will of her own. Stereotyped with titles like the "weaker sex" and the "second sex" the women are adorned with adjectives like sensitive, emotional, debilitated, tender fragile, feeble, indecisive, submissive, etc. because "to be feminine is to show oneself as weak, futile, passive, and docile" (Beauvoir 402).

Polygamy in traditional African society also acts as a tool of exploitation and domination of women by women as hatred, jealousy and feeling of insecurity on the part of senior wives are obvious as evident in the text where Ngbeke, the first wife of Okonkwo, "did not like Ma Blackie and was very jealous of her" (32) for becoming the fourth wife of her husband. She does not even like Aku-nna, Ma Blackie's daughter and says that "Aku-nna will come to no good" and calls her "ogbanje", a "living dead" (32). Actually, "An ogbanje doesn't belong in this world. They all die young, usually at the birth of their first child. They have to die young, because their friends in the other world call them back" (33).

Aku-nna's miserable plight and perturbing sense of alienation after their dislocation from Lagos to Ibuza consequent upon her father's death, can be understood owing to the fact that her own mother never supports her and prefers to side with Okonkwo's family every time the daughter needs her support. During an incident concerning visit of young boys to the house of a young girl who attains puberty, which is a tradition of community, Okoboshi tried to molest Aku-nna who "screamed, and Chike hit Okoboshi in the face" (52). Even during this incident, Ma Blackie reprimands Chike saying "If you must fight, do it somewhere else!" (52). Despite Aku-nna's telling her mother that Okoboshi is horrible and tore her shirt, the mother instead of supporting and consoling her daughter, says: "'Don't be so shy and silly. How can he harm you with all those young men watching? I suppose you'd rather let a slave touch you!" (52).

Such a callous attitude shocks her as it was totally unexpected of her own mother. But the fact of the matter is that African women themselves play a major role in inflicting pain on their fellow women. Mothers are not exceptions in this sense. It is sad but true that Aku-nna's first brush with oppression starts at her own home by her mother. Osa feels that she suffers a "psychological feeling of inadequacy at home because she is a girl" (33). She suffers psychological trauma at the hands of her own mother. She is "alone in her private world of tears and loneliness" (40). Her own mother has become an important tool of patriarchal oppression as far as Aku-nna's miserable plight is concerned.

Oppression and subordination of women in African society takes intricate forms as it is grounded in the traditional culture wherein women themselves become the agents of patriarchal exploitation as echoed by Adeola James, who states that "half of the problem rests with women, they are busy bitching about one another" and situation is such that when changes are suggested, "our women don't like it" (36). In the novel, Ma Blackie comes to Ibuza after the death of her husband and wears a new sari for mourning that is objected by the females who want that "she must wear the old one" and they "had prepared an old, torn dress for her to wear" (26). Ngbeke, "Okonkwo's first wife" (31), out of sheer jealousy instigates her family members against Aku-nna and Ma Blackie, and says that "Aku-nna will come to no good, I tell you. She and her mother are too proud" (32). Ngbeke's poisoning against Aku-nna prepares the foundation for her tragic experiences and ultimate death as Okonkwo is so frustrated with Aku-nna that he even tries black magic against her and does not accept the bride price. It affects Aku-nna psychologically and leads to her eventual, untimely death. Ma-

Blackie's role also cannot be ignored in causing this tragedy as rather than standing by Aku-nna, she alienates her further to find solace in her relationship with Chike. Therefore, it won't be an exaggeration to claim that women are more responsible than men for Aku-nna's tragic death. This is true for the entire female community.

No doubt, she is closer to her father, but such crude behaviour from her mother is beyond her expectations. That is why Aku-nna feels like an orphan and totally alienated as Ma Blackie becomes totally engrossed in her newly found motherhood by accepting Okonkwo as her husband as "he has made her dreams come true" and hence she "won't be able to refuse him anything" (53). Her ecstatic condition is natural as her newborn baby has erased the stigma of an incomplete or failed woman from her life. Alienated, Aku-nna finds support in the company of Chike, an Osu man and falls in love with him. She even hates her mother for being so passive about her life and relation with Chike She wanted her mother to support her. Ma Blackie did not like Chike which becomes evident in her reaction on seeing him in her house with Aku-nna. She "gave him a long, hard look that said, 'Be careful!'" (44). Of course, she knew that "there was a kind of bond between her and her father which did not exist between her and her mother" (12). Therefore, Nwapa, a feminist is right in observing that "the oppression of the woman starts in the home" (James 113). Why women who themselves are victim of oppression victimize other women is, indeed, beyond ken.

This theme of the bride price is developed further when the heroine, Aku-nna, attains her puberty. Her entire family is happy for her readiness to accept the responsibilities of wifehood and motherhood. For Okonkwo, it is time to get good amount of bride price which will help him become Chief, an Obi. He shares his plan with his son Ibuza and says: "'Don't you know that I hope to become a chief, an Obi?' To become an Obi a man had to offer a large, expensive gift to the gods" (28). Aku-nna's marriage and the procured bride price will furnish the title of Obi that Okonkwo covets desperately. Ma Blackie plans to send her son, Nna-nndo to college. Thus, Aku-nna's marriage has put double burden on her shoulders. She has to provide means to send her brother to college and raise the entire Odia family from poverty to prosperity. Her own readiness to start this new chapter of life is of least concern to anyone in the family. She wants to be self-reliant and therefore thinks: "'Ma promised me that I could teach for a year or two before marrying. She will never let my uncle marry me off so soon"' (49-50). But, like other women of the society, she has to surrender to the customs and bow to the commands of the elders in the family.

The complications in the story arise from the heroine's clash with and defiance of the unwritten law that forbids a marriage between a free-born and a person of slave ancestry as Chike was the son of a slave. She is told that "No girl from a good family like yours could possibly marry a slave" (61). Her modern upbringing and social exposure in town and her education forbid her to marry a person she does not like. She wants to sail the boat of her life herself. Rather than sitting passively and lamenting on her life, she demonstrates courage and decides to fight for her life and choose her own husband.

Chike was also "falling in love with his fifteen-year old student. He was helpless to stop himself" (34). Both were warned by their families but there was no moving back for them. Chike had not only helped Aku-nna in her studies but also had also provided her care and affection that was missing in her family. Due to her alienation from her mother, Ma Blackie and confused state of mind due to adjustment problem in rural surroundings, she finds solace in Chike's company. Emecheta portrays these characters convincingly in the backdrop of regressive socio-cultural traditions. They have boundless love for each other.

Through the careful depiction of love between Aku-nna and Chike, Buchi Emecheta ensures the audience's sympathy for them. Thus, emotional, psychological and physical support she expected from her mother during the period of her transformation into a woman is provided by Chike. Okoboshi's inhuman treatment of Aku-nna contravenes that of Chike who is humane and gentle in his handling of her. Okoboshi mistreats her during his visit to Aku-nna's house upon her attaining puberty. Later, his family kidnaps Aku-nna for a forced marriage and she gets ill-treated in a ruthless and uncouth manner after knowing about the fact that she has lost her virginity to Chike. Thus, Emecheta weaves the narrative of this boundless and undying love between Aku-nna and Chike beautifully and imbues it with powerful human emotions such as love and affection.

Aku-nna's short stay in Okoboshi's house after her kidnapping for forced marriage is like a horrible nightmare. The pain of indignity of attempted sexual assault is followed by humiliation at the hands of his family members after the revelation of her moral laxity. Akku-nna's fortitude and strength of mind to save her honour deserves appreciation. Upon finding herself in a difficult situation in Okoboshi's house, she figures out a way to play traditions prevalent in her community to bravely escape his ultimate defilement bid. According to the Igbo tradition, "All girls must be virgins when they go to their husbands" (47). She mocks at Okoboshi by saying, "Am I the only bride you can get – the girlfriend of a slave?" She further says: "You think I am a virgin?" (63), and tells Okoboshi falsely that she is not a virgin. Okoboshi believes her and "hit her across the face with all his strength" (64), spits on her, curses her and beats her so ruthlessly that her mouth got "sore and swollen" (66). He asks her to get out of his bed, and "hit her once more. She fell onto the floor and lost consciousness" (64). Actually, a woman is "obliged to defend her virtue, her honor; if she "gives in" or if she "falls," she arouses disdain" (Beauvoir 444). Aku-nna sacrifices her pride and her reputation of being a virgin, highly valued in the Igbo culture, and thereby succeeds in keeping the supposed marriage from being consummated. Whereas the tradition of forced marriage pushes her into a difficult situation, the other traditional belief of giving excessive importance to virginity helps her overcome the situation. She saves her honour by insulting Okoboshi, and it enables her ultimate escape to freedom.

However, the short sigh of relief that Aku-nna heaves after eloping with her lover to neighbouring Ugheli is engulfed by her dilemma because of the bride price which Okonkwo denied to accept from Chike's father. In this way, the ritual confirmation of the marriage cannot be achieved. Eventually, the curse of unconsummated marriage in the absence of the bride price keeps hanging on the life of the married couple even though the couple settles down after marriage. Thus, like other heroines in Emecheta's fictional world, Aku-nna's roller-coaster journey of life also shows a continuous and steady transformation from a meek and scared girl to a strong-willed person who could fight against adverse circumstances she encounters to eventually dare and go against the societal norms that form an integral part of their upbringing. The institution of marriage acts as a springboard for the growth of her heroines as they confront the problems rather than simply buckle and perish and thus show the strength of their individuality.

Aku-nna in the story also rises from a powerless and passive position to a position of self-awareness and confidence where she is able to take decision against the oppression and break shackles of male-dominated traditions. This is evident in her rejection of her forced marriage with Okoboshi and eloping with Chike, her lover. Though Aku-nna is unable to totally rise above the limitations of tradition against which she has rebelled, she shows reflective but dynamic attitude towards them. She oscillates between modern and native traditions where she is neither able to uproot ancient traditions from her heart and mind, nor is she able to persuade/ convince other people to eradicate these regressive traditions. Her nightmares and hallucinations about the consequences of the unpaid bride price become real enough to haunt her and rattle her psychologically.

Although Chike protects her through a continuous reinforcement of his love, regressive social traditions and customs are so profoundly ingrained in her mind that she finally becomes a victim of the fear and psychological torture that she constantly undergoes. Aku-nna's death is result of her broken will more than outside factors as the author says in "Buchi Emecheta: The Yoke of Womanhood", that "the failure or success of a character depends not only upon extraneous factors but also upon the character's individual strength of will" (Chukurere 206). Nevertheless, her losing the battle "against entrenched notions of female subjugation through limiting social norms has not been wholly successful" (Chukurere 206) as Aku-nna gave birth to her first child, a beautiful girl and wished to "call her "Joy" too, the same name that we gave our marriage bed" (83) and thereafter she dies very "softly and peacefully"(85). Whether it was her malnourishment or unripe age as the doctors suggested, or the myth coming true, it cannot be established but this incident of Aku-nna's death somehow validates the traditional superstitions regarding the bride price. It renders the struggle of the couple to eradicate regressive traditions and myths futile and confirms its validation in the mind of the people of Ibuja:

> Afterwards every girl in Ibuza was told the sad story of Aku-nna and Chike. 'If you want to live a long time,' they were told, 'you must accept the husband that your people choose for you, and your bride price must be paid. If it is not paid, you will never survive the birth of your first child.' (83)

Therefore, mythical and traditional beliefs are difficult to eradicate owing to their deep psychological hold on people. Abrams too observes that "Myths provide a rationale for social customs and observances, and to establish the sanctions for the rules by which people conduct their lives" (170). This, however, is not to condone the unacceptable socio-cultural and traditional practices like bride price as practiced in Igbo society. Emecheta's narrative brings into question an entire way of life that is overtly as well as covertly anti-women and deeply patriarchal.

Aku-nna revolts against ingrained notions of female suppression by choosing her life partner and marrying without the bride price. She was supposed to marry the husband chosen for her by her people and thus provide financial benefit/ support to her parents in the form of bride price. Her death while giving birth to her first baby results in the failure of her struggle but not before demonstrating their (Aku-nna and Chike's) deep and unconditional love for each other. Rather than encouraging Aku-nna to break chains of regressive traditions to live a whole life, the community scares them of grave consequences. It confirms and validates such prejudiced practices against women. Aku-nna's death also confirms how traditions/ traditional beliefs grip lives of people who despite repeated efforts cannot break free of them. In spite of her modern outlook, Aku-nna cannot come out of the guilt and fear of having gone against established norms and ends up embracing death eventually. Lloyd Brown echoes the same idea: "Her death is itself a demonstration of the degree to which her will is dominated despite her conscious act of revolt" (52).

Another Igbo traditional belief is that in case a man cuts and keeps a lock of a girl's hair, she would forever belong to him irrespective of her consent. In Aku-nna's case too, Okoboshi uses the same tactic to spoil Aku-nna's life for eloping with her lover. Okoboshi falsely convinces everyone that he had cut the lock of hair of Aku-nna. Therefore, everyone thinks that Aku-nna belongs to Okoboshi which automatically nullifies her marriage with Chike. It is because of this reason that Okonkwo denies accepting the bride price from Chike's father and that is why Aku-nna could not come out of the notion of failure of consummation of her marriage. Her dilemma between tradition and modernity and the state of extreme psychological despair that it causes contributes majorly to her untimely demise.

Acceptance of European customs undoubtedly has increased in the life of natives of Igbo community as these seem more liberating than their indigenous traditions. The incident of christening of Aku-nna and Chike's English bed by Chike's friend Ben Adegor as "Joy" clearly indicates this inclination. Actually, the only way to awaken people from the slumber of superstitious traditional clutches is through educating them. Victimized by indigenous and regressive and patriarchal traditions steeped in sexism, people like Chike, a slave child and Aku-nna, become prey despite their belief in and practice of the liberal western education system. Aku-nna and her brother in the novel get divided between "two sets of traditions" after coming from Lagos to their native place, Ibuza, which is a "home to the countless, unchanging traditions of their own people." Both of them "were trapped, like two helpless little fish" (35). Aku-nna's growing dilemma between suffocative living as per the framework of community norms and her instinct as a woman to revolt to follow her own feminine aspiration for a free identity serves as the pivot around which the whole narrative moves. The enlightenment due to education, traditionally a male bastion, enables her to pierce through the ironic reality of her socially defined inferior status, even though like other female protagonists of Emecheta, she also lacks the guts to oppose and eradicate deep-rooted traditional beliefs and customs altogether as tradition is not an easy enemy to deal with/ fight against.

Thus, time and again, we come across foreign and indigenous cultures along with subjugating and male-defined traditions that are seen at loggerheads with one another in Emecheta's representation of cultural and traditional setup of her society. It is quite distressing to observe that most of the customs are against women in African society where they are denied freedom and individual identity. Aku-nna, the protagonist's life is an apt example to underscore this point. The fate of the protagonist throws light on Emecheta's ambiguous stance which oscillates between rebellion against and acceptance of the traditions. Her ending of the narrative with Aku-nna's death, to some extent confirms her acceptance of dominating and demeaning patriarchal culture of African society. It appears as if Emecheta remains passive toward exploitation of women who seem to prefer being non-responsive to their ill-treatment by the patriarchal society. One may also feel that sustained manifestation of partial behaviour of society for ages has made women internally accept this notion as natural that their fate cannot be changed. The same gets in a way endorsed when Aku-nna says: "This is the end of all my dreams" when she is being kidnapped (56). At this juncture, it seems as if she has accepted her fate. Raphael seems right when he observes: "Perhaps this outright collusion with oppression is a necessary evil in this society" (28). However, oppressive and regressive patriarchal and traditional practices that deprive women of their due and deny them their right to freedom of choice and living must be done away with as it is only then that we can envision an exploitation-free society form the viewpoint of women.

Summing up, we can say that *The Bride Price* is a layered text that powerfully yet realistically portrays women in Igbo society as subjugated and subordinated entities devoid of any will of their own. Besides portraying suffering of women under regressive patriarchal traditions wherein women are demeaned, objectified and marginalized through and through, this novel also depicts as to how women are denied their identity as individuality. In case someone like Aku-nna resists and revolts against the patriarchal norms of the Igbo society, everyone turns against her including her mother and uncle who does not accept the bride price, which is a must to lend her marriage the tag of a 'successful marriage.' Thus, we see how African women in patriarchal, socio-cultural setup have been shown through marriage and other rituals associated with it such as the bride price. The social evil of the bride price has in fact resulted in the commodification of women as through this they are deprived of their right to live as self-respecting individuals having their own identities. Through the individual tragedy of Aku-nna, Emecheta has brilliantly universalized the inequality prevalent in African culture and brought to the fore the evil of social acceptance of women to male subjugation in marriage. Her life and her dreams are at the mercy of a man always who can be her father or her husband for that matter. Her existence and her identity are totally negated. What can be more painful than this? Emecheta, being a native of Igbo socio-cultural setup, has experienced these feelings herself, which accords her narrative a sense of depth and credibility. Even though her characters do not exhibit a strong revolting attitude, one may observe a glimmer of hope in her narrative to change the system which impedes women's dreams and kills their aspirations. Her characters like Aku-nna emerge stronger in adverse and hostile situations and try and live life as per their wish not how society wished it for them. Even marriage between Aku-nna and Chike may be viewed as a symbolic pointer towards slow but sure transformation that seems in the offing in a society as regressive as Igbo.

Works Cited

Abrams, M. H. *A Glossary of Literary Terms.* Thompson Business International India, 2006.

Beauvoir, Simone de. *The Second Sex.* Vintage Books, 2010.

Bernard, Jessie. "The Good Provider Role: Its Rise and Fall." *American Psychologists,* vol. 36, no. 1, 1981, pp. 1-12, doi:10.1037/0003-066x.36.1.1.

Boehmer, Elleke. "Stories of Women and Mothers: Gender and Nationalism in the Early Fiction of Flora Nwapa." *Stories of Women: Gender and Narrative in the Postcolonial Nation.* Manchester UP, 2005, pp. 88-105, *JSTOR,* www.jstor.org/stable/j.ctt155j4ws.

Brown, L. *Women Writers in Black Africa.* Greenwood P, 1981.

Chukukere, Gloria C. *Gender Voices and Choices: Redefining Women in Contemporary African Fiction.* Fourth Dimension, 1995.

Emecheta, Buchi. *The Bride Price.* George Braziller, 1976.

"Emecheta, (Florence Onye) Buchi 1944." *Contemporary Authors, New Revision Series. Encyclopedia.com.* 15 Apr. 2021 <https://www.encyclopedia.com>.

Fonchingong, Charles C. "Unbending Gender Narratives in African Literature." *Journal of International Women's Studies,* vol. 8, no. 1, 2006, pp. 135-147.

James, Adeola. *In Their Own Voices: African Women Writers Talk.* J. Currey, 1990.

Kolawole, Mary E. Modupe. *Womanism and African Consciousness.* Africa World P, 1997.

McEmrys, Aaron. "Engaging the Sacred Wisdom of Our Sisters in the Wilderness: A Unitarian Universalist/Womanist Dialogue." *The Journal of Liberal Religion,* vol. 7, no. 1, 2006, pp-1-17.

Mezu, Rose Ure. "Buchi Emecheta: A Biographical Sketch." Introduction. *The Writings of Buchi Emecheta: A Comparative Study. Rosey Blog,* www.roseyblog.com/buchi-emecheta-comparative-study. Accessed 23 Jan. 2021.

Millett, Kate. *Sexual Politics.* Doubleday, 1970.

Osa, Osayimwense. *African Children's and Youth Literature.* Twayne Publishers, 1995.

Raphael, M.G.M. *Tied to Tradition: The Silenced Rage of the African Women in Selected Novels of Buchi Emecheta.* Edith Cowan U, 1992.

Wentworth, M.L. "What is Patriarchy and Why Is It the Most Powerful Force in the World Today?" *Global-Sisterhood-Network,* 2005, pp. 1-12.

CHAPTER 14

Education as Empowerment: Exposing the Real Infertility in Lola Shoneyin's *The Secret Lives of Baba Segi's Wives*

Varnika and Hem Raj Bansal

Infertility is a health issue that has affected all the spheres of human society. It is a gender neutral issue which is often perceived as woman's problem. The patriarchal society lays the burden of barrenness on women. Men seek to assert their manliness through procreation. When a woman fails to conceive, she is blamed by the society as well as by her husband. Women are viewed as objects in marriage and if a woman turns out to be infertile, she has to undergo unbearable pain and social stigma. Regardless of the fact that infertility can be on the part of man as well, it is always a woman who bears the brunt of barrenness. In African culture, marriage is only fulfilled if a couple conceives and bears children. Women face societal criticism because of childlessness while men try to hide their own impotency many a time. Lola Shoneyin's novel *The Secret Lives of Baba Segi's Wives* (2010) is an example of unbearable pain that the African women are subjected to on the basis of barrenness. Society constructs man as a powerful perfect being; he is expected to be fertile. Infertility is, therefore, a stigma describing woman's imperfection. Shoneyin subverts this socially accepted norm by presenting an impotent male character. The stereotypes against women in procreation are irrational since having a baby depends on both man and woman. Education is presented as fundamental for women to challenge the dominated social order and system which undermines them.

The WHO defines infertility as "a disease of the reproductive system defined by the failure to achieve a clinical pregnancy after twelve months or more of regular unprotected sexual intercourse" (web. n.pag.). It is a serious issue affecting all the spheres of human society. Female partners are often blamed for barrenness in patriarchal communities because it is believed that men cannot be infertile. There is a high level of stigma against infertile men because they are seen as transgressing the constructed form of idealized masculinity. Stacy Elliot writes: "Regarding men as infertile is a taboo because it forces the embodiment of an alternative masculinity that is outside hegemonic norms" (300). Men who do not achieve this idealized form of masculinity are viewed as deviant from other men because they do not fit within the rigid norms of hegemonic masculinity. Stacy Elliot also adjoins, "A man's sense of masculinity, his ability to perform sexually and his capacity to be a biological father are a large part of what constructs a man's concept of his own masculinity" (297).

The fact that male infertility is equally responsible for the inability of a woman to conceive is rejected by the patriarchal mentality. Men are viewed as powerful perfect beings and are expected to be fertile; infertility is, thus, a stigma describing a woman's imperfection. Simone de Beauvoir (1908-1986) in her essay *The Second Sex* (1949) says, "Women have been reduced to the position of inferiority in the male dominated society. Even when her rights are recognized in the abstract, long standing customs prevent their full expression..." (35). Women are viewed as objects in marriage and if a woman turns out to be infertile, she is subjected to scathing societal criticism. Women suffer at the hands of their husbands, in-laws and society. The consequences of being barren result in countless agony to women. Regardless of the fact that men can also be impotent, it is always a woman who bears the brunt of barrenness. Women face societal disparagement because of childlessness while men try to hide their impotency many a time. The identity of women in many African societies is determined by their ability to bear children. If a woman fails to fulfil this role, her identity as a woman is threatened and if a woman is barren, she is not considered a complete woman. A woman is not only blamed by her partner but she also curses herself for not being able to bear a child. Life without a child is not perceived worth living. A marriage is only deemed successful if a couple conceives and bears children. The stereotypes against women in procreation are irrational since having a baby depends on both man and woman. Adrienne Rich (1929-2012), as cited by Rosemarie Tong, suggests that "men have convinced women that unless a woman is a mother she is not really a woman" (13).

Motherhood is a very important aspect in the lives of women in general and African women in particular. Adrienne Rich (1929-2012) in *Of Woman Born: Motherhood Experience and Institution* (1976) says, "There is nothing revolutionary whatsoever about the control of women's bodies by men. The woman's body is a terrain on which patriarchy is erected" (55). Many women live under the fear that their marriage will collapse if they are unable to give birth. Men who learn that their wives are infertile replace their wives to prove their virility while women who discover that their husbands are infertile stay silent to save their husbands from disgrace. "Infertility poses a serious threat to one's masculinity since the diagnosis is antithetical to the values of hegemonic masculinity (Griel et al. 741). A woman without a child in this society is seen as incomplete and becomes what John Mbiti defines as the "dead end of human life, not only on genealogical level but also for herself" (144).

The Secret Lives of Baba Segi's Wives is an example of unbearable pain that African women are subjected to on the basis of childlessness. The novel depicts a culture where a woman's worth is measured by her children. When Baba Segi's first wife, Iya Segi discovers that her husband is impotent, she secretly dates Baba Segi's driver Taju to avoid being termed barren. It is with Taju that she conceives and delivers a baby. Iya Segi later shares this secret with her co-wives Iya Tope and Iya Femi. Learning the truth, Baba Segi's second wife Iya Tope starts an extra marital affair with a meat-seller and becomes the mother of his children. This affair with meat seller produces three girls. Iya Femi, Baba Segi's third wife also gets pregnant with her former boyfriend to retain her position in her husband's household. She maintains her past relationship with Tunde and gives birth to two children. Adultery is consciously committed by these women in order to fulfil a dream of procreation and is used as a solution to their husband's impotency. Getting pregnant becomes so important for the first three wives of Baba Segi that they move out of their roles as virtuous housewives to conform to patriarchal dictates. Baba Segi is himself unaware of the fact that he is not the biological father of the children that his wives had.

Everything in the household functions well until Baba Segi brings in Bolanle as his fourth wife. Bolanle's prolonged barrenness invites trouble for the first three wives as well as for Baba Segi. Baba Segi saw nothing valuable in Bolanle except that she is a woman whom he had married to give birth. Being the patriarch of the household, he is least concerned about her educational qualifications. Baba Segi does not feel that pain that his wife is going through but he is disturbed because it makes people think that he is no longer a man. He says, "Your barrenness brings shame upon me. And I am sure that you, as well, are saddened by it" (15). Baba Segi follows a belief system where the inability of the couple to conceive is faulted on women. Baba Segi is more concerned about his virility than the pain that Bolanle is going through. He says:

> Does your blood not boil when you see other women carrying babies on their backs? Do tears not fill your eyes when you see mothers suckling infants? You of all people should be willing to trying everything! Offsprings make your visit to this world complete! Do you want to remain a maggot? (46)

Baba Segi no more loves Bolanle because she is unable to give him a child. He only comes to her to fulfil his desire of having a child from her. Bolanle says, "Baba Segi only comes to deposit his seeds in my womb" (46). She further goes on saying "He emptied his testicles as deep into my womb as possible. It was as if he wanted to make it clear, with every thrust, that he didn't make light of his husbandly duties. He wanted to fuck me pregnant" (47). Bolanle's barrenness causes a feeling of fear among the other wives of Baba Segi. They fear that the truth of Baba Segi as not being the father of their children is now going to come out. Iya Segi says, "That Bolanle is a trouble maker" (59). Baba Segi's other wives want Bolanle to leave that house as they do not want their secret to be revealed. Iya Segi goes on saying, "She will destroy our home. She will expose our private parts to the wind. She will reveal our secrets. She will bring woe" (59). They plot against Bolanle so that she is compelled to leave the house. Iya Femi acts as an enemy of Bolanle, "Of what use is she? She cannot have children. Her womb is dead" (61).

Bolanle being educated wants to get medically examined to find out the cause of her barrenness. Baga Segi is very confident of his virility because he thinks that he already has seven children so he is ready to get his fertility test done when Bolanle insists him in doing so. Through the fertility test, Baba Segi discovers the shocking fact that the problem lies with him. This test opens up all the secrets, deception and lies. Bolanle is the representative of the promising Nigerian woman whose reliance on education and scientific thinking destroys the power of her husband. The test reveals that Baba Segi is impotent. "There's nothing! Not a solitary sperm swimming around" (206). The news of being sterile shatters Baba Segi. Shoneyin presents Baba Segi as an impotent being who possesses neither the skill of pleasing his wives' sexual desires nor the capability of impregnating them.

Women in the novel are depicted as commodities and their existence in the household is limited to sex and reproduction. Initially when Baba Segi's second wife who is offered to him as a compensation for the crop failure is unable to conceive, he threatens her: "If your father sold me a rotten fruit, it will be returned to him" (88). Iya Tope is even compared to an animal by her father when he offers her as a compensation. He says, "But she is as strong as three donkeys" (86). Iya Femi too is objectified by her uncle first and then by her husband. After the death of her parents, Iya Femi is denied the right to her father's property. Her uncle sold her into house slavery and the woman whom Iya Femi's uncle had courted says, "This is not your home and it will never be. A girl cannot inherit her father's house because it is everyone's prayer that she will marry and make her husband's house her own" (128). Bolanle, Segi's fourth wife is blamed to be barren and for this reason she is not entitled as "Iya". Atanda (Baba Segi's friend) says – "'Baba Segi, I think you should drag her to a medicine man if she doesn't follow you. You are the husband and she is a mere wife, and the forth one at that! If you drag her by the hair, she'll follow you anywhere, I swear it!'"(5). Each wife in Baba Segi's household endures pain.

Religion is also used as a tool by men to oppress their wives. Abiding by the Islamic law, Baba Segi simultaneously holds four wives. He rests his polygamous stance on third verse in Surat An-Nisaa in the Holy Quran which sanctions a man the right to marry four women at the same time. The same verse sets a condition to have this right. The verse says, "If you (men) fear that you shall not be able to deal justly (with those wives), then only one... That is nearer to prevent you from doing injustice" (Al-Hilali and Khan105). Even the sacred texts are twisted and manipulated by men in order to oppress women.

After learning the truth of his impotency, Baba Segi initially denounces his unfaithful wives but later he calls them and says, "Neither is it every day that a man finds his children are not his own" (259). He tells that they are now free to go. He says, "'I want you to know that you can go. The door is open. I will not stop you" (260). The first three wives beg Baba Segi to keep them as his wives and Iya Segi even says that the secret that Baba Segi is infertile and the children have different fathers must be kept within the family. It is only Bolanle who asks for divorce. For Bolanle living under humiliating circumstances means losing self-dignity. She divorces him once she rediscovers her own powers and her own ability to heal from past traumas. She believes that life can give her better alternatives. She interrogates the culture from within and shakes the presumption of ascribed identities and rigid cultural norms. Living in this family, Bolanle realises how important it is to be educated. She says:

> Living with them has taught me the value of education, of enlightenment. I have seen the dark side of illiteracy. So deep seated in their disdain for my university degree that they smear my books with palm oil and hid e them under kitchen cupboards. I have often found missing pages from my novels in the dustbin, the words scribbled over with charcoal. (9)

Bolanle is determined to educate her co-wives to understand their roles not only as wives but also as human beings. Through Bolanle, Shoneyin emphasises the importance of achieving economic independence for women.

Bolanle realises that illiteracy is chiefly responsible for excessive erratic behaviour of her co-wives. Good education is a horizon of opportunities for Nigerian women, for when a woman is educated; the family in particular and the country in general is strengthened. Women must empower themselves before they empower others. They must stand before they can help other people to stand. Women should not accommodate others but should ensure that they achieve recognition for themselves.

Education is presented as fundamental for women in order to challenge the dominating social order which determines them. Education provides power to overcome the fear to open up and be able to speak their minds, voice their own opinions about issues concerning their own lives. There is a famous African proverb by which says that "to educate a man is to educate an individual but to educate a woman is to educate a nation" (qtd. in Aggrey). Being educated, Bolane stands in sharp contrast to the other women. Bolanle feels that she has "woken up from a dream of unspeakable self-flagellation" (263). The act of realization leads Bolanle to no longer accept her subjugated and silenced position. She is ready to face all the challenges ahead in her life. She declares, "People will say I am a second-hand woman. Men will hurt and ridicule me, but I won't let them hold me back. I will remain in the land of living. I am back now and the world is spread before me like an egg cracked open" (264).

Through education a new social verve, consciousness and awakening has taken birth which is altering the mindset of budding minds to reject male superiority and to create new self-definitions that liberate masculinities from patriarchal, homophobic, and capitalist power. Dewey elaborates that "the incalculable facts of birth and death of each one of the constitute members of a social group determine the necessity of education" (45). It means that education guides human's life. Education enables humans to connect to their experiences and their surroundings in order to improve their lives. In *African Gender Studies: A Reader*, Oyeronke Oyewumi suggests ways in which women can attain power to strike a gender balance. Oyewumi suggests the formulation of "different groups of marginalized women [that] can create new spaces and social locations for themselves within the dominant culture [...] By creating these new spaces and locations, women take the margins to the centre and vice versa" (273).

Iya Segi works hard and helps Baba Segi set up his business and buy a new house for themselves. Even after being economically independent, she thinks that she needs a man by her side to be regarded as a good woman in the society. She has internalised patriarchy by accepting a position of inferiority and by becoming subservient. In a patriarchal society women are made to internalise unconsciously that they must the family and if they fail to do so then it will bring disgrace to the family. Being outspoken or questioning on the part of women is considered to be disrespectful. Women live in this oppressive system because of the fear of the repercussions. This fear leads to strict implementation of patriarchy and thus women blindly carry this burden in the name of the dignity of the family. Remaining silent and completely submissive have become the virtues by which women are defined.

The novel also highlighs another important concern about women.When women are under the threat of patriarchal institution of motherhood, they resort to anything to save their marriage. It is what happens when the three wives of Baba Segi they turn to different men to avoid the stigma/trauma of being barren. They transcend their high status/class and share physical relations with men below the rank of their husband. They identify with men of lower class because somehow their inferior position in the marriage brings them closer to these men.

Works Cited

Al-Hilali, Muhammad T and Muhsin Khan, Muhammad (1993). *Translation of the Meaning of Meanings of the Noble Quran: KSA (Madin): King Fahd Complex for the Printing of the Holy Quran.*

Beauvoir, Simone de. *The Second Sex*. Harnondsorth, 1949.

Dewey, John. *Democracy and Education*. Macmillian, 1916.

Dudgeon, Matthew R., and Maria C. Inhorn. "Gender Masculinity, and Reproduction: Anthropological Perspectives." *International Journal of Men's Health*, vol. 2, no. 1, 2003, pp. 31-56.

Elliott, Stacy. "The Relationship between Fertility Issues and Sexual problems in Men." *The Canadian Journal of Human Sexuality*, vol. 7, no. 3, 1998, pp. 295-303.

Greil, Arthur, Julia McQuillian, and Kathleen Slauson Blevins. "The Social Construction of Infertility." *Sociology Compass,* vol. 5, no. 8, 2011, pp. 736-46.

Oriel, Jennifer. "Sexual Pleasure as a Human Right: Harmful or Helpful to Women in the Context of HIV/AIDS?" *Women's Studies International Forum*, vol. 28, 2005, pp. 392-404.

Oyewumi, Oyeronke. *African Gender Studies: A Reader*. Palgrave Macmillian, 2005.

Rich, Adrienne. *Of Women Born: Motherhood as Experience and Institution*. Norton, 1996.

Shoneyin, Lola. *The Secret Lives of Baba Segi's Wives*. Serpents Tail, 2010.

CHAPTER 15

Ruptures, Wounds and Convalescence: Analyzing Complex Contours of Slavery in Yaa Gyasi's *Homegoing*

Prajya Parmita Mishra and Roshan Lal Sharma

Slavery has been a historic blow to human civilization – a wound that may perhaps never heal. Richard Hellie views slavery as a "condition in which one human being was owned by another" (n.pag.) It implied "dependent labour... usually, but not always, involuntary" performed by the slave who was "deprived of personal liberty and the right to move about geographically as he desired." This chapter paper seeks to look into the complex contours of slavery, its 'whys' and 'hows' alongside its devastating impact on several African generations in general and the way it impinged on the lives of black women and their achingly glorious survivance in particular. It will also try and encompass the indigenous life with its richness of customs and rituals and a dignified Black existence until it was disrupted by slavery. The wounding effect of enslavement and sturdy surviving instinct of the black populace and especially the black women will be the major point of consideration in this chapter. An attempt has been made to compassionately grasp and study the ruptures, the wounds and the scope of subsequent reconciliation and convalescence in Yaa Gyasi's novel, *Homegoing* (2016) in which slavery is the common thread that interlaces a series of interconnected stories to form an empathetic fabric of the novel.

Slave trade, which signifies "the capturing, selling, and buying of enslaved persons" (Britannica), has always engendered illimitable curiosity and has supplied infinite material for writers like a bottomless well of tragic curves. Many a writer has documented the epic dimensions and uncharted secrets of slave trade. Achebe narrated the woeful tale of colonization in *Things Fall Apart*, Edward P. Jones questioned the Black slave owners of Virginia in *The Known World*, Toni Morrison palpably described the tale of slaves who kill their children to set them free in *Beloved*, Colson Whitehead wrote about how the Black slaves tried to attain freedom in *Underground Railroad*, and Bernardine Evaristo in *Blonde Roots* upended the transatlantic slavery wherein the Blacks enslave the Whites. Thus, the list of literary representation of black enslavement goes on and it is into the desolate waters of this same well that the debutant Ghanaian novelist, Yaa Gyasi dives into to narrate the story of *Homegoing*, portraying the role of West Africa in the transatlantic slave trade to depict how cruel, unfair, debased and horrific the institution of slavery was. Gyasi, however, is distinctly unique in conveying the impact of slavery on modern life too. According to Laura Miller, this novel is a "sprawling tale of a family split between Africa and America" and its title has been taken from "an old African-American belief that death allowed an enslaved person's spirit to travel back to Africa" (n.pag.).

As a contemporary African woman writer, Yaa Gyasi builds a narrative that challenges and counters the historiography of slavery to straighten the eschewed and garbled official record. Her foray into literary arena makes a significant political intervention to upstage the hegemonic/ preponderant gaze and facilitate the convalescence, wholeness and reclamation of disregarded abject black body especially the female black body. She revisits the sites of exploitation to transform/ sanctify by reconnecting and reconstituting the matrix of ugliness and disempowerment into sites of empowerment and self-enunciation. It is an enormous achievement for a new writer to narrate and weave a story of seven generations but Gyasi rises to the challenge. Each deftly crafted narrative episode/ chapter has a central character, a carefully crafted, clearly shaped and defined protagonist who we sympathise with largely because of the extent of her suffering. The life stories of seven generations are bound and glued together with love. The chapters flow and have been structured in such a way that one makes way for the next in line. As the generations come into being, one finds them helpless in the face of the course of history but despite their powerless and crushing situations they have their small resistances/ rebellions giving them the solace of having some sense of existence/ being, and thereby leading them to wholeness through healing.

Whereas the story is located in the late 18th century when inter-tribal wars were fought for supremacy, the novel is set in the Gold Coast, present-day Ghana where the British colonial troops began trading in slaves in 1562 and managed to have monopoly in the slave trade by 18th century. It is a tale of two sisters Effia Otcher and Esi Asare born of the same mother, Maame, but begotten through two different fathers. Maame worked as a house girl/slave in Fante land and was raped by her master, Cobbe. She rebels against Cobbe's invasion/violation by lighting a fire and disappearing thereafter leaving her female infant behind namely Effia. She flees and seeks anchorage in Asante land with the big man, Asare and gives birth to Esi. Out of the two sisters, Effia is bartered off to James (governor of British slave traders) as a bride by the step-mother Baaba, and is taken to Cape Coast Castle (a place to keep the women slaves) to live with him. Esi, who is fifteen-year-old is caught as a prisoner of inter-tribal war in a sudden attack on her village and sold off as a slave. She is brought to the same castle and kept in the women's dungeon as cargo in transit to be transported to America as a slave. Unlike Cellie and Nettie of *Color Purple* who despite being distant remained in perpetual correspondence with each other, these two sisters never meet, and it is only Esi who comes to know about the existence of another sister without knowing her whereabouts. Dove, the house girl of Maame, says about the separated sisters: "They are like a woman and her reflection, doomed to stay on opposite sides of the pond" (84).

It turned out to be true in case of Effia and Esi too – one stayed in Africa and the other lived off her life at cotton plantations of America. The consequences of their fate reverberate through the generations that follow, from the Gold Coast of Africa to the plantations in America. The bloodlines of these two sisters are traced spanning three continents and through their lives the corresponding histories of the US and Ghana up to the turn of the 21st century. The trajectory of future generations intersects at Stanford in the US when the seventh-generation progeny finally meets and comes together embodied as Marcus and Marjorie in their mother continent, Africa.

Inter-tribal wars between Fantes and Asantes along with regional wars yielded the bulk of usual domestic helps as houseboys or housegirls and the surplus prisoners/ unlucky captives of tribal and regional wars were sold to the Europeans for money and goods. Esi and Tansi too, become victims of inter-tribal war. Tansi tells Esi that white men will eat them as they "buy us from these soldiers" (44). After each capture, the prisoners were put on display at the centre of the village square where anybody could walk and stare at them while taking them home as houseboys or housegirls. Along with the virile warriors, the women and children were also taken as prisoners.

Slavery, in fact, existed even before the advent of the British as slave traders as the prisoners of the tribal wars were absorbed as domestic helps in the African households like Abronoma is kept as a slave by Maame. While Asantes do not sell their prisoners to the British, Fantes trade with the British. Esi and Tansi are sold off to the whites by Fante chief Abeeku risking the fury of Asante allies for dealing with their enemies. But the chief is driven by greed for material wealth and that is why Abeeku says: "Today their enemies pay more, Fiifi….Tomorrow, if they pay more, we will work with them too. This is how you build a village…" (45). Money and goods thus propel the Fantes to sell their own.

Women have always occupied the central position in slave trade as Kirsten E. Wood observes: "Women and ideas about them shaped slavery from beginning to end." Women slaves were in great demand because of the "non-pecuniary returns" (Beckles) that came in the form of rape and physical assault. Representation of women slaves in the novel is poignant as well as harrowing. They could scarcely see the sunlight and their bodies were stacked on top of one another's. When governor James comes to inspect the women slaves, the Fante soldiers undress the women for inspection. He inspects them by running his hands on their breasts and between their thighs without any hesitation or self-reproach. Esi protests by spitting on Fiifi's face and gets smacked for it.

Gyasi palpably captures the harrowing tale of women slaves who were regularly raped/ sexually assaulted. Esi is physically violated twice like many others. Women go on shushing and silencing each other because if they make noise, they will be collectively flogged. Extremely afflicting is the way Esi is raped by one of the soldiers: "His foot at the base of her neck so that she couldn't turn her head to breathe anything but the dust and detritus from the ground" (30). Esi keeps bleeding and watching herself. The cruel violation diminishes Esi not just to a body, but a part of it – a plain simple hole.

The narrative also textualizes the unscrupulousness of the white soldiers in using and abusing the enslaved women's bodies amidst the most degrading and dehumanizing surroundings. Sometimes, the predating white men who manoeuvre such situations become even more abject than their poor preys. Second time when another soldier takes Esi to his room and rapes her, he is utterly "horrified, disgusted with her", and Esi spells out this "[a]s though he were the one who had something taken from him. As though he were the one who had been violated…. He looked at her like her body was his shame" (48). The way the onus/blame comes on the victim instead of the contrite victimizer is exemplary. Mar Gallego aptly observes: "It also reveals how Esi is able to question that hegemonic racist and sexist order by feeling more human than her sexual predator, thus demonstrating her keen awareness of the need for self-healing and self-protection despite the horrid mistreatment and abuse" (49). The governor smiles at Esi after checking. She finds the smile kind and pitying but now she had understood that white man's smile meant more evil was coming. The whites thus inflict unprecedented cruelty, inhumanity and barbarism on the women slaves while indigenous people connive with them.

Owing to Baaba's artful design Effia could not get married to Abeeku, the chief as promised and wished by her father, and is finally married off to James Collins. Effia goes to Cape Coast Castle and has her first tangible encounter with the slave trade when she discovers that several people especially women were kept as captives in the dungeon for flourishing slave trade, and questions James: "How can you keep them down there crying, enh?" She further says, "You white people. My father warned me about your ways" (17). She starts screaming and James puts his hand on her lips, and she realizes that he was a man capable of hurting and she should be glad to be on his side of meanness. Ironically, Effia doesn't come to know that her own sister Esi captured in the inter-tribal war was kept in the dungeons meant for women slaves under the supervision of her husband James.

The portrayal of dungeon is absolutely heart-wrenching as it is shown to be a place where women are forced to live in the most inhuman conditions. Piss, puke and shit put together creates the unbearable stench where the women are kept as captives. Afua, the lactating mother, has nothing to feed to her baby as her milk has dried up due to starvation. The baby howls incessantly and the soldier on duty plucks the baby away from the mother. Esi is not able to stop herself and asks: "Where are they taking the baby?" (29). Tansi, a co-captive, answers: "They will kill it, I'm sure" (29). The baby was conceived before the marriage ceremony of Afua and therefore the village chief as punishment sold her to the traders, she was sure that her parents would come to her rescue but her hopes were shattered. The man who was responsible for the baby obviously goes unscathed/unpunished; it is only Afua who bears the brunt. Thus, women inevitably become the worst victims. As captives, they receive food (mushy porridge) once a day and at times, not even that: "[T]heir stomachs were empty more days than full" (29). The new women were brought in the dungeon wailing and unconscious. Esi and others had to lie down on their stomach so that the women could be piled up on them: "Esi could feel the woman on top of her peeing. Urine traveled between both of their legs" (31). Afua is not able to endure this and hence chooses death to a life of sheer shame: "Her skin was purple and blue, and Esi knew that she held her breath until Nyame took her" (30).

Esi is sold and transported across the Atlantic to the US as a labourer for cotton plantations in Alabama. When it was time to deliver, Esi went behind a tree alone and revelled in her private moment of motherhood with her newly born baby before anyone came to snatch both her joy and her baby. The slaves recall that before Ness's wail they had heard a strange unfamiliar sound. The slaves believed that the sound had come from Esi herself: "The sound, that slave had said, was of Esi laughing which was why they hadn't recognized it" (84) because she was never seen smiling or laughing. Esi was a solemn, solid woman who was never known to smile or tell a happy story and was called "Frownie" by other slaves. Esi's suffering had numbed her to the extent that when Ness, her daughter, was sold in 1796, her lips stood in the same thin line. Ness tried to reach out, flailing her arms and kicking her legs, fighting the man who had come to take her away but Esi neither moved nor reached out for her daughter. Ness would remember her mother as the one with a gray rock heart and would associate real love with hardness of spirit like her mother. Such fortitude to stay stoical was Esi's way to keep herself intact and heal. Esi recalled her horrific transatlantic journey as a slave to narrate bedtime stories to Ness which were full of the images of "the big boat" from where the men were thrown into the Atlantic Ocean "like anchors attached to nothing: no land, no people, no worth" (70). They were stacked ten high and when a man died on top, his weight pressed on the pile "like cooks pressing garlic" (70). The slaves lived in perpetual fear of inhuman atrocities committed by their owners and pushing their progeny into slavery. Hence, maternity came with fears of seeing their children separated either by sale as it happened with Ness and Esi or whipped to death or demeaned or overworked or raped and buried. Sexual maturity of a slave girl could not be celebrated as per the African tradition because it enhanced the fear of inter-racial rape by the owners. That is why many enslaved women either killed their child, as Ness and her husband Sam pretend when caught by the owner, or resisted child bearing through contraception. Gynecological resistance was the most effective gendered resistance practiced by enslaved black women because they were acutely conscious of the fact that they would reproduce bondage which will further enrich the owners.

Gyasi vividly narrates the life of women slaves working on the plantations in southern states of the US. The whites as slave owners castigate and ridicule the colour, rituals, beliefs and even the language of the indigenous people. It was a documented slavery, the owners possessed legal papers of ownership as Ness belonged to Tom Allan Stockham. Slaves were openly sold and bought, and an existence bereft of dignity was given to them. They were beaten regularly by their owners, lashed for conversing in their mother tongue or for not talking in English. In Mississippi, when Esi was caught by her master speaking in Twi with her daughter, she was given "five lashes for every Twi word Ness spoke" (71). Ness witnessed the beating of her mother and was very scared to talk but the master beat Esi for Ness's silence too. Prior to whipping, Esi used to call her daughter 'Maame' after her mother but the master objected to this and whipping followed until she cried "My goodness." These were the only English words that escaped Esi's mouth, and the beating stopped so she thought this must be something divine like the gift of her daughter. The daughter was named 'Goodness' which turned into simply 'Ness.'

The slave owners created a subordinate status for the slaves religiously, linguistically and culturally as well. They coerced them to lapse into forgetfulness as they were whipped for conversing in Twi or any African language because learning English would take a while and until then they had to remain meek and halting. The communication gap would persist, and the slaves would be forced to follow their dictates without understanding. Ness tried to remember the Twi that Esi used to speak to her, "a tongue that Ness could no longer quite grasp. Phrases and words would come to her, mismatched or lopsided, wrong" (75). The owners want the slaves to unlearn things associated with their African identity. Any unchristian belief would be black magic or voodoo and was considered inferior to their Christian beliefs.

The life of the women slaves on American plantations was even worse compared to their male counterparts. Women slaves were supposed to cater to every need of their masters including the physical/sexual needs. Ironically, the women slaves vied for the attention of the master because his attention made their life less difficult. As Henrice Altink argues that some enslaved women chose to enter into sexual relationship with their owners/ white men in the hope of material favours. According to him, "Many colonialists addressed relations that were initiated by white men, had the consent of the slave women and were relatively permanent" (99). It is evident from Margaret's statement when she watches Ness putting on her clothes after the master's disgustful screaming, "It a shame, really. For a second, I's thought you mighta been prettier than me" (74). Tom Allan, the owner, found Ness to be too pretty to be a field nigger but he was advised by his friend to use her only in the field. Allan thought his friend must have made some kind of mistake and therefore agains decides to keep Ness as a house nigger at his friend's advice and takes out an outfit that he liked his house niggers to wear.

To keep Ness as a house nigger meant easy accessibility for the owner but when Ness appeared in the outfit given to her, shoulders bared as well as the bottom halves of her calves, Susan, the wife of the owner fainted outright. Tom Allan could barely catch his wife while shouting at Margaret to ask Ness to change. If Susan would have been like other master's wives, she would have known that her husband's bringing a new nigger meant she ought to pay attention to him. Susan was a woman of poise and grace, so she allowed her husband to keep a new house nigger. Ness went to change and stood in the center of the room "running her hands along her body, reveling in her ugly nakedness" (73). She knew it was the intricate scars on her shoulders travelling the full length of her back touching the top of her buttocks that had alarmed them. The scars were the ghosts of her past but seeable in the present. She rejoiced in the brutal reminder of her past and derived pleasure and satisfaction from her ugliness because now she was of no use to her owner except as a field nigger. Her ugliness saved her from sexual exploitation which would accompany back-breaking labour in the field.

Even ugliness too becomes a form of resistance in the context of slavery and therefore some of the tribes had intentionally adopted the practice of tattooing the face of their children so that they could look ugly and become unsuitable for sale as slaves and also for identification. The scars were not merely physical and would manifest in the conduct and disposition of the slaves such as Esi who could never smile and likewise sleep became a rarity for Ness owing to the harrowing images that danced behind her closed eyelids. Even the slave kids were made to toil right from morning to evening on the plantation. Tim Tam's mute hiccupping child Pinky was the water girl, on a regular basis she had to make as many as forty trips to the creek at the edge of the Stockhams' plantation to fill the large water buckets kept in the porch, to fill the basins for the afternoon baths of Stockham children, to water the flowers that were kept on Susan Stockham's dressing table and then two pailfuls to Margaret for cooking. At the end of the day, Pinky's arms used to throb so hard that Ness could feel her heartbeat in them when the girl crawled into the cot with her. Ness and Pinky's relationship leads them to healing. Pinky fills the void created by the absence of Ness's son, Kojo.

In general, the life of slaves on the plantations in the south of the US was harsh and ruthless. They were asked to pick the sun-scorched cotton which burned their hands as Ness recalls: "Holding those small white puffs almost felt like holding fire" (74). But they were not supposed to drop it and hold it at any cost because the owner was extremely vigilant. Ness was born into slavery in the American south. She withstands the full atrocity of a life in which whippings were rife and random, and a five-minute break every three hours when picking cotton was a sign of "a good master", and where attempts to escape were harshly punished, as Ness's Yoruba husband, Sam discovers. Ness had met Sam in the Hell. She called it "Hell" as it was the place she had learned to eat standing up – "Picking cotton with her right hand, shoveling food in with her left" (74). In Hell, even the sexual acts between the slaves were planned and enforced by their masters. So marital togetherness was coerced and thrust on Ness and Sam to produce new chattels for the owner. The controlling authority of the owner terrorized the slaves and confirmed their helplessness and inferiority. The compelled togetherness between Ness and Sam resulted in Kojo's birth.

Ness was convinced that a child cannot be raised in the Hell, so she decides to escape from the plantation/ Hell with the help of Aku. But it was destined not to be, the devil/the owner comes looking for them with the dogs and Ness and Sam understood that it was time for them to sacrifice their lives to save Kojo and Aku's so they surrender and Aku escapes with Kojo. Sam gets hanged and Ness gets ruthless beating and since then sleep becomes a rarity for her. Aku escapes with Kojo to Baltimore. The city was known for more freedom for negroes. Some of them were slaves, others ex-slaves and the rest as free as can be. Whenever Kojo aka Jo saw a slave in Baltimore, he saw himself and realized what his life would have been had Ma Aku not taken him to freedom. His free papers named him Kojo Freeman. Half the ex-slaves had this name Freeman. He did not know much about his parents, Ness and Sam, except through the stories Ma Aku told him about South and them. Ma Aku registers her resistance by helping the slaves to escape from the plantations and merciless clutches of the slave owners. Her absolute integration with Kojo as the foster mother is a reclamation of her maternity and motherhood as it heals her as a woman.

Baltimore gave that quantum of solace to both Ma Aku and Jo until the Fugitive Slave Act was passed. Their life turns in a muddle, Jo's pregnant wife Anna goes missing along with the baby H to be born. Anna was sold off to another owner as a slave though she was set free along with her mother by her owner/ father. But freedom did not mean much for blacks as it was governed by the whims and fancies of the whites. Their kids were born free in Baltimore and hence did not fall within the ambit of this law, but Ma Aku and Jo did. There were rallies and protests throughout North, and not just among the Negroes but the Whites also joined them despite the fact that the Whites could be fined for giving meal/ job/place to stay to a runaway Negro. It was known as the 'Bloodhound Law'. When the kids got married and settled with a job in Baltimore, Jo plans to move to further North or to Canada along with Ma Aku who resists the move because it was after being an Asante slave and then American slave that she had found freedom and she would not let go of it at any cost. From Baltimore, she could only move to Gold Coast and therefore Jo stayed on until Ma Aku lived and then moved to New York to do odd jobs of carpentry and plumbing.

Meanwhile, Anna who was sold to another master died giving birth to H who worked for the old master until the war against slavery ended and he walked free from his old master's plantation. He walked from Georgia to Alabama as a free man but it did not last long as he landed himself in jail. From jail he was sold by the state of Alabama to work in coal mines outside Birmingham as part of his sentence. Thus, despite being free, he was sold. In the mines the conditions were inhuman, they had to work shackled on their knees the whole day and deliver the ten-ton quota of coal every day. And if they were not able to deliver, they were whipped to death. Even during the night, they were kept chained with ten other men so they could not sleep laterally, they could only sleep on their backs. Horrific images of coal mining slaves are evoked by Gyasi to bring home the point that freedom for the blacks was elusive despite the end of the war and proclamation of the same. H after the completion of his sentence in 1889 moved to Pratt city, the town made up of ex-cons white and black alike who were free miners now. Ethe joins H there and Willie comes in the world.

Willie's metamorphosis from H's baby to Ma Willie exemplifies struggle and grit of a woman to live with self-esteem. In comparison, her husband, Robert Clifton appears to be small and feeble. They move from Pratt City to Harlem where she aspires to be a singer. But colour discrimination in Harlem stifles her growth; Robert is treated as a white man because of "more white" in him. Colour chasm between the two of them results in the failure of their marriage. Colour too has its own hierarchy such as black, less black, brown, light coloured etc. especially with reference to women. Within the ambit of black colour, people with beautiful black complexion are object of rejection/ disdain and the ones with light colour are preferred. Willie is denied entry in the auditions for Jazzing, "A very slender and tall man held a paper bag up to her cheek. 'Too dark', he said." Willie insisted that she can sing but the man said, "Jazzing's only for the light girls" (209). She pointed that she had seen a man dark as midnight walk in with a trombone, and he answered: "I said girls, honey. If you were a man, may be" (209). Thus, black women were the worst sufferers. Willie is insulted by Robert's white friends. He is asked by his friends to enter her in front of them and Robert instead of defending her, plays in their hands and then breaks down while announcing his final departure from her life. It is difficult to achieve social security as a black person and if it is a black woman, the situation aggravates all the more. After Robert's departure, she is left with their son, Carson to rear as if she was the only one responsible for his birth. Her family perforce becomes matrifocal due to the absent father. However, she continues to live with self-respect. Eli, the romantic, comes in her life with his erratic poetic sunshine. She would tell the landlord that her husband was a famous poet, though she knew he was neither husband nor famous, for social security. Willie becomes a sterling example of a black matriarch who takes care of the family as well as the community. She chooses to stand by her drug addict son, Carson aka Sonny, financially and emotionally and at the same time supports little Josephine. Willie rises to sublimity when she forgives Robert for dumping her and marrying a white woman. She smiles at him and purges herself of negativity and initiates healing. In her black matrifocal family, she is the key element in keeping her family united. Every weekend she organizes dinner for the whole family asserting and underscoring the familial ties. For Sonny's son, Marcus too, Willie the grand mother is a shield that protects him, even from his own heroin addict mother, Amani. She is a perpetual source of strength for Marcus. She reclaims not only her dignity but also lends dignity to others. This reclamation of dignity, space and self-esteem is the affirmation of black identity.

Gyasi successfully creates an alternate slave narrative by giving an account of the impact of slavery on the present day modern life in addition to showing its horror, cruelty and unfairness. Navigating through an assemblage of lives and array of emotional landscapes, Gyasi brings us to the contemporary closing characters of Marcus, who is sixth generation of Esi, and Marjorie carrying forward the bloodline of Effia. Marjorie comprehends the pain and scars of her father, Yaw and her grandmother, Akua and therefore, never complains of her pain even when the ring worm spreads from her thigh to knee. She understands the ruins of her father, grandmother and ancestors' lives. She poignantly experiences the rootlessness / loneliness of the migrant slaves when her teacher, Mrs Pinkston ruthlessly tells her: "[H]ere black is black is black" (273). She further tells that blacks get dumped for whites of which Graham is a perfect example. He appreciates Marjorie but when it comes to taking her for

Prom, he prefers a brunette for it will be socially appropriate. Marjorie has not suffered like her grandmother or her ancestors but surely bears the brunt of contemporariness of slavery in another form and finds her people "still bleeding" (282). She articulates the scarred soul of an African American in the poem she writes and recites in the black cultural event of the school. She ropes in the emotional interiors of black humanity across the continents in the poem:

> We, two, black.
> Me, you.
> One grew from
> Cocoa's soil, birthed from nut,
> Skin uncut, still bleeding.
> We, two, wade.
> The waters seem different
> But are same. (282)

She thus connects the continents, merges all blacks whether born in Ghana or in the US as African American or 'Akata', and lends them identity and commences the convalescing of the ruptures created by slavery. Convalescence is also sought through "Our same, Sister skin" (282). She does not exercise the option of escape and rather accumulates and assimilates the past and affirms its existence in the current scenario. Her choice to work on African / African American works of literature owing to the fact that "those were the books that she could feel inside of her" (295), and this is what exemplifies the process of reconciliation and healing.

Marcus, too, wants to unlayer the past to find his lineage. In his research project to be submitted in Stanford, he wishes to recapitulate the times that stretched back far to trace that he and everyone else existed in it "not apart from it, but inside of it" (296). He had heard stories about his great-grandpa "Two shovel H" who worked in Pratt city from Ma Willie and the stories made him cry and filled him with pride. He feels that they were products of their time and today he is the cumulation of those times and the present. He carries all of them inside him. He goes to Ghana with Marjorie and when he visits the castle and the dungeons, a sickness overtakes him. He runs out to the beach to overcome his sickness. The catharsis comes when he wades into the waters of the Atlantic at the behest of Marjorie and triumphs over his painful affliction of fear of water. Both Marjorie and Marcus conquer their fears, after complete knowledge of the layers of past and eventual acceptance of it, to feel at home in their mother continent Africa. This acceptance and reconciliation sets them free to chart new course. The remarkable and the courageous feat in the narrative is the ability to visit the wounds/ ruptures inflicted by exploitative oppression.

Customs and traditions in a typical African society were gender-specific. The Asante puberty rites were a serious matter. A week-long ceremony was held to bless the girl's fresh womanhood and after this the rules were strict. For instance, the menstruating women could not visit the "stool houses" (where the king stayed) and cross certain rivers. They lived in separate houses and painted their wrists with white clay on the days they bled. If anyone found out that the woman had bled but did not disclose, the punishment was great. The coming of blood and burgeoning womanhood was declared with a week-long ceremony and this was kind of an invitation to the suitors. The suitors came with gifts in order to woo and win the family of the girl whom one wanted to marry. The practice of giving gifts to the family of the girl was called bride price. Cobbe was happy to see his daughter growing up and the interest she generated among the young men in the village. He had big plans of marrying off Effia in a prestigious African family, "a man of our village" as Cobbe puts it.

In the late 18th century, slavery was deep rooted and the white slave traders wanted to mingle with and marry the local girls; therefore, they lured the families of the girls by hefty bride price which included money, fabric, millet, gold, and iron. Adwoa Aidoo was the first girl to be proposed by a British soldier. Cobbe detested the British enslavers and never wanted his daughter Effia to get married to a British soldier because he knew that the "white men live in the Cape Coast Castle. There, they trade goods with our people" (7). Iron and Millet were given in return of African people as slaves. Thus, despite the large bride price offered by the British slave traders, they preferred an African as is evident from Millicent's mother's gloating on marrying off her daughter to chief Abeeku: "To be sure, my sister, the money is good, but I for one glad my daughter has married a Fante" (9).

Keeping two wives had become a norm for the British soldiers, one in England and the other in Africa. The African wives were called "wenches" (12) because wife was a word reserved for white women across the Atlantic. The soldiers kept their hands clean as they claimed to have only one wife who lived in England so that they would not get into trouble with their god too. They avoided the sin of polygyny which is not sanctioned by Christianity, and therefore, the African wives were "wenches". This in fact was also a way to distinguish themselves from polygynous Africans who they looked down upon. Polygyny was a norm among Africans. According to John T. Dalton and Tin Cheuk Leung, "Skewed sex ratio" in fact played a significant role in the "emergence and strengthening of polygyny" (n.pag.). Each wife had her own hut in the big campus maintained by all the wives. Bigger the status and prestige of a man, higher the number of wives. The first wife, however, enjoyed more power and authority.

The prevalence of any tradition has its pros and cons and likewise prevalence of polygyny helped the motherless child, Effia. It was because Cobbe Otcher's several wives collectively took care of Effia who "was born of fire" (3) in which her mother disappeared. The happening on the day of her birth was shocking and destructive in nature but none mentioned it as Cobbe had instructed them not to. Baaba, the first wife, had no milk to feed the newly born and so the second wife fed her. However, the rivalry among the various wives was widespread, the junior wives often went to the apothecary ("Mampanyin") when they wished to quietly kill the senior wives. Baaba's antagonism for Effia is an obvious outcome of polygyny which deshapes the future of Effia and her progeny forever.

Jealousies, rivalries and contempt among the wives were common in a polygynous setup. Baaba's son Fiifi candidly concedes that his mother hated Maame (Cobbe's wife who ran away in the middle of the night amidst raging fire) and her daughter Effia and after their father's death she had told Fiifi that "she was not truly my sister, I owed her nothing" (68). Therefore, for many years, Fiifi believed this but now with time and age, he is wiser and wishes to follow the tradition of Africa wherein "mothers, sisters, and their sons are most important. If you are a chief, your sister's son is your successor" (68). If one wife died or disappeared (as in this case), the other wives were encumbered with the rearing of other woman's kids. Polygyny cannot be glossed over for the simplistic reason that other wives were available to look after the motherless child in the absence of a biological mother. The African women writers inadvertently or maybe just to validate the custom/ culture in which they trace their mooring, mute these emotions of rivalry, jealousy or at times pure hatred among the many wives and thus, deny the space they deserve in howsoever oppressive familial setup. Gyaasi too ignores/ does not attempt to voice or dissect the pain of Baaba in rearing the child of a slave woman with whom her husband committed adultery and compromised her position as his first wife. Though, Gyasi does momentarily dwell on the antipathy of Baaba for the child of another woman but does not convey the hurt and humiliation she must have felt as a wife, and thereby justify the system of polygyny which diminishes women as it happens in Mabel Dove Danquah's story "Anticipation" where the chief remarries one of his wives again out of his forty wives when he sees her dancing, for he had not seen this wife for a long time and he failed to recognize her. Effia's life is a perfect example of disruptive effect of polygyny. As Naana Jane Opoku-Agyemang states in her article "Recovering Lost Voices": "[B]y denying voices to her women characters about subjects that influence their lives, the writer unwittingly denies the story a powerful effect. More than this, her failure to include women's voices reflects the writer's subconscious identification with an essentially male view of marriage" (71-72).

African societies had a deeply patriarchal setup where in a family situation, man would eat first followed by women. The roles of men and women were well-defined. For instance, women's domain was confined to kitchen, kids and home while men ventured out working in the farms, fighting wars for defending their tribe. War and its machinations were the domain of men whereas women were supposed to focus on domestic affairs as pointed by Esi's mother Maame when the former quizzes her about the fate of prisoners: "Mama, what happens to all the prisoners after they leave here?" She answers: "That's boys' talk, Esi. You don't need to think about it" (34-35). Both Effia and Esi are wont to asking blatant questions and that is why, the former asks Abeeku, the would be chief of the Fante tribe: "Will you work for the British when you become chief?" (7). Abeeku answers Effia smilingly, "We work with the British…not for them" (8). When the British started trading with Americans, Asante and Fante tribes too made an alliance with each other to sell slaves to the British as Fiifi says: "We will help them sell their slaves to the British" (12). Abeeku and the Fante tribe thrived on slave trade and became the leading slave market in all of the Gold Coast.

In the marriage too, patriarchy has a well-defined role for woman and hence the failure to conceive has always been the woman's fault – more often than not an outcome of infidelity or loose morals as per the African beliefs. Gender anatomy of patriarchal and imperialist structure exhibit the concurrent avouchment and disruption of the system by women. The cliché of motherhood in individual, religious and nationalist narratives conceal the fears, vulnerability, upheavals, upsets, disruptions, and ambivalence of personal and collective histories. Child-bearing is seen as a way to keep a marriage strong. Adwoa, another one married to a British soldier, advises Effia to bear children for James as it is the duty of a woman and it will also ensure the continuous affection and attention of the husband. So accordingly, Effia pursues James Collins not only to keep him romantically entangled but also to overcome the falsehood created by Baaba that she is cursed, and nothing will come out of nothing. She tries to conceive by placing large, swirled roots under the bed and when James sees the roots, he calls it black magic or voodoo. Until this moment she did not know that magic had a colour. The impulse to label things as good or bad and white or black respectively was incomprehensible to Effia.

The very concept of labelling/berating anything and everything as black and unchristian exemplifies typical attitude to otherwise everything Black/ African. This episode of roots can be interpreted firstly from the Eurocentric male point-of-view, as dominance of a woman in sexual relations evokes the connection between black women and beastliness because the white men are used to timid and virtuous women as their wives. Secondly, a sexually active woman is considered a deviant from a sexist viewpoint too. However, if it is explicated in view of African parameters, Adwoa's advice is in sync with the positive facets of femininity and matrilineage which enable African women reproduce descendants and consolidate their socio-cultural positions in African societies. In a way, this depicts an assertion of autonomy against the sexist and racist order. These women derive strength from their traditional beliefs to counter their weakness and powerlessness and thus affirm a viewpoint about the importance of mothers as ancestors of posterity. Hence, motherhood arguably becomes a means of healing for these women, both individually and communally.

To briefly sum up, one may concur with Toni Morrison who aptly observes thus: "There is no time for despair, no place for self-pity, no need for silence, no room for fear. We speak, we write, we do language. That is how civilizations heal" (n.pag.). In the like manner, Gyasi too seeks to unearth the healing strategies black women have been developing and employing in order to deal with the traumatic and devastating effects of patriarchal oppression, structural commodification and socio-cultural exploitation of women by both slave traders as well as their own men. Almost all the women characters in *Homegoing* are intent on visiting their wounds and ruptures to thereby initiate healing and convalescing of their badly bruised interiorities via challenging the prevalent hegemony be that through the ploy of motherhood, or by forgiving the deserter/exploiter, or helping the slaves in escaping, or by going back to the roots from where it all began. These women reclaim not only their bodies but also their identities and dignity.

Works Cited

Achebe, Chinua. *Things Fall Apart.* Anchor Books, 1994.

Altink, Henrice. "Representations of Slave Women in Discourses of Slavery and Abolition, 1780-1838." 2002. U of Hull, PhD Dissertation. *Core: The World's Largest Collection of Research Papers*, Core.ac.uk/download/pdf/2731539.pdf.

Beckles, Hilary M. "Plantation Production and White 'Proto Slavery': White Indentured Servants and the Colonisation of the English West Indies, 1624–1645," *The Americas*, vol. 41, no. 3, 1985, pp. 21-45.

Britannica, The Editors of Encyclopaedia. "Slave Trade." *Encyclopedia Britannica*, 14 May. 2020, www.britannica.com/topic/slave-trade. Accessed 3 December 2021.

Dalton, John T., and Tin Cheuk Leung. "Why Is Polygyny More Prevalent in Western Africa? An African Slave Trade Perspective." *Economic Development and Cultural Change*, vol. 62, no. 4, U of Chicago P, 2014, pp. 599–632, doi: 10.1086/676531.

Danquah, Mabel Dove. "Anticipation." *The Literatures of Asia and Africa*, edited by Carolina R. Duka, Rex Book Store, 2001, pp. 10-14.

Dove, Mabel, Audrey Gadzekpo, and Stephanie Newell. *Selected Writings of a Pioneer West African Feminist.* Trent Editions, 2004.

Evaristo, Bernardine. *Blonde Roots.* Hamish Hamilton, 2008.

Gallego, Mar. "Sexuality and Healing in the African Diaspora: A Transnational Approach to Toni Morrison and Gyasi." *Humanities*, vol. 8, 2019, pp. 1-12, doi: 10.3390/h8040183.

Gyasi, Yaa. *Homegoing.* Penguin, 2017.

Hellie, Richard. "Slavery". *Encyclopedia Britannica*, 24 Aug. 2020, www.britannica.com/topic/slavery-sociology. Accessed 3 December 2021.

Jones, Edward P, and Kevin R. Free. *The Known World.* Harper Audio, 2003.

Miller, Laura. "Decendants: A Sprawling Tale of a Family Split between Africa and America". *The New Yorker.* 30 May 2016. www.newyorker.com/magazine/2016/05/30/yaa-gyasis-homegoing.

Morrison, Toni. "No Place for Self-Pity, No Room for Fear," *The Nation*, 23 Mar. 2015. www.thenation.com/article/archive/no-place-self-pity-no-room-fear/

---. *Beloved.* Vintage Classics, 2007.

Opoku-Agyemang, Naana J. "Recovering Lost Voices: The Short Stories of Mabel Dove-Danquah." *Writing African Women: Gender, Popular Culture and Literature in West Africa,* edited by Stephanie Newell, Zed Books, 1997, pp. 67-80.

Walker, Alice. *The Color Purple.* Harcourt, 1992.

Whitehead, Colson. *The Underground Railroad: A Novel.* Knopf Doubleday, 2016.

Wood, Kirsten E. "Gender and Slavery". *The Oxford Handbook of Slavery in the Americas*, edited by Mark M. Smith and Robert L. Paquette, Oxford UP, 2012, doi: 10.1093/oxfordhb/9780199227990.013.0024.

About the Contributors

1. **Archana Thakur** is an Assistant Professor of English at RGM Govt. College Jogindernagar, H.P. She has earned her PhD on women studies from Central University of Himachal Pradesh, Dharamshala. Her research interest areas include – African feminism, gender studies and post-colonial literatures. She could be reached at archana.17@hotmail.com.
2. **Bipasha Som Gune** is a faculty in the Department of English in Gautam Buddha University in national capital region, India. Her specialization is in colonial and post-colonial studies, literary theory, Indian Writing in English and Indian *bhashas* and British literature. Dr. Bipasha is a bilingual creative writer, writing poems and short stories in English and Bengali.
3. **Deepshikha Sharma** is a Teaching Fellow in Krea University. She is a recent postgraduate from Department of Philosophy, University of Delhi and holds Bachelors in philosophy from Kamala Nehru College, University of Delhi. Her research interests lie on the intersections of social epistemology, science and technology studies, and gender.
4. **Kanu Priya** is currently working as Assistant Professor in the Department of English, School of Humanities at K.R. Mangalam University, Gurugram. She is also the Academic School Coordinator of School of Humanities. Her research and interest areas are Gender Studies, Autobiographical Studies and Women's Writing.
5. **Khem Raj Sharma** is an Assistant Professor of English in the Department of English, Central University of Himachal Pradesh, Dharamshala. As a researcher, his areas of interest include Postcolonial Literatures, Indian Writing in English, Folk Literature, Diasporic Literature, Comparative Literature and Translation Studies. He has published numerous research papers

in national and international journals of repute, including two co-edited book, *Critical Voices on Toni Morrison* (2015) and *Cats Talk* (2018). His PhD is a postmodern study on Toni Morrison and V. S. Naipaul.

6. **Neha Arora** is an Assistant Professor in the Department of English, Central University of Rajasthan. Her areas of interest are Dalit literature, Comparative literature, Indian Writings, and Literatures from the Margins. She has one authored book to her credit and has co-edited two anthologies on New Literatures and Mahesh Dattani. Her forthcoming anthology is *Understanding Marginality: Cultural and Literary Perspectives*. She has also contributed several research papers in reputed journals and books. Two research scholars have been awarded PhD degree under her supervision.
7. **Pallavi Mishra** is an Assistant Professor of English at Government PG College, Doiwala, Dehradun. She has published numerous papers in journals of repute and has also two books to her credit: *Disdain: A Fiction* and *Mahasweta's Literary Canvas – A Critical Reading*. Her areas of interest include Postcolonial Literatures, African Literature, Gender Studies, Modern British Literature, Translation Studies and Disability Studies. Her forthcoming book is an edited volume on *The Dynamics of Folklore and Orature in Culture*.
8. **Prajya Parmita Mishra** is Principal, KDC Government Degree College, Jaisinghpur, District Kangra (HP). She has done her PhD on "Politics of Activism: A Study of Arundhati Roy's Non-Fictional Writings" from the Department of English, Himachal Pradesh University, Shimla. An avid reader, Mishra's areas of interest include World Literature, Literary Theory and translation from Hindi to English and vice versa.
9. **Prakash Kumar Meher** has done his PhD on Life Writings (Autobiographies and Memoirs) from Central University of Himachal Pradesh, Dharamshala. He has qualified UGC NET examination. His areas of research interests include Resistance Studies, Comparative Literature, Dalit Literature and African American Literature. He is also an alumnus of Indian Institute of Mass Communication (IIMC) Odisha.
10. **Priti Verma** is presently working as Lecturer in English at GSSS, Kothi, Dist Solan (HP). She has done her PhD on Salman

Rushdie's fiction from the Department of English, Himachal Pradesh University, Shimla. She is a committed researcher and has published few research articles in journals of repute along with book chapters. Her areas of interest include World Fiction, Indian Writing in English along with Communication Studies.

11. **Sheelpa Sweety** has obtained her PhD from Centre for Linguistics, Jawaharlal Nehru University. Her teaching interests range from English Language Teaching to Gender and Language. Currently, she is working as an Assistant Professor in the School of Humanities at KR Mangalam University, Gurugram.
12. **Shweta Tiwari** is an Assistant Professor in Amity Institute of English Studies and Research, Amity University. A gold-medalist in M.A., she is the recipient of Certificate of Excellence under the category "Indian Women Rising Star Award" by Asian Literary Society. She has also received several scholarships like Indraprastha Research Fellowship and Prof. V.K. Dublish Memorial Scholarship, to name a few. Her areas of interest include Indian English and Postcolonial Literature.
13. **Shikha Thakur** is currently working as an Assistant Professor in the Department of English, at Lovely Professional University, Jalandhar. Having studied PhD English from Central University of Himachal Pradesh, she has qualified UGC-NET and HP-SET. Other than having nine (9) conferences to her credit, she has published fifty (50) plus research papers. Her area of interest ranges from gender studies to mythological studies to postmodernism. Having previously taught at DAV University, Jalandhar, Shikha has a teaching-experience of three (3) years in total. Other than supervising four (4) PhD scholars, she has one (1) PhD awardee to her credit. Being an established creative-freelancer on UPWORK, Shikha is an avid researcher and thus, wishes to expand her credentials infinitely.
14. **Subhash Verma** is an Assistant Professor of English at RNT Government College Sarkaghat, Mandi (HP). He did his M.A., M. Phil. and PhD from Himachal Pradesh University, Shimla. He has thirty five research articles to his credit and has presented many papers at national and international conferences in India and abroad. He has supervised two PhD and one M. Phil. Dissertation. His areas of interest include Australian Drama, Aboriginal Literature, Canadian Drama, Postcolonial Literature and Contemporary Literature. He has also worked as Project

Associate in the Centre for Australian and New Zealand Studies at H.P. University Shimla-5.

15. **Varnika** is doing her PhD on Contemporary African Women Writers from the Central University of Himachal Pradesh, Dharamshala. She has also presented a couple of papers at International conferences.
16. **Vinod K. Chopra** earned his PhD from Himachal Pradesh University, Shimla in 2002 on the topic "Community, Communalism and Gender: A Study of Short Stories on Partition." He is an independent researcher. He is also honorary faculty, Career Point University, Kota, Rajasthan. He has guided thirteen M. Phil scholars and at present is supervising four PhD scholars. He has published a book *Partition Stories: Mapping Community, Communalism and Gender* in 2009 and has translated into English a monograph on Inderpal, a freedom fighter from Himachal Pradesh, *Saga of a Revolutionary Hero: Pt. Inderpal, a Freedom Fighter.* He has contributed about twenty papers and chapters to journals and books and has presented ten research papers in national and international seminars.

Index

E

F

G

H

I

L

M

N

O

P

R

S